A BOOK OF BRITISH MUSIC FESTIVALS

for Minoru Hayashi

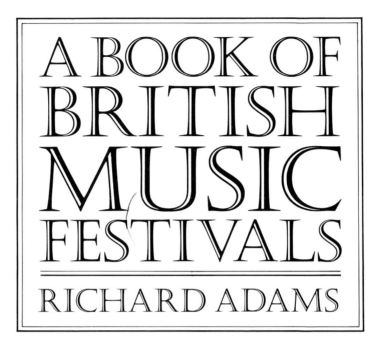

A BOOK OF BRITISH MUSIC FESTIVALS

RICHARD ADAMS

ROBERT ROYCE LIMITED

Picture Credits

The author and publishers would like to express their special thanks to Shigekazu Tanaka and Mrs Ralph Vaughan Williams not only for the loan of their photographs but also for the advice and information they have provided.

17: *Illustrated London News*; 19: BBC Hulton Picture Library; 20: *Illustrated London News*; 27: East Cornwall Bach Festival; 29: Paul Wigmore; 32: Lichfield Arts Festival/ Rackhams of Lichfield; 35: Christopher J. Roberts; 42: Stour Music; 44: both Mrs Ralph Vaughan Williams; 46: Cladonia Resources/David Bryson; 47: Chester Music; 50: Tilford Bach Festival; 54: Dunfermline Abbey Festival; 58: both Aldeburgh Foundation; 62: both Aldeburgh Foundation; 64: Salomon Quartet; 67: Bath Festival; 71: both Brighton Festival/Paul Myatt; 77: City of Cambridge/N. S. Mason-Smith; 81: Shigekazu Tanaka; 87: Glyndebourne Festival Opera; 89: Clive Barda Photography; 92: Roderick Cameron; 95: Harrogate International Festival; 98: Henley Festival of Music and the Arts/Paul Terian; 101: Nigel Luckhurst; 102: Music at Leasowes Bank; 106: C. W. Baynon; 107: Air Photographs; 108: English String Orchestra; 115: Newbury Spring Festival; 118: City of Nottingham; 123: Shigekazu Tanaka; 125: Stogumber Music Festival; 129: Keystone Press Agency Ltd; 130: *Curlew River* by Nigel Luckhurst; others by Alan Holland-Avery ARPS; 133: Shigekazu Tanaka; 135–6: both Mrs Ralph Vaughan Williams; 137: Clive Totman; 141: both Almeida Theatre; 148: EMI/Peter Vernon; 152: City Arts Trust/Bill Mackenzie; 154: both Tom Morris; 155: Nettlefold Festival; 159: all Shigekazu Tanaka; 162–3: all Stately Homes Music Festival; 165: English Bach Festival; 170: both Shigekazu Tanaka; 172: Noël Goodwin; 179: Aberdeen International Youth Festival; 181: Cleveland Inter-TIE; 182: Deal Summer Music Festival; 183, 187: both Concertworld; 189: John D. Sharp; 191: York Early Music Festival; 193: Mrs Ralph Vaughan Williams; 195–6: both Cheltenham International Festival of Music; 197: (left) Zoë Dominic; (right) J. A. Batten; 200: Christian Avril; 201: Huddersfield Contemporary Music Festival; 206: Cardiff Festival of Music; 210: EMI; 216: Swansea Festival of Music and the Arts.

First published in Great Britain 1986
by Robert Royce Limited,
93 Bedwardine Road, London SE19 3AY

Copyright © Richard Adams 1986

British Library Cataloguing in Publication Data

Adams, Richard
A book of British music festivals.
1. Music festivals—Great Britain
I, Title
780'.7'941   ML37.G7
ISBN 0 947728 22 8

Designed by Roger Walker

Phototypeset by Input Typesetting Ltd,
London SW19 8DR
Printed in Italy by New Interlitho S.p.a.

THE RIVERDALE COMPANY, PUBLISHERS

COPUBLISHERS / DISTRIBUTORS

5506 KENILWORTH AVENUE, SUITE 102
RIVERDALE, MARYLAND 20737
(301) 864-2029

Contents

ACKNOWLEDGEMENTS

My grateful thanks to the many directors and organizers of festivals who gave up valuable time to meeting and entertaining or writing to me and answering my many questions. Without their ready co-operation this book could never have been undertaken, let alone completed.

And special thanks to Michael Berkeley, Geoffrey Burgon, Teresa Cahill, Noël Goodwin, Linda Esther Gray, Richard Hickox, Robert Saxton and Simon Standage for agreeing to share with me some of their festival thoughts, experiences and anecdotes.

No writer about festivals in this country can fail to be indebted to the pioneering work of Vincent Jones (his *Festivals in Britain* was published in 1978 by Charles Letts and Co.) and to Sheena Barbour's annual list of *Festivals in Great Britain* (published by John Offord Publications on behalf of the Arts Council). Theirs is the credit for a mass of information, mine the blame for any errors in transcription or interpretation.

Richard Adams
Thame – San Francisco
1985–6

Festivals in England, Scotland and Wales

ST MAGNUS (ORKNEY)

ABERDEEN

DUNKELD & BIRNAM
DUNDEE
PERTH
ST ANDREWS
DUNFERMLINE
STIRLING
MONKLANDS
EDINBURGH
GLASGOW
EAST KILBRIDE

AYR

DUMFRIES

ASHINGTON
NEWCASTLE
HOUGHTON
DURHAM
CLEVELAND
LAKE DISTRICT
SWALEDALE
RICHMONDSHIRE
HELMSLEY
GRASSINGTON
HARROGATE
YORK
LEEDS

MANANAN

SADDLEWORTH
CROSBY
MANCHESTER
WARRINGTON
DISLEY
ST ASAPH
CHESTER
MANSFIELD
LINCOLN
BUXTON
LLANGOLLEN
NOTTINGHAM
FAKENHAM
WREKIN & TELFORD
KEELE
CHARNWOOD
BARMOUTH
LEASOWES BANK
BIRMINGHAM
LEICESTER
KING'S LYNN
NORWICH
CHURCH STRETTON
BROMS-
GROVE
BADDESLEY
CLINTON
CORBY
MILDENHALL
PRESTEIGNE
WARWICK
ALDEBURGH
LLANDRINDOD WELLS
WORCESTER
CHARLECOTE PARK
LUDLOW
CAMBRIDGE
BURY ST
SNAPE
LEOMINSTER
STRATFORD-
UPON-AVON
WAVENDON
EDMUNDS
MALVERN
FISHGUARD
ROSS
PHILOMUSICA FESTIVALS
LLANTILIO CROSSENNY
GUITING
HARPENDEN
WOOBURN
SWANSEA
RHYMNEY VALLEY
STROUD
HENLEY
WINDSOR
VALE OF GLAMORGAN
LLANDAFF
LONDON
CARDIFF
BRISTOL
BANSTEAD
GILLINGHAM
THORNBURY
BATH
NEWBURY
BRACKNELL
GREAT COMP
BROADSTAIRS
GLYNDEBOURNE
CANTERBURY
MINEHEAD & EXMOOR
SALISBURY
BATTLE
PETWORTH
CHIDDINGLY
RYE
STOGUMBER
CHICHESTER
ST LEONARDS
DOLTON & DOWLAND
WIMBORNE MINSTER
ARUNDEL
BRIGHTON
EXETER
PORTSMOUTH
SIDMOUTH
ASHBURTON
DAWLISH

ST IVES

GUERNSEY

Not to Scale

ST MAGNUS
(ORKNEY) ✛

Specialist Festivals
Youth Festivals
Competitive Festivals
Festivals in Churches &
 Cathedrals
Organ Festivals

ABERDEEN △

DUNFERMLINE ✺✛

KEY:
○ Specialist Festivals
△ Youth Festivals
□ Competitive Festivals
✛ Festivals in Churches and Cathedrals
✺ Organ Festivals

CLEVELAND ◪

● Windermere
□ MARY WAKEFIELD
HARROGATE △
HUDDERSFIELD ○   ○ YORK
              LEEDS

✺ MANCHESTER

● Chester
● Stoke on Trent   ✛ BOSTON

LLANGOLLEN ◪

△   ✺ OUNDLE   ○ NORWICH
SHREWSBURY ✛ LICHFIELD   ✛ PETERBOROUGH ✛ GORLESTON

                                    ✛ WANGFORD

WORCESTER ✛
HEREFORD ✛   △ MILTON KEYNES
      PERSHORE ✛   ○ COLCHESTER
MADLEY ✛   ✛ ○ CHELTENHAM
GLOUCESTER ⊕ ✛ BARNWOOD   ✛ ASHWELL
LLANTILIO CROSSENNY ✛   ST ALBANS ✺
              ✛ LEONARD STANLEY   ✛ LITTLE MISSENDEN
LLANDAFF ✛   ✛ BATH   LONDON ◐△ ✛   CANTERBURY
              ✛ CRICKLADE   (KING'S WEEK)
BRISTOL   LEITH HILL □   ◐
(ST MARY   ✛ EDINGTON   BOXHILL △   △ DEAL
REDCLIFFE)   ○   SEVENOAKS ⊕ STOUR
SALISBURY ✛ HASLEMERE ○ ✛ TILFORD   MAYFIELD
      WINCHESTER ✛   □ PETERSFIELD
MILTON ABBEY ✛   ✛ CHICHESTER

✛ ST ENDELLION
      ✛ ST GERMANS
✛ TRURO

GUERNSEY
✛

Not to Scale

A Festival Calendar

Key: L = London; S = Scotland; W = Wales

Festival dates naturally vary from year to year. The following list, however, gives some idea of the time of year at which individual festivals take place, and of their order in relation to each other. Up-to-date information may be obtained by phoning or writing to the festival office in question (see Index).

JANUARY
Park Lane Group Young Artists and 20th Century Music Series (L)

FEBRUARY
Broadstairs Festival of Music
Leeds Twentieth Century Music (biennial – 1987)
St Andrews Festival (biennial – 1987) (S)

MARCH
Leith Hill Musical Festival
Camden Festival (L)
Petersfield Musical Festival
Harrogate International Youth Music Festival
St Endellion Festival of Music and Drama (Easter Festival)
Barnet Festival (L)
Cleveland Music Festival (biennial – 1987)
Keele – British Music Week (biennial – 1987)

APRIL
London Handel Festival (St George's, Hanover Square) (L)
Thornbury Arts Festival
Colchester – Essex Festival
Leeds – City of Leeds College of Music Festival
Gillingham Arts Festival
Bromsgrove Festival
Covent Garden Proms – Opera (L)
Ashwell Music Festival
English Bach Festival
Monklands Community Festival (S)

MAY
Llantilio Crossenny Festival of Music and Drama (W)
Brighton Festival
Lincoln Festival
Mayfield Festival of Music and the Arts (biennial – 1986)
Warrington Festival
Glasgow – Mayfest (S)
Barnwood Festival of the Arts
Newbury Spring Festival
Bury St Edmunds Festival
Bristol Proms
Newcastle Festival
Wrekin and Telford Festival
Battle Festival
Charnwood Festival
Aberdeen – Scottish National Orchestra Music Week (S)
St Germans – East Cornwall Bach Festival
Ayrshire Arts Festival (S)
Dundee – Scottish National Orchestra Proms (S)
Dolton and Dowland Festival
Malvern Festival
Perth Festival of the Arts (S)
Bath International Festival of Music and the Arts
Dumfries and Galloway Arts Festival (S)
Exeter Festival
Gloucestershire and Worcestershire – Philomusica Festivals
Nottingham Festival
Ross and District Festival of the Arts (biennial – 1986)
Swaledale Festival
Glyndebourne Festival Opera

Spitalfields Festival (Christ Church) (L)
Greenwich Festival (L)
Stately Homes Music Festival
Tilford Bach Festival
Wavendon Summer Season
Piccadilly Festival (L)
Ashington Festival (biennial – 1987)
Banstead Arts Festival (biennial – 1987)
Fakenham Festival of Music and the Arts
(biennial – 1987)
Lake District – Mary Wakefield Westmorland
Music Festival (biennial – 1987)
Richmondshire Festival (biennial – 1987)

JUNE

Portsmouth Festival
Boston Festival
Edinburgh – Craigmillar Festival (S)
East Kilbride Festival (S)
Edinburgh – Scottish National Orchestra Proms
(S)
Aldeburgh Festival of Music and the Arts
Boxhill Music Festival
Merton Festival (L)
Leominster Festival (biennial – 1986)
Mildenhall – Forest Heath Arts Festival
Almeida Festival (L)
Leicester Proms
Sidmouth Arts Festival
Baddesley Clinton Festival
Pershore Festival
Aberdeen – Bon-Accord Festival (S)
Edinburgh – Wester Hailes Festival (S)
Dawlish Arts Festival
Truro – Three Spires Festival
Llandaff Festival (W)
Manchester – Hallé Proms Summer Festival
Orkney – St Magnus Festival (S)
Grassington Festival
Stour Music – Festival of Music in East Kent
Ludlow Festival
Birmingham – CBSO Proms
Sevenoaks Summer Festival
Mananan International Festival of Music and the
Arts
Dunkeld and Birnam Arts Festival (S)
Glasgow – Scottish National Orchestra Proms
(S)
Bracknell – Wilde Festival of Music
Stogumber Music Festival
Leonard Stanley – Music at the Priory
Petworth Festival
Harpenden – Bourne Music Festival
Dunfermline Abbey Festival (S)
Rhymney Valley Arts Festival (W)
Wimborne Minster Arts Festival

York Festival and Mystery Plays (quadrennial –
1988)

JULY

Guernsey – Notre Dame Festival de Musique
Norwich Festival of Contemporary Church
Music
Covent Garden Proms – Ballet (L)
Lichfield Festival
Ashburton Festival
Warwick Arts Festival
York Early Music Festival
Cheltenham International Festival of Music
Chichester Festivities
City of London Festival (L)
Llangollen International Musical Eisteddfod (W)
Henley Festival of Music and the Arts
National Festival of Music for Youth (L)
Shrewsbury International Music Festival
Glasgow – Easterhouse Summer Festival (S)
Richmond Festival (L)
Canterbury – King's Week
Stratford-upon-Avon Festival
Wangford Festival
Bristol – Redcliffe Music Festival
Minehead and Exmoor Festival
Shrewsbury – Music at Leasowes Bank
Chester Summer Music Festival
Haslemere Festival
BBC Henry Wood Promenade Concerts (L)
Fishguard Festival (W)
Buxton Festival
Cambridge Festival
Cleveland Inter-TIE (biennial – 1986)
Oundle International Organ Week
Guiting Festival of Music and the Arts
Church Stretton and South Shropshire Arts
Festival
Charlecote Park Festival
Southern Cathedrals Festival
King's Lynn Festival
Deal Summer Music Festival
Helmsley Festival
Harrogate International Festival
Aberdeen International Youth Festival (S)
Great Comp Festival
Madley Festival
Peterborough Cathedral Arts Festival
St Albans International Organ Festival

AUGUST

Stirling District Festival (S)
Royal National Eisteddfod of Wales (W)
Snape – Maltings Proms
Disley – Lyme Park Festival
Arundel Festival

St Endellion Festival of Music and Drama
  (Summer Festival)
Worcester Entertains
Edinburgh International Festival (S)
Vale of Glamorgan Festival (W)
Edington Festival
South Bank Summer Music (L)
Barbican Summer Festival (L)
Three Choirs Festival
Milton Abbey Music Festival
Presteigne Festival (W)
Rye Festival
Aldeburgh – Rostropovich Festival (next is 1987)

SEPTEMBER

St Ives September Festival
Barmouth Arts Festival (W)
Llandrindod Wells Festival (W)
Salisbury Festival
Lake District Festival
Wooburn Festival
St Leonards Festival
London Dance Umbrella (L)
St Asaph – North Wales Music Festival (W)
Canterbury Festival
Windsor Festival
Swansea Festival of Music and the Arts (W)
Cricklade Music Festival

Manchester Festival and International Organ
  Competition
Saddleworth Festival of the Arts (quadrennial –
  1987)

OCTOBER

Chiddingly Festival
Bath – West of England Organ Festival
Houghton Feast
Stroud Festival
Crosby Arts Festival
Mansfield Festival
Little Missenden Festival
Early Music Centre Festival (L)
Nettlefold Festival (L)
Milton Keynes Festival
Corby Festival
Hackney Festival (L)
Durham Music Festival
Norfolk and Norwich Triennial Festival of Music
  and the Arts (triennial – 1988)

NOVEMBER

Gorleston – St Andrew's Festival of Music and
  the Arts
Huddersfield Contemporary Music Festival
Cardiff Festival of Music (W)
Leeds Musical Festival (biennial – 1987)

Introduction

'Festivals,' declared Sir Thomas Beecham, 'are bunk!' It was a strange judgement, perhaps, coming from the man responsible for the influential Delius festivals in London in 1929 and 1946, but one with which other people – music-lovers as well as musicians – have been known to sympathize. Festivals, it has been maintained, can trivialize great art, reducing it to the status of a glittering accessory for inflated social occasions, blunting its impact by placing it in a wholly irrelevant context of flower-shows and fireworks. 'You know the definition of a music festival?' a cynic once asked. 'A festival is a garden fête with string quartet.' But that, happily, is not all there is to be said on the subject. For one thing, music festivals provide a hardly equalled opportunity for people to attempt the unusual: maybe by gathering forces to rehearse and perform a Schubert mass or a Mendelssohn symphony in some ill-lit, draughty church or community centre, miles from the nearest concert hall; maybe by raising the money to engage a pianist of international standing to play live, in the same draughty church, music that in the normal run of things is only available to his audience on the radio or on disc; maybe by tapping the latent talent of an entire community or turning a listening ear to new music – perhaps even music written with local resources in mind. The actress Joan Plowright pointed out recently that there are three prerequisites for a festival of the first order: one – it should focus on the special; two – it should be brief and uncluttered; and three – the celebration in which it unites performers and audiences should derive from a sense of passionate and shared commitment.

It was a deeply felt desire to celebrate that prompted the great outburst of new festivals at the end of the Second World War. In the drab austerity of the late forties, men and women throughout Britain sought ways of rekindling spirits, of injecting new colour into their monochrome lives. Festivals – culminating in the hugely ambitious Festival of Britain in 1951 – provided something of an answer, assisted by the funding policy of the infant Arts Council. A second surge of festivals, in the sixties and early seventies, was more concerned with self-help than with jubilee. The feeling of the time was that the country's major artistic centres were becoming increasingly remote and self-absorbed, and that it was up to members of outlying communities to develop their own cultural resources if they were to keep pace with their city-dwelling brothers and sisters. A significant number of new festivals from this period were modest undertakings, located off the beaten track.

Cultural enrichment is not, of course, supplied by classical music alone and few of the festivals launched in Britain since 1945 are devoted wholly and exclusively to music. The present survey covers events in which a substantial musical input is combined with interests as diverse as architecture, sport, the visual arts, fell-walking, kite-flying, steam traction, theatre and *haute cuisine*. They come in all shapes and sizes, from the gargantuan such as Edinburgh to the intimate such as Guiting, which for a few days each July provides yet another good reason for motoring deep into the Cotswolds. I cannot pretend to have said something about every event that takes place in England, Scotland and Wales: I have not, for instance, included one-off festivals – with the single exception of Stephen Pile's hilarious Nether Wallop International Arts Festival (1984) – or those which are of shorter duration than two days. Nor have I paid much attention to brand new festivals, my review being confined in the main to events with an established annual (biennial, triennial or – in one case – quadrennial) pattern. Purely competitive festivals are not included, though Leith Hill and Petersfield, venerable institutions that have shifted focus over the years from competition to performance, receive the attention they deserve.

When one considers the nearly two hundred British festivals covered here, the thing that strikes most forcibly perhaps is the richness and variety of their music-making. There are festivals devoted to church music, to early music, to the most radical of contemporary music; festivals of opera and of chamber music; festivals that celebrate the English or Scottish or Welsh tradition; festivals for the organ, for choirs, for young people; festivals that each year devise and work to a specific theme, festivals that explore the music of a single composer; festivals that have no fixed abode and festivals that are closely associated with particular buildings. I have attempted to highlight some of these features in the way I have organized the various sections of the book. Scattered among these sections there are several 'private views' of the festival scene, volunteered by well-known musical figures – composers Michael Berkeley, Geoffrey Burgon and Robert Saxton, singers Teresa Cahill and Linda Esther Gray, critic Noël Goodwin, conductor Richard Hickox and violinist Simon Standage. The book concludes with a calendar of festivals, in the approximate order in which they take place each year, together with contact addresses and telephone numbers.

It takes little more than a glance at this calendar to appreciate that – rather as with pilgrimages in the time of Chaucer – there is very much a season for festivals in Britain today. Though there is a trickle of activity during the winter months, it is only when April's sweet showers are past and gone that the current begins to flow in earnest. From the beginning of May until the end of October there is no letting up: carnivals and concerts, barbecues and bunting remind the world that festivals are somehow more festive when the sun is high in the sky.

Some festivals are born of pure love – that of Mstislav and Galina Rostropovich for the Aldeburgh of Britten and Pears, for example – others owe their being to the happy accident that someone with the necessary dedication and drive was in the right place at the right time – Ruth, Lady Fermoy in King's Lynn, Pat Harrison at Little Missenden, Russell Brandon at Guiting, Netlam Bigg in Stroud. Some, like Canterbury, spring fully grown from the minds of resourceful directors, others have more tentative beginnings. One English festival developed from a highly successful performance of *Trial by Jury*, one in Wales started life as a carol concert. Some – Glyndebourne, Great Comp, the Stately Homes Music Festival – depend on the generosity of the owners or trustees of fine houses, others on the architectural and acoustic properties of an ancient church or cathedral. There is a festival in Scotland that came about because of a bypass, and another – south of the border – that developed from celebrations surrounding the unveiling of a new town plan. In short, there are as many reasons for festivals as there are festivals. And the firmest based are those events which demonstrate, to some degree or other, that passionate commitment to an ideal – whether it is reviving old music or exploring new, encouraging the young or motivating an entire community – in the absence of which the sounds of celebration ring hollow and fade all too quickly.

It is a commitment which shows itself in a hundred different ways – from the enthusiasm of the amateur who gives his all in the once-yearly *Messiah* or stays up half the night helping erect a platform for a visiting string quartet, to the generosity of the professional who waives her fee for a recital that costs more effort and trouble and patience, and offers a good deal less in terms of glamour, than a South Bank appearance. 'Let's play *all* the repeats,' conductor Jeffrey Tate was overheard to say while rehearsing the Mozart *Jupiter* Symphony with the English Chamber Orchestra. 'After all – it's a festival!'

—I—
Origins

The word 'festival' derives from the Latin *festivitas* and a sense of celebration still exists at the heart of any festival worthy the name. But as celebrations, festivals are neither spontaneous nor haphazard, the cultural equivalent of dancing in the fountains at midnight. They require careful preparation. They are calculated affairs, deliberate in their marking of men, of achievements, of occasions, and – even today – many of them retain something of the sense of ritual from which they draw their origins.

Music was very likely an important though secondary aspect of the earliest festivals, which were first and foremost religious occasions. They grew out of the cycle of the year, as special and sometimes spectacular reminders to the gods of the people's need for good crops or success in the season's battles, or as a means of registering gratitude for benefits already received. In ancient Greece, in settings of breathcatching magnificence, men gathered to pay their respects to the guardians of their destiny with solemn ritual: Artemis at Ephesus, Apollo at Delphi, Zeus on the plain at Olympia. Music, dancing and display played their part in the ritual, but they were not its *raison d'être*. In modern times, the positions have been reversed: now the music festival is, more often than not, an independent cultural enterprise in which – as the latest edition of Grove points out – 'it is still often possible to discover some vestige of ancient ritual in its celebration of town or nation, political or religious philosophy, living or historical person'. The wreath-bearing, banner-waving, anthemsinging Last Night of the Proms bears eloquent witness to the idea that ritual, in the context of the music festival, is still very much alive and well – as indeed it is in the wreath-bearing, banner-waving, anthem-singing ceremonial of the modern Olympic Games. It is maybe a shorter step than we think from the arena in Kensington Gore to those in Moscow or Los Angeles or Seoul.

It was in late-mediaeval times in Europe that the festival took on a more secular identity. Now, instead of honouring the gods, music was employed to celebrate the greatness of men. The Italian *festa* combined courtly entertainment for the nobility with processions to amuse the ordinary people. Music and pageantry joined together to celebrate the meetings, marriages and coronations with which kings and emperors fuelled the flame of their earthly glory. The series of wood-engravings executed around the turn of the fifteenth century to immortalize the triumphs of Maximilian I depict instrumentalists on horseback enlisted to accompany – in more senses than one – the imperial progress. When, in 1520, Henry VIII of England and François I of France met formally in the lavish pavilions of the Field of the Cloth of Gold, each was attended by his own domestic and court musicians, whose tasks ranged from singing daily services to providing entertainment at and between meals. No less a composer than Lassus was employed to compose suitable music for the eighteen days of festivity that surrounded the marriage in 1568 of Duke Wilhelm V of Bavaria to Renata of Lorraine. Not surprisingly, perhaps, the Renaissance princes of the Roman Church sought to match their temporal counterparts by ordering music in 'festal' style for important occasions. Elaborate and extended settings of the mass added to the high solemnity of great feasts and saints' days.

In late seventeenth-century England, one particular feast – that of Saint Cecilia, patron of music, on 22 November – was appropriated by the laity. The occasion was quickly turned into a celebration not of the lady, but of the gift of music itself: it was probably the first annual festival to shrug off its specifically religious associations. Each new year produced verses by poets of the calibre of Dryden set to music by composers of the calibre of Purcell, Handel and Blow.

In 1713, Worcester Cathedral was the setting for the singing of a grand *Te Deum* in celebration of the signing of the Treaty of Utrecht. In the years that followed, that occasion became the pattern for annual gatherings at which the choirs of Worcester, Gloucester and Hereford Cathedrals joined together to make festive music. By 1724, what was later to become known as the Three Choirs Festival had ceased to be simply celebratory, having also taken on the charitable function of raising funds for the maintenance and education of the orphans of poor clergy in the three dioceses. The notion of enlisting music to help raise money for deserving causes goes back earlier than the Three Choirs, however. In 1655, the London-based Corporation of the Sons of the Clergy had the idea of an annual service for the relief of distress among clergy families. By the last decade of the century, the so-called 'Festival of the Sons of the Clergy' was being celebrated annually – each May – in Saint Paul's Cathedral. It was the precursor of those mammoth concerts – the largest on record employing some six thousand performers – given by the children of the London charity schools, which attracted the praise of composers as widely different in their backgrounds and tastes as Haydn and Berlioz. The charity pattern was repeated many times outside London. A large number of festivals established during the second half of the eighteenth century in rapidly expanding provincial centres such as Leeds (1767), Birmingham (1768), Norwich (1770), Chester (1772), Newcastle (1778), Liverpool (1784), Manchester (1785), Sheffield (1786) and York (1791) had as their explicit object the founding or financial support of new hospitals.

In 1887, Dr A. H. Mann, the organist of King's College, Cambridge, got together a choir of townspeople to take part in festival concerts to mark Queen Victoria's Jubilee. Addenbrooke's Hospital benefited by over two hundred pounds from the

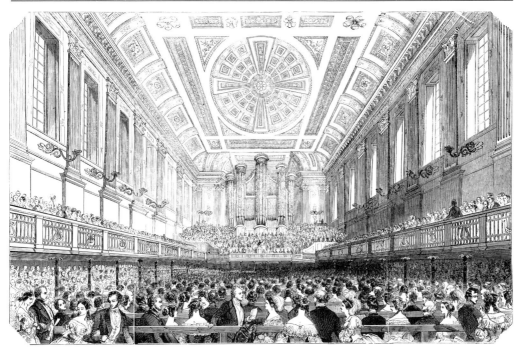

First performance of Mendelssohn's *Elijah* in Birmingham – from the *ILN* of 29th August 1846.

venture, and such was the enthusiasm of the amateur participants that 'festival services' were held each June for the next fifteen years. What is more, the festival choir formed itself into an association for 'the advancement of musical taste and the cultivation of musical talent in the town and neighbourhood of Cambridge' which later became the Cambridge Philharmonic Society. Festivals had come to mean more than simply celebrations and good deeds: they had acquired a social importance in bringing people together and encouraging them to share in the enjoyment and making of music. Indeed, such had been the case as early as 1812, when a certain Daniel Lysons, writing about the 'annual musical meeting' of the Three Choirs, had described an institution 'which, at the same time that it provides relief for so large a portion of the children of misery, promotes the ends of social intercourse and affords the lovers of music an opportunity of hearing the most exquisite harmonic performances'.

There has always been a strong sense of the local in festival music-making. The focus is on a particular town or village, sometimes even on a particular building. But above all it is on a particular community of people, whether they are involved as performers – and many festivals rely heavily on homegrown talent, especially in the choral field – or as members of the audience. When, in 1938, D. G. Stoll published his survey of European music festivals, he painted a picture of an international festival audience constantly on the move, engaged in a never-ending musical pilgrimage to hear fine performances by the best musicians. Though the more well-heeled and musically motivated among us may still set off on this seasonal quest, today's festivals – particularly those run on a more modest scale – tend to attract the bulk of their audiences from the near neighbourhood. Indeed, many festivals have as their avowed aim the bringing of live music of all kinds– jazz, chamber and orchestral, folk, opera – to parts of the country otherwise rather barren of musical activity. That is not to say, however, that festival organizers are blind to the tourist potential of their enterprises. All festivals have to pay their way and it is presumably no accident that so many take place in the spring and summer months in areas of Britain which have more than a little attraction as holiday resorts. The idea of combining music with tourism actually goes back well over a hundred years: to 1859 and the Handel Centenary Festival held in London's Crystal Palace, whose organizers, in an effort to drum up custom, arranged for the printing of some fifty thousand prospectuses to be circulated in the European offices of the railway companies whose lines served the Crystal Palace. In modern times, improved communications and tourist promotion have helped raise some of the larger, longer-established British festivals – such as Edinburgh, Bath, Cheltenham – to international status.

Handel has always been one of the most popular of festival composers. A number of festivals started life with the aim of performing his – and only his – music. They were to be celebrations of England's greatest, though adopted, musical son, with renderings of *Messiah* and others of his large-scale oratorios and operas as their centrepieces. Most notable of these heroic occasions was the Handel Commemorative Festival initiated in 1784 in Westminster Abbey. Everything was on a grand scale, from the setting to the size of the forces employed – over five hundred performers descending on the capital from all parts of England. During the century and a half that followed, this trend developed apace: the word 'festival' became synonymous with vast cohorts of singers and instrumentalists in overblown performances, regardless of their suitability to the music programmed. As late as 1926, the last of the series of triennial Handel festivals that had begun with that well-publicized Crystal Palace jamboree of 1859 featured no fewer than four thousand performers.

Though the festival he organized at the Paris Opéra late in 1840 employed a more modest force of six hundred, Berlioz claimed – with considerable pride – that it was the largest concert yet seen in the French capital. He went further, lamenting the way in which the term 'festival' – 'which I was the first to employ on the posters in Paris' – had subsequently become debased:

> This word . . . is now used indiscriminately in the most ludicrous contexts. We have 'festivals' of music and dancing in the meanest pleasure gardens, with three violins, a drum and two cornets.

For Berlioz, festivals meant magnificence. He saw no incongruity in using, at his Opéra concert, the huge choir he had mustered for the Dies Irae and Lacrimosa movements of his own *Requiem*, to perform unaccompanied Palestrina.

Though he may well have been the first, Handel is by no means the only composer to have been fêted in concerts devoted exclusively to his music. The achievements

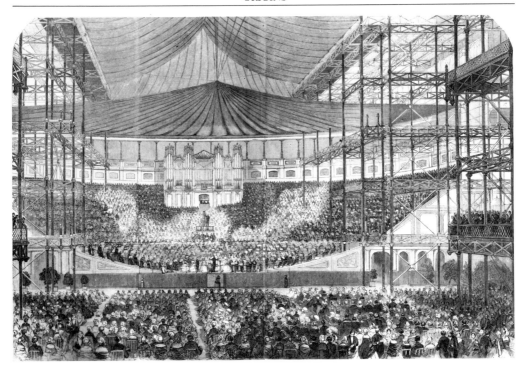

The first Handel Festival at the Crystal Palace in 1859.

of others have been honoured with their Bach or Delius or Beethoven or Stravinsky festivals. In 1871, the Royal Albert Hall in London was the scene of a Wagner festival, in which the composer himself participated. Its aim was to raise money to pay off the huge debts incurred in the building of the new opera house at Bayreuth. It was not, however, a success and it was not repeated. On the other hand, there are several notable examples of festivals associated with living composers which have – in their time – become splendid beacons on the British musical landscape: the Three Choirs with its encouragement of Elgar, Vaughan Williams and many others; Leith Hill, where for forty-eight years Vaughan Williams was resident conductor; Thaxted, inspired and guided by Holst; and – perhaps most brilliant of all – Aldeburgh, raised to world renown by its association with Britten. Festivals such as these, in providing composers with the occasion to write and perform new works, to meet and talk music with players and listeners alike, to share their gifts and their experience, have made a huge contribution to our cultural heritage. And the tradition is very much alive in Peter Maxwell Davies's Orkney festival of St Magnus.

The encouragement of amateur music-making which is today an intrinsic feature of many festivals derives in part from the competitive events which became especially popular in England in the middle of the nineteenth century – though the comparable traditions of the Welsh *eisteddfod* and Irish *feis* reach a good deal further back into mist-wreathed history. The setting of choir against choir in friendly rivalry created a demand for a good deal of new choral music. It also provided suitable occasion

THE THREE CHOIRS FESTIVAL AT GLOUCESTER

The Triennial Musical Festival at Gloucester has, as usual, been favoured with brilliant weather, and nearly all the prominent stars of the musical world of England have been present.

1.—Sir Edward Elgar well wrapped up on Monday, when he conducted rehearsals of his works.

2.—Mr. Geo. Bernard Shaw, wearing a steward's badge, leaving the Cathedral on Wednesday.

3.—Mr. W. H. Reed (left), leader of orchestra and solo violinist, with Mr. H. W. Sumsion, organist of Cathedral.

4.—Miss Elsie Suddaby (solo soprano) (left) and Miss Muriel Brunskill (solo contralto) (right).

5.—Dr. Percy Hull, organist of Hereford Cathedral.

6.—Mr. Horace Stevens (solo bass) and Mr. Heddle Nash (solo tenor) at the "Elijah" performance.

7.—Dr. Vaughan Williams, the composer.

8.—Sir Ivor Atkins and Sir Walford Davies in front. Col. Frank Isaac, of Worcester, behind.

9.—Mr. A. F. Watts and Dr. Lee Williams.

10.—Mr. S. A. Pitcher and Professor Herbert Howells.

11.—Mrs. Croft and Miss Doris Leach.

["Cheltenham Chronicle" Photos. Copies 1s. and 1s. 9d. each.]

The Three Choirs Festival at Gloucester in 1928 – from the *Illustrated London News*. The 'prominent stars of the musical world of England' included Elgar, William Reed (the violinist, composer and author), Heddle Nash (the tenor), Vaughan Williams and Herbert Howells.

for promoting new techniques. It was in 1860, for instance, that John Curwen launched his Crystal Palace festivals with the aim of popularizing his tonic sol-fa system. The movement came to its peak in the Mary Wakefield competitions founded in Kendal in 1885. Today, there are still festivals which – like Leith Hill at the height of Vaughan Williams's reign – invite individual choirs to compete against each other during the day, and then to join together in perfect amity for an evening performance with professional soloists and orchestra. There has, over the years, been a good deal of public debate as to the merits or otherwise of competitive festivals. Some hold that competition is the only way to ensure continuing improvement in standards of performance, while others believe that it blurs recognition of what ought to be the proper objective of all festivals – the performance of music for its own sake.

During the past forty years, festivals of all sorts – not just the musical variety – have proliferated in this country as never before. They come in all shapes and sizes, draping themselves over great cities or tucking into village corners, and they fill a wide range of needs. Music festivals in particular are closer to the centre of our cultural life than is perhaps the case in any other country in the world. Before the Second World War, D. G. Stoll expressed the view that they ought to be essentially educative – the means of reviving a healthy curiosity in, an ability to wonder at, our musical heritage. Acknowledging that few festivals, if any, can hope to be financially self-supporting, he maintained that we should regard them 'as investments which will show no interest save wiser, happier, and more rational men and women'. His sentiments will undoubtedly strike a chord with those who devote so much in the way of time, resources and passion to the success of music festivals today.

—2—

Festivals in Churches and Cathedrals

Abbeys, minsters, cathedrals, royal peculiars . . . priory churches, collegiate churches, parish churches . . . chapels great and small – throughout the length and breadth of Britain, ecclesiastical buildings of every description provide the focus and inspiration for festival music-making: from the Cathedral of St Magnus in the Orkneys to the Church of Notre Dame du Rosaire in Guernsey; from Truro's three spires in the West to St Andrew's, Gorleston, in the East. And just as festivals themselves vary enormously in scale – try putting the modest activities of Madley alongside the Three Choirs in full cry – so their settings range from the dauntingly vast (St Paul's Cathedral in London) to the intimate (the Church of St Endelienta in North Cornwall). They may possess the elegant proportions of King's College, Cambridge, or the more tattered majesty of Christ Church, Spitalfields; they may be riotously Baroque like St George's, Hanover Square, or purest Early English like Salisbury Cathedral. They may be masterworks by celebrated architects like Wren or Hawksmoor or the quiet achievement of some unknown mediaeval mason.

Some festivals were born in church – maybe thanks to the cultural farsightedness of a parish priest, maybe because the whole point of their existence was to fund the restoration of the organ or the provision of new hassocks – and have remained firmly rooted in their parent soil ever since. Spitalfields, Llantilio Crossenny and Dunfermline Abbey are all cases in point. Others, more secular in origin perhaps, have taken advantage of the space and facilities that churches have to offer in the same way that they have cashed in on such amenities as school halls or the drawing-rooms of country houses. Newbury, for example, employed no fewer than seven different churches and chapels in its 1985 programme. There are festivals that have outgrown the churches that originally gave them being. It did not take long for that at Gorleston, founded in 1969 and held at the beginning of November, to spread its influence and activities across the River Bure into the cultural vacuum of Great Yarmouth. Others – like that at St Mary Redcliffe in Bristol (mid-July) – have sprung up and flourished in buildings famed for high standards in music-making for many years. There are village festivals like that which grew in the mid-fifties out of an informal gathering of choristers and choral scholars at Ashwell Church, near

Baldock in Hertfordshire, and which devotes a week or so in late April to furthering the cause of church music. And there are much more ambitious affairs, like the one which started in 1985 in Peterborough Cathedral and is now to become a biennial event celebrating English music from all periods.

The reasons for the popularity of ecclesiastical buildings as festival venues are not hard to determine. In the first place, the Church has had an important influence on the development of the British musical tradition by providing a constant demand for new choral settings of its various offices. All our major composers, from Byrd to Britten, by way of Purcell and Handel, Elgar and Vaughan Williams, have felt this influence. On the Continent, the choral masterpieces of Bach and Mozart, of Berlioz and Verdi also sprang from a religious impulse, and it is these works that – on account of their celebratory and uplifting nature – have found special favour with festival organizers and audiences alike. And where better to perform them than in church?

Of course, the reasons for mounting a concert or recital in church may sometimes be more fundamental, more practical: an organ is needed and the only one in the area is at St Miriam's; or we want to put on a Brahms symphony and the only place that can possibly house a ninety-piece orchestra, let alone an audience of more than forty, is Barchester Cathedral. That is not to say that churches or cathedrals always make ideal concert halls. Seasoned festival administrators know exactly the sort of problems that they present: where are the players to change and store their instruments between the afternoon rehearsal and the evening performance? where is the temporary staging to come from and how can it be assembled without disrupting normal services? what on earth can be done about the lighting? Audiences have their problems too. They have to learn to equip themselves with cushions (against those narrow, penitential pews) and rugs (against the unaccountable chill that seems to descend on all churches about Compline time, even in high summer), to survive the interval without refreshment and make prior arrangements so as to avoid having to queue indefinitely for the vestry's one lavatory. And, having come to terms with such minor irritations, they have to deal with that vague, nagging worry about the propriety of clapping in church – though, happily, the days are long past when Sir Adrian Boult used to give his audiences short homilies on the subject.

But such inconveniences do little to dampen the enthusiasm of audiences, largely because they are mightily outweighed by the grandeur and sense of occasion that a church setting can add to the simplest recital. What great music does for the ear, a fine church does for the eye. Where better to lose oneself in the echoing spaces of the *Tallis Fantasia* or in the intellectual labyrinth of *The Well-Tempered Clavier* than beneath such airy vaults, amid such deepening shadows, watching the light fade slowly beyond the ornate tracery of a great rose window? Where indeed? – unless, of course, as happens increasingly at the more prestigious festivals, the atmosphere is destroyed by glaringly insistent television lighting, by cables and gantries, by cameras sidling back and forth between listeners and music. But that is another story.

BARNWOOD

St Lawrence's Church, Barnwood, dates from Norman times and in its early years had close links with the great Abbey of St Peter – now the Cathedral – in nearby Gloucester. Barnwood has itself long since been absorbed into the Gloucester suburbs, but it proclaims its individualism and independence through the modest week-long festival that occupies the church, and sometimes one or two other local buildings, in early May. The festival – started in 1964 by the then Vicar of St Lawrence's, the Revd Michael Seacome, himself an artist and musician of note – exists with the sole idea of providing a few days' concentrated cultural activity in a notably beautiful setting.

There is no expectation of financial gain – not even for charitable purposes – no hidden motive of luring reluctant church-goers into the fold. Barnwood is a festival very much for its own sake, recognized throughout the Gloucester area for the contribution it makes to the city's cultural life. Events tend to be on a small scale, the Cathedral being left to put on the big shows at appropriate times. Drama is catered for largely by local amateurs who specialize in anthology evenings and poetry readings rather than major productions. Exhibitions of painting and photography attract widespread interest and entries come from throughout the county, while illustrated lectures on topics ranging from 'Manuscript Paintings of the 14th and 15th Centuries' to 'Swan Rescue' regularly draw good crowds. Music is featured most days, with mainly professional performers, and recitals for piano, organ or harp are the festival staple. The organizers make a point of encouraging young musicians early in their careers – partly because the festival budget does not run to big names, but also because they see Barnwood as an ideal platform for some of the many developing artists in need of concert experience. That said, the list of past performers includes some conjurable names: Philip Fowke, Anthony Peebles, Richard Markham, Robert Spencer, Alexander Kok, Penelope Walker, Susan Drake, Harry Gabb, Walter Landauer and Joseph Cooper.

Very much a parish festival, Barnwood is nevertheless very welcoming to visitors, whether it be to listen to an illustrated talk on christening customs, followed by a glass of fruit wine in a local living-room; to spend a Sunday afternoon listening to the Mercia String Quartet play Beethoven, Brahms and Dvořák; to attend a recital by the German organist Magnus Jacobs; or to support one of the Occasional Players' Elizabethan evenings.

BOSTON

Plus ça change . . . Boston Festival, as it is today, is the direct descendant of an earlier event, founded in 1969, centred on this ancient Lincolnshire town's handsome Church of St Botolph and consequently known as the 'Stump Festival'. 'Consequently' because for centuries the 'Boston Stump' has been the name popularly applied to the church's superb octagonal tower, which rises to 272 feet and dominates both town and countryside. Seafarers plying the Wash of old used it as a beacon and it can be seen for miles across the Fens and even from parts of Norfolk. The Stump Festival revolved mainly around amateur artists and performers, and was designed in part to provide each June a fortnight's entertainment and activity for the benefit of the flocks of tourists that come to rest in the town – many of them from that other Boston, founded by Lincolnshire emigrants, on the other side of the Atlantic. However, in 1978, a special festival was devised, employing imported professionals alongside the talented locals, to inaugurate the Sam Newsom Music Centre, housed in a converted eighteenth-century grain warehouse, and the following year it was decided to repeat the formula for the first official Boston Festival.

The Boston Festival has, in many ways, taken over where the Stump Festival left off: the dates have remained the same – celebration of St Botolph's Day, 17 June, occupies the centre of each season; the mixed-arts pattern with a healthy fringe involvement has not altered; St Botolph's itself continues to play host to major concerts. But important changes have also taken place: new venues have been developed, such as the Blackfriars' Arts Centre – a converted early-mediaeval friary – the fifteenth-century Guildhall and Fydell House, an elegant pilastered town-house dating from 1726, which is the home of Pilgrim College and has one of its rooms permanently reserved for visitors from the Massachusetts Boston; while the shift towards greater professional participation, especially on the musical front, has if anything been more pronounced in recent years.

Programmes are generously varied: from large-scale concerts, featuring orchestras such as the English Sinfonia (under Steuart Bedford), the then BBC Northern Symphony Orchestra (under Janos Furst) and the Northern Sinfonia conducted by Rudolf Schwarz, to specialist recitals performed by groups like the London Baroque Soloists, the Landini Consort and London Collegiate Brass. Solo recitals have been given by Malcolm Binns, Osian Ellis, Michel Dalberto, Craig Sheppard, David Wilde, Carlo Curley and Pascal Rogé, while the Allegri, Alberni, Coull and Delmé Quartets (the last named with Jack Brymer as guest clarinettist) and the Borodin Piano Trio have drawn appreciative audiences to chamber concerts. Among the big names, recent visitors have included Boris Belkin (playing the Tchaikovsky Violin Concerto), Radu Lupu and Carlos Bonell (in Rodrigo's *Concierto de Aranjuez*). A special, but by no means surprising, feature of the Boston Festival is the regular participation of American groups, such as the Radcliffe Choral Society from Harvard, who gave a concert ranging from Monteverdi and Weelkes to American spirituals in 1979, the Brainerd High School Choir from Minnesota or the McFarlin United Methodist Choir and Handbell Ringers of Normanton, Oklahoma. Jazz also puts in a regular appearance (the London Ragtime Orchestra, Butch Thompson, Humphrey Lyttelton, Sammy Rimington) as does brass band music. And there is a miscellany of folk music, music from the shows, light-hearted lecture recitals (Brian Kay or John Amis, Richard Baker or Fritz Spiegl) and country music.

The programming, on the other hand, tends to be predictably mainstream. Boston is not, on the whole, the place to go to hear new commissions or first performances

– though Paul Parkinson's *Dream Gold*, written for choirs of local schoolchildren, was premièred at the 1984 festival and Paul Patterson's *European Variations* received their first English performance by the European Community Chamber Orchestra under Yitkin Seow the following year.

And as far as local contributions are concerned – well, they are still there from the 'Stump' days, if more than a little overshadowed now by imported attractions. The Boston Choral Society, the Boston Operatic Society and the Lincolnshire Sinfonia all get a look in from time to time, but – by and large – Boston is now a festival at which the townspeople sit in the auditorium rather than on the platform.

CRICKLADE

London is not the only place that can boast a concert hall on the south bank of the Thames. True, it is an infant river that chatters past the handsome Wiltshire town of Cricklade, and true, St Sampson's Church is more than just the main venue for the town's festival concerts. But for a week each autumn the music-lovers of Cricklade embark on a venture which is as important to them as anything that goes on in the Royal Festival Hall or the Purcell Room.

The Cricklade Festival started, like so many country-town festivals, in a modest but determined way: three concerts by good amateurs arranged to test the water, so to speak, to see just how much support the town was likely to give this sort of cultural enterprise. The answer was 'plenty'. Within three years professional artists were being sought to take part in what had become a regular eight-concert series. From the start, the organizers were anxious that audiences should commit themselves to supporting the entire festival, not just one or two chosen concerts. So they devised an attractive concessionary scheme whereby for £15 (the 1985 figure) – half price for pensioners and children – individuals can attend as many or as few of a total of twelve concerts as they wish. Needless to say, the concerts are usually sell-outs.

Cricklade specializes in chamber music and the first weekend always features music from a specific period (Renaissance, Baroque, Classical, Romantic and, in 1985, the years 1890–1930). A recent innovation has been the focus each year on a specific instrument, such as the recorder, with recitals and master-classes conducted by well-known performers. Musicians and actors (there is usually a poetry or drama evening) who have appeared at Cricklade in the past include Nigel Kennedy, Judi Dench, Michael Williams, the Nash Ensemble, the New London Consort, Emma Kirkby and David Wilson-Johnson. Young artists from the International Musicians' Seminar at Prussia Cove are also regular visitors.

The repertoire is very broad and generally enterprising. For example, in 1985, Peter Csaba (violin) and Susan Tomes played Elgar, Debussy, Bartók, Stravinsky, Gershwin and Ravel; the Franz Schubert Trio of Vienna gave performances of music by Zemlinsky, Bloch, Shostakovich and Rachmaninov; the Fauré *Requiem* was included in a concert by the St Cecilia Singers; Esther Lamardien from France sang twelfth-century monody with harp, lute and organ accompaniment; and the Endellion

Quartet included in their programme quartets by Haydn, Britten and Smetana. The festival has made it policy to commission new works from British composers – Patrick Piggott, Elizabeth Maconchy and Imogen Holst (her Concerto for Recorder and Nine Strings) among them.

Cricklade looks for outstanding artists and outstanding performances – and it casts its net widely to get them. The result is a festival notable for the vigour and excitement of its music-making. Definitely worth a detour!

EAST CORNWALL BACH FESTIVAL

St Germans sits on a hill, overlooking a small harbour, at the end of one of the arms of the Tamar Estuary that separates Cornwall from Devon. Now an unassuming village with thatched and colour-washed houses, it was until shortly before the Norman Conquest Cornwall's cathedral city. The Normans built an imposing monastic church on the site of the Saxon cathedral, with twin west towers and a fine doorway. This, in turn, was extensively refurbished in the late sixteenth century. Not far distant stands Port Eliot, one of the region's most impressive country houses and seat of the Earls of St Germans.

Church and house are the focal points for an enterprising music festival which in 1985 celebrated its twentieth birthday. The festival's policy has been to present, for two days each May, programmes in which the music of Bach is set beside that of

Nigel Amherst and the East Cornwall Bach Choir, away from their normal concert platform at St Germans, during a concert at St Endellion (see page 39).

other composers, particularly those of the present century. It largely relies on singers and players who live within the region, but also attracts and encourages young professionals from the capital. The choir, which numbers about fifty amateur singers and rehearses from October to May in nearby Liskeard, also gives concerts at other times of the year. The orchestra is made up largely of professional music teachers. This grand co-operative exercise was originally set in motion by James Sargeant, then Cornwall's assistant music adviser, who was also the festival's first music director. He was succeeded about ten years ago by Nigel Amherst, from Dartington.

One of the refreshing things about St Germans is the programme-planning. Of course, the Passions and the B Minor Mass put in statutory appearances, but there is also plenty of exploration of less-trodden paths. The festival takes seriously its responsibility for bringing before the public music from the vast treasury of Bach's church cantatas and has, indeed, programmed over fifty of them to date. The tercentenary year was devoted to performances of all the Brandenburg Concertos, interspersed with cantatas, of contrasting moods, noted for their inclusion of movements well known in other versions: No. 174, with the first movement of the Third Brandenburg employing five additional wind parts added to the existing ten for strings, and No. 110 containing the Overture from the Fourth Orchestral Suite with independent additional parts for chorus.

Other major works performed over the years have included Purcell's *Fairy Queen*, Handel's *Saul* and *Hercules* (as well as the perhaps inevitable *Messiah*), Haydn's *Creation*, the Mozart *Requiem*, and – from the twentieth century – Britten's *Saint Nicholas*, *Rejoice in the Lamb* and *Ceremony of Carols*, Kodály's *Missa Brevis*, Vaughan Williams's *Serenade to Music*, *Flos Campi* and *Five Mystical Songs*, and the Bliss *Pastoral*, as well as shorter works by composers ranging from Bartók to Sculthorpe, from Finzi to Stravinsky.

The East Cornwall Bach Festival has the distinction of combining real musical enterprise with the provision of a much-needed cultural outlet in a beautiful, but remote, part of England.

EDINGTON

The village of Edington nestles just below the northern edge of Salisbury Plain, four miles to the east of the Wiltshire town of Westbury. It boasts a grand, battlemented parish church dedicated to St Mary, St Katharine and All Saints and originally founded in the 1350s by the Augustinian Order of Bonshommes for the singing of the daily liturgy. At one time divided into two parts – the nave serving as parish church, the chancel with its canopied niches and statues of the evangelists reserved for the monastic choir – this beautiful cruciform building, slumbering in a peaceful treescape, is an ideal setting for a festival of liturgical music.

For a week each August, there descends on Edington a group of singers and instrumentalists from the great cathedrals and collegiate chapels of England and Wales whose aim is to sing the daily offices of Matins, Eucharist, Evensong and

Compline to the glory of God and the highest standard of which they are capable. In 1984, boys came from as far afield as Guildford, Lichfield, Lincoln, Llandaff, Salisbury and St Paul's Cathedrals and from New College, Oxford, the adult singers being lay clerks and past or present choral scholars from Oxford or Cambridge. For those who sing the daily services the year round, Edington is something of a busman's holiday – though in no way the less valued or enjoyed for that; for those who have moved into some other walk of life (no fewer than three BBC studio managers were listed in the 1985 programme) it is a not-to-be-missed opportunity to keep in touch and in voice. Good relations between festival and village are reflected in the fact that the singers are accommodated, free of charge, in private houses in the vicinity, and catering is handled by the Wiltshire County Council.

The closing prayer outside Edington Priory Church.

The range of music at Edington is wide and is in no way limited to the Anglican tradition. Messiaen and Widor appear alongside Howells and Lennox Berkeley, Couperin and Victoria share services with Byrd and Tallis. There is also a sound tradition of commissioning new music, the list of composers who have been asked to write specially for Edington including Philip Radcliffe (*O Bone Jesu* and *Missa Brevis Edingtoniensis*), Simon Preston, John Joubert (*Proper Anthems for the Feast of Saint Augustine*), Patrick Gowers and John Harper. John Rutter's *Series Three Service* was also given its first performance at the festival.

Ever since its foundation in 1956, Edington has been renowned for its high musical standards and for the excellence of its performers, many of whom – Simon Preston, Richard Seal, Neil Jenkins, Rogers Covey-Crump, Simon Carrington – have subsequently achieved considerable distinction in the musical world. The festival has also benefited from the commitment of individuals who have returned to offer their services to the maintenance of its ideals year after year. The present director, Geoffrey Webber, for example, first came to the village as a young chorister from Salisbury Cathedral, and has stayed, in one capacity or another, ever since.

Edington is unusual in many respects. Audiences (or congregations) are welcome, but their support is not essential to the festival: there are no admission charges, no reserved seats, very few ancillary facilities (though snacks are served at a hut in the church car park, and a local family offers cream teas). The performers, most of whom receive no payment, are of course important, but the festival is not just an excuse for an annual get-together of old friends and does not exist for their benefit. The music, too, has its place, but is never performed for its own sake – rather as a means of worshipping God and enhancing the Anglican liturgy.

GUERNSEY

The Church of Notre Dame du Rosaire in St Peter Port, Guernsey, dates from 1829 and has associations with Victor Hugo. Restructured in 1962, it is not a large building, but it has fine acoustics and a justly celebrated organ. For twenty-one years, Notre Dame has been the home of a music festival, designed by its founder Père Maurice Lecluze 'to bring some French culture to this lovely island'.

Père Lecluze was trained at the seminary in Coutances on the French mainland, and it was from Coutances that in 1964 he invited the then director, Père Kuhn, to join forces with the blind organist Antoine Reboulet and two Guernsey musicians in a series of five concerts entitled *une semaine musicale*. His aim was to use music as a means of breathing new life into his somewhat flagging parish, and the success of this initial venture led to more ambitious plans in ensuing years. In 1965, Père Lecluze persuaded the distinguished French pianist, Eric Heidsieck, with whom he has family connections, to give the first of what has since grown into a total of over twenty recitals on the island. He also conceived the idea of inviting a symphony orchestra of classical proportions to perform in his church, housing and feeding its members in his own shambling presbytery. In recent years, however, he has been relieved of this particular administrative chore by a generous grant from the French government, enabling him to lodge visiting musicians and employ a French chef to feed them during the festival period. But there is still plenty for the indefatigable rector to do behind the scenes each year: 'If I send one of the children from my school down to the shops with posters, the assistant will say "yes" and put the poster away in a cupboard; if I go myself with a roll of sellotape and my own scissors, they will say "Of course, Father, put the poster wherever you like!"'

To date, Notre Dame has seen well over two hundred festival concerts, with a current average of fifteen per season. Though the French connection remains vigorous, musicians now come to perform from England, Germany, Holland, Belgium, Sweden and even further afield, and the festival which usually runs from mid-July to mid-August attracts large numbers of visitors. Among the artists who have, over the years, played or sung on the altar steps, under Notre Dame's resonant barrel vaulting, are L'Ensemble Ars Antiqua de Paris, L'Ensemble Instrumental de France, the Taffanel Wind Quintet, the Enesco and Parrenin String Quartets, the Ravel Trio of Paris, Gabriel Tacchino, Martine Geliot, Jean-Marc Luisada and Bruno Rigutto. Programmes are well planned, wide ranging and seldom dull – from Renaissance and Baroque music played on original instruments to the modern repertoire.

LEONARD STANLEY
MUSIC AT THE PRIORY

It was the then Vicar of Leonard Stanley, the Revd Gordon White, who in 1979 conceived the idea of a festival to raise funds for the rehanging of the bells in his beautiful Norman (1129) Priory Church of St Swithun. A man of broad musical tastes, he was aware of the excellent acoustic in this unusually large village church and realized that it was well suited to be a vehicle for achieving two long-standing ambitions: to bring classical music to people in this quiet nook of the Cotswolds, especially those who found it difficult to get to concerts in nearby Cheltenham or Gloucester, and to encourage young musicians who were embarking on careers in music, giving school choirs and orchestras the opportunity to perform away from their own home ground.

The pattern of the festival, which occupies two to three weeks in midsummer, is to interweave appearances by visiting performers (in 1983, for example, the pianist Janusz Stechley and the Caerphilly Male Voice Choir; Angela Lear, the New Orleans Jazz Band and the Risca Male Voice Choir two years later) with those by local ensembles (the Little Orchestra of the Cotswolds, the Cheltenham Sunday Players directed by Mark Foster, the Painswick-based Beacon Singers, the Cotswold Savoyards, the Capella Singers, the Cinderford Band and groups from Selwyn, Marling, Maidenhill and Stroud High Schools). Many of these choirs and instrumentalists support the festival by offering their services without fee. Nestling under the Cotswold escarpment not far from Stroud, Leonard Stanley Church is an idyllic setting at any time. It has a special magic, however, on a still summer's evening, when the music of Ravel or Chopin, Handel or Schubert swirls round the nave or drifts through the porch to mingle with the soft shadows of the churchyard. Worth looking up.

LICHFIELD

Lichfield lies at the very heart of the Midlands; the three sandstone spires of its thirteenth-century Cathedral, known popularly as 'The Ladies of the Vale', are visible from miles around. And it is 'The Ladies' that since 1982 have presided over a mainly music festival that has grown steadily in its drawing-power and appeal. In

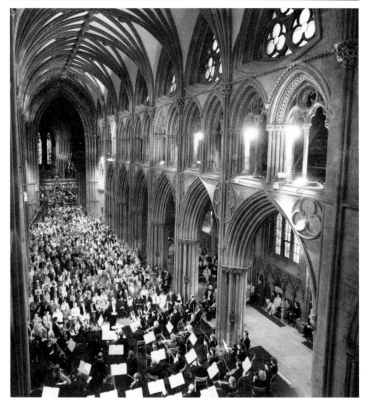

View from the clerestory of Lichfield Cathedral during a concert given
by the Philharmonia Orchestra conducted by Andrew Davis.

1984 over 15000 visitors attended the ten-day event, some of them from as far afield
as Europe and the United States. What brought them? Perhaps it was the serenity
of the deep-lawned Cathedral Close through which audiences stroll on their way to
and from the various concerts and recitals. Perhaps it was the fascination of the
city's many historic buildings, its associations with such figures as Addison, Garrick
and – most celebrated of all – Samuel Johnson. Perhaps it was the varied festival
fare on offer, for although music dominates, there are also exhibitions, theatre,
dance, puppetry, cabaret and a fringe which relies largely on local talent. Perhaps it
was the opportunity to hear musicians of international note, many of whom were
engaged to make not just one but a number of appearances during the ten days.
Perhaps it was the way in which the festival activities were woven into the daily life
of the Cathedral, concerts and recitals alternating with Sung Eucharist or Choral
Evensong as if it were the most natural thing in the world.

An idea of the quality of the Lichfield music can be gained from a glance at what
happened in 1985. Things got off to a resounding start with a concert in which
André Previn led the Royal Philharmonic Orchestra (with Emanuel Ax as solo
pianist) in a programme which included music by Handel, Bach and Elgar. This
was counterpoised towards the end of the festival by a visit from the BBC Philhar-

monic Orchestra under Bernhard Klee and performances of works by Mozart, Strauss and Brahms. The orchestra-in-residence, however, was the Chamber Orchestra of Europe, whose members gave no fewer than four concerts in the company of such distinguished soloists as George Malcolm (harpsichord), Heinz Holliger (oboe), Aurèle Nicolet (flute), Andras Schiff (piano), Yuuko Shiokawa and Sandor Vegh (violin). These performers also joined together, in varying combinations, to give instrumental recitals from time to time during the festival. A second resident group was the Lindsay String Quartet who played three programmes of Mozart and Haydn. Jazz was also strongly represented in 1985, with Oscar Peterson playing in the Cathedral, and the Ronnie Scott Quintet, Humphrey Lyttelton and his Band, Bireli Lagrene and the Diz Disley Trio holding the stage in the Civic Hall. Other music came from the Birmingham Bach Society Choir and Orchestra conducted by Richard Butt (in Bach's B Minor Mass with soloists Gillian Fisher, Charles Brett, Neil Mackie and David Thomas) and the boys of Lichfield Cathedral Choir with Jonathan Rees-Williams (organ). The festival came to a euphoric conclusion with a supper party at Shugborough, the family seat of Lord Lichfield who chairs the festival committee, to the accompaniment of Guillermo Fierens (guitar) playing Sor, Moreno Tórroba, Villa-Lobos and Albéniz. A magical way to round off ten happy July days.

LITTLE MISSENDEN

Where do you begin in describing a festival like Little Missenden – that sprang to life in 1960 with Louis MacNeice reading his own poetry, Rubbra accompanying Rohan de Saram in a performance of his own Cello Sonata, Helen Watts singing Bach and Lennox Berkeley with the Geraint Jones Orchestra and an exhibition of eighteenth- and nineteenth-century drawings and watercolours from the collection of Sir Bruce Ingram, and that celebrated its twenty-fifth anniversary in 1984 with first performances of music for ondes martenot and piano by Elmer Bernstein and Richard Rodney Bennett and a set of variations specially commissioned from Geoffrey Burgon, John Tavener, Richard Drakeford and Neil Saunders?

Little Missenden, a Buckinghamshire village with a population of less than 300, is situated in the deep Chilterns about thirty miles from London. The idea for a festival there came just before Christmas 1959 when Pat Harrison, a musician who has lived all her life in the village, was driving Rohan de Saram back to Oxford after a weekend's music-making at her home. She expressed some frustration at the fact that she had managed to do precious little for music in the course of her life – some teaching, a little composition, no more. Her companion's reply that she should start a festival, that Little Missenden had the right sort of harmonious atmosphere, that he would be glad to be involved, quickly led to her exploring possibilities. Soon she was talking to the Arts Council, the Ralph Vaughan Williams Trust, potential patrons, potential helpers, influential friends. A steering committee was set up, which included a number of distinguished musicians then living in the area, and a festival policy was formulated. First, the physical setting was to determine the scale of the under-taking: the beautiful but small ten-centuries-old Church of St John the Baptist clearly lent itself to chamber music and solo recitals rather than orchestral concerts. Next, programmes should reflect an awareness of contemporary developments in the arts and should bring in the younger generation as performers and creators as well as listeners. Third, the highest possible standards should be maintained at all times, and last but not least, *everyone* – audience, performers, organizers – should enjoy themselves!

For all that it attracts interest and admiration from supporters from all over the country, Little Missenden started life as, and has remained, a festival in a village. The church, with its resplendent fourteenth-century fresco of St Christopher domi-nating the entrance, is the main auditorium, though local houses – several of them fine eighteenth-century buildings – are also brought into use for poetry recitals, lectures and small exhibitions. The not very prepossessing village hall serves for some master-classes and concerts, while the school turns into the festival club for the serving of hot meals and refreshments. And whenever something needs doing – manning the bar, ushering, preparing food, fixing the lights – there always seems to be someone from the village ready and willing to help out.

The festival takes place around harvest time, for ten days or so in early October, when the hazel hedges and beechwoods are at their most amazing. Then the village buzzes with visitors come to see a Henry Moore, a Ben Nicholson or a Barbara Hepworth exhibition, or to hear Marie Rambert, Roger Smalley or Sir Michael Tippett talking about music. St John's is packed to capacity for the Elizabethan Singers, the Janáček Quartet, the Melos Ensemble, the Purcell Consort of Voices, the Academy of St Martin-in-the-Fields or the John Alldis Choir. Many of the festival's early supporters remember with nostalgia some of the sixties line-ups – Gerald English, Ian Harwood, Rohan de Saram and Ivor Keys in a mostly English evening; Dennis Matthews, Howard Ferguson and John Shirley-Quirk in an all-Schubert programme; Janet Baker, Wilfred Brown and Richard Drakeford in a recital which started with Purcell and ended with Britten's Second Canticle, *Abraham and Isaac*. Sometimes the concerts are given by candlelight, as when in 1980 Diana Cummings and Rohan and Druvi de Saram concluded a colourful programme with a crisp account of the *Archduke Trio*, or when, three years later, Richard Jackson (baritone) and Graham Johnson (piano) led the way from Haydn to Finzi via Brahms and Bizet. There have been special schools' concerts and concerts given by Bucking-hamshire Young Musicians (the names Christopher van Campen and Richard Deakin appear on programmes from the late sixties); in recent years students of the Yehudi Menuhin School have paid regular visits and Timothy Walker, Andrew Marriner and Albert Ferber have conducted junior master-classes.

And throughout its entire existence, Little Missenden has been true to its ideal of encouraging new music: a number of important works by Richard Drakeford and Neil Saunders have been premièred at the festival (including the former's First

Interior of Little Missenden Church showing the fourteenth-century
wall paintings.

String Quartet, *Festival Jubilate* and opera *The Sely Child* and the latter's *Three Psalms of David* and Cello Sonata). Other 'festival firsts' have been John Caldwell's Second String Quartet, Tony Osborne's Piano Trio, Richard Benger's Concerto Grosso and *Robert Frost Songs*, and John Tavener's Aria for Solo Cello, *My Grandfather's Waltz* (for piano duet) and *To a Child Dancing in the Wind*. The catalogue of riches could go on, with scarcely space to mention the poetry recitals with Alvar Liddell, Margaret Rawlings, John Westbrook, Jill Balcon, Denys Hawthorne, Gabriel Woolf, or Ian Rodger's play *Paul*, first seen in 1963, or the contributions of Moira Shearer and Michael Bakewell.

With Little Missenden, once you *have* begun, it is difficult to know where to stop.

MADLEY

Madley is a charmingly secluded village about six miles from Hereford, cooled by the sauntering Wye, in the shadow of the Black Mountains. It is dominated by a splendid parish church – dedicated to the Nativity of the Blessed Virgin Mary – whose origins go back to Norman times. The building as it stands today is, however, the result of extensive refashioning during the thirteenth and fourteenth centuries. Of particular note are the polygonal apse, the mediaeval choir stalls, and the fine nave arcades. Many of the windows are of clear glass, giving the interior a light spaciousness, but some magnificent jewel-like roundels of stained glass survive from the thirteenth century.

For twenty years this has been the setting for a festival which aims to bring professional music, poetry and art to the inhabitants of a part of Herefordshire not really touched by the Three Choirs. Local volunteers are responsible for making all the arrangements – from putting up the staging on which performances take place, to preparing interval refreshments, to finding beds for visiting musicians.

Music at Madley tends to be on a smallish scale and takes up five days in a single week in mid-July. There might well be a concert of ancient and modern by the Fine Arts Brass Ensemble or a Baroque evening with the London Harpsichord Ensemble. There is very likely to be an appearance by the English String Orchestra under William Boughton, playing a programme with appropriately pastoral overtones – Finzi (say), Elgar and Vaughan Williams in a near perfect setting. Solo performers who have visited Madley in past years include Michael Thompson, Jack Brymer, Anthony Peebles and Timothy Walker, while Doreen and Michael Muskett have delighted young and old alike with their lecture recital 'Flutes, Reeds and Whistles'. Each festival concludes on Sunday afternoon with a special service sung by the Madley Festival Choir. All in all, a venture well scaled to the community from which it has grown.

MAYFIELD

The festival which takes place every two years in the picturesque, timbered village of Mayfield, in Sussex, started life in 1970 as part of an attempt to raise funds for the building of a parish hall. The guiding spirit was the vicar, the Revd Donald Carter, who, with members of his parochial church council, played an important role in organizing events enough to fill a fortnight. The hall was, in fact, never built, but the festival – now reduced to a week's duration – goes on, thanks to the continuing enthusiasm and imagination of its musical director, Kenneth Pont, and to the willingness of audiences to come together from all over the South-East, to hear fine performances in especially attractive settings.

Most of the festival concerts and recitals take place either in St Dunstan's Church or in the Old Palace, which now houses a Roman Catholic girls' school. The spacious, fifteenth-century church, with its massive Parvis Tower from whose roof May carols ring out at the start of each festival, is dedicated to a saint who had close associations with Mayfield. Dunstan was Archbishop of Canterbury during the tenth century, and was responsible for the building of many churches around the country – including that at Mayfield, a place for which he had a particular fondness. Legend has it that he also kept a forge in the village, which was the scene of his celebrated contest with the devil, whose nose he pulled with red-hot tongs. After a considerable struggle, the devil managed to free himself and escaped in a single leap to Tunbridge Wells, where he cooled his nose in the famous spring. Dunstan was also responsible for the building in Mayfield of a palace for the use of the archbishops of Canterbury. The chapel, courtyard, community room and old kitchens together with the school refectory are fourteenth-century remains of a stone palace built on the site of

Dunstan's wooden original. In 1930, Adrian Gilbert Scott was responsible for the fashioning of a new, acoustically impressive, school hall.

The co-operation between the Anglican and Roman Catholic traditions which has always been a part of the Mayfield spirit is nowadays best summed up in the figure of Kenneth Pont, who is both organist of St Dunstan's and director of music at the Old Palace School. In the early years, the festival relied for its choral concerts on amateur singers from all over East Sussex, but in 1978 Pont formed the Mayfield Festival Chorus which is made up almost exclusively of local people. Another important contribution to festival music-making comes from the village's own prize-winning brass band.

Over the last decade, Mayfield has attracted a growing number of internationally known professional musicians, many of whom have been inspired by the nature of the festival to perform for reduced fees. Past programmes are scattered with names such as Colin Horsley, Dennis Matthews, Ilse Wolf, Ruggiero Ricci, Paul Tortelier, Isobel Baillie, Jan Latham-Koenig, Bernard d'Ascoli and Christopher Hogwood. In 1972, Malcolm Williamson spent the festival week in Mayfield organizing an opera workshop and supervising a performance of his opera *Dunstan and the Devil*, while the 1976 festival saw the British unveiling of his *The Terrain of Kings*. Neither of these works was actually written for Mayfield, though it can boast the commissioning of Paul Patterson's Humoresque for Wind Quintet (1972). In 1976, Sir David Willcocks began an association with the festival which still continues today: he conducts one large-scale work each year, making the occasion an opportunity for introducing young professional soloists and for bringing to Sussex members of his Bach Choir and Royal College of Music Orchestra. The full-blown choral concert is one of the highlights of the Mayfield season, and works performed over the years include *Dixit Dominus* and *Israel in Egypt* (Handel), the B Minor Mass (Bach), *The Dream of Gerontius* (Elgar) and Mozart's *Requiem*. Perhaps one of the most moving evenings, however, was provided in 1972 by the London String Quartet, when they gave performances of three chamber works written in 1918 by Elgar while he was living in his cottage near the not-so-distant Sussex town of Pulborough.

MILTON ABBEY

Milton Abbas was built as a 'model' village in the heart of Hardy country during the eighteenth century. Its gently curving main street is lined with thatched cottages and rowan trees. But its chief claim to architectural fame is Milton Abbey, a cluster of fine Gothic buildings comprising an unfinished late-mediaeval church and the grand house built for Lord Milton in answering style towards the end of the eighteenth century by Sir William Chambers (architect of Somerset House in London) and James Wyatt. The house, which incorporates some of the original abbey buildings including the Abbot's Hall (1498), is now a school. Both church and house provide the setting for the Milton Abbey Festival, which has occupied the last few days of August each year since 1979.

One of the central concerns of the festival is the performance of church music in the context for which it was written, with choral services – Mass, Matins, Evensong, Compline – providing the backbone for four or five days of intense activity. The musical tapestry is broad and rich – ranging from Byrd and Palestrina to Poulenc and Britten. Alongside the services there are major choral concerts (Haydn's *Harmoniemesse*, Brahms's *German Requiem*, Vivaldi's *Magnificat*, the Mozart *Requiem* or the Monteverdi *Vespers of 1610*) performed by an *ad hoc* professional orchestra and festival choir, which also supplies the soloists. Each year choirs and instrumental groups from other parts of the country are invited to perform, and these have included Pepys Music, the Pisces Ensemble, the Choir of St Catharine's College, Cambridge, and students from both the Guildhall and the Royal Academy of Music. Chamber concerts usually take place in the Abbot's Hall or in the eighteenth-century King's Room and Ballroom of the house – particularly apt settings for listening to music by Haydn, J. C. Bach, Mozart and Beethoven. Occasionally programmes feature performers of wider repute, as when Fritz Spiegl gave his one-man entertainment 'Music as she is spoke' and Barbara Leigh-Hunt, Richard Pasco, Jill Nott-Bower and Robert Spencer presented their celebrated portrait of Elizabeth I in words and music, entitled 'Gloriana'.

Milton Abbey is a devotional and celebratory festival which makes good use of the facilities available to it and performs a very useful function in bringing music of all kinds to a grandly beautiful corner of England.

PERSHORE

Pershore is a tourist's delight – a sunny market town set among the woodlands and plum orchards of Worcestershire, it is one of fifty or so that have been designated as being of outstanding architectural and historical interest. Many of the domestic buildings are Georgian, but the six-arched bridge that spans Shakespeare's Avon dates from the fourteenth century and the great torso of the Abbey Church goes back even further. Much of the original Abbey building was savaged at the time of the Dissolution, so that only the south transept and the magnificent Romanesque Lantern Tower plus the Presbytery lopsidedly remain, now serving as the town's parish church. It is in the Abbey that most of the musical events of the annual Pershore Festival take place.

The festival was founded in 1961 with the twin aims of bringing out all that is best in the arts of the region and of attracting to the town professional performers of national and international standing. The early festivals lasted only five days, but increased confidence and success have led to welcome expansion. Nowadays, the last two weeks of June are regularly filled with a hectic round of events for all ages and tastes.

Solo performers in recent years have included Christopher Dearnley, Nigel Kennedy and the flautist Paul Edmund-Davies, while the Serenata of London, the Albion Ensemble, and the Fitzwilliam and Medici Quartets have been among visiting chamber groups – the Fitzwilliams giving the first performance of a piece by Bernard Rands. Orchestral and choral concerts are, on the whole, kept to a modest scale, with important contributions from the locally based Hereford and Worcester Youth Orchestra and the Pershore Choral Society. For the last eight years, a special feature of the festival has been a competition for young pianists.

ST ENDELLION

If you drive the North Cornwall coast road west from the unlovely, straggling slate town of Delabole and make in the direction of Wadebridge, a quarter of an hour – more or less – of dipping and winding between hedgerows pruned and sculpted by the sharp northerlies will bring you to the old elvan-stone Collegiate Church of St Endelienta. It was a route that Sir John Betjeman took as a child: in *First and Last Loves* (1952) he recalls his first impression of the church – 'it looked, and still looks, just like a hare. The ears are the pinnacles of the tower and the rest of the hare, the church, crouches among wind-slashed firs'.

The festival at St Endellion started in 1959 when the Revd Roger Gaunt gathered a few friends together for a summer house-party with poetry and madrigals. The idea was a great success and the next year there were string quartets. And so things naturally developed until, by 1984, the festival was occupying twelve days in early August with *The Dream of Gerontius* as its centrepiece. In 1974, a younger sister was born in the form of an Easter festival – just a couple of performances of the *St Matthew Passion* that first year, but now running to a full week of very varied concerts and recitals. The artistic director of both festivals is Richard Hickox, who shares the concerts with a number of other young conductors – Richard Cooke, chorus master of the London Philharmonic Choir, Martin Merry (one of the founders of the Chester Festival), Louis Carus, Gareth Morell.

The philosophy of St Endellion is to invite singers and instrumentalists, both amateur and professional, from all over Britain, to enjoy a busman's holiday of highly polished music-making in an austerely beautiful part of Cornwall. No one is paid; in fact, everyone is expected to make a financial contribution to festival funds in return for board and lodging, either at the festival's own Trelights Farm or in one of the many holiday homes made available by friends in the area. Guest soloists – who, over the years, have included John Shirley-Quirk, John Amis, Wendy Eathorne, Sir William Glock, John Graham-Hall, Stephen Varcoe, Stephen Roberts, Marjorie Biggar and the members of the Endellion Quartet – receive no fees, but perform in return for a free holiday and travel expenses. And *everyone* is expected to help with festival chores, which range from car park duty to washing up. About a hundred and twenty musicians come together for each Easter and summer season to rehearse and perform the festival repertoire from scratch.

The Easter programmes tend to lean towards the Baroque and Classical periods – the Mozart *Requiem*, Handel's *Dixit Dominus*, the Bach *Magnificat* or B Minor Mass – while in the summer there is a rather greater catholicity. August 1984, for instance, began with a Holst-Berlioz-Beethoven concert (including the *Pastoral* Symphony); the Endellion Quartet (former members of the festival orchestra) played Haydn, Britten and Elgar; elsewhere there was Rossini, Delius, Duruflé, Fauré, Purcell and Vaughan Williams, and the final concert brought together Respighi (the *Three Botticelli Pictures*), Mozart's Clarinet Concerto (with David Rix) and Schubert's Mass in E Flat. Both Easter and summer festivals usually include one concert in Truro Cathedral – generally a large-scale choral piece, such as *The Creation*, Brahms's *German Requiem* or *Dona Nobis Pacem* by Vaughan Williams. There are also programmes of light entertainment, talks, anthologies of words and music and even opera (*La Clemenza di Tito* in 1971, Holst's *Savitri* in 1981), and each summer also sees a drama production.

Though this is quintessentially a performers' festival, at which old friends get together both to work and to relax (Richard Hickox leading his football team into action on one or other of the local beaches is a not uncommon sight), it depends very much on attracting large and regular audiences. It is a mark of its success that such audiences have been homing in on St Endellion for a quarter of a century.

SOUTHERN CATHEDRALS

Though in its present incarnation it dates from 1960, the Southern Cathedrals Festival can be traced back to 1901 when the cathedral choirs of Chichester, Salisbury and Winchester took part in celebrations to mark the unveiling of a statue of King Alfred in Winchester. The 1960 gathering, brought about by the efforts of the three cathedral organists of the day – John Birch (Chichester), Christopher Dearnley (Salisbury) and Alwyn Surplice (Winchester) – had as its objective the performance of church music of all periods and backgrounds in the context of concerts as well as services, both pieces already in the repertoire of the individual choirs and those better suited to their combined strength. The festival visits each city in turn – 1984 Winchester, 1985 Salisbury, 1986 Chichester, and so on – giving audiences the chance to enjoy their many and fascinating beauties. The three cathedrals alone are fine examples of mediaeval ecclesiastical architecture at its grandest – Chichester with its Library and Treasury; Salisbury, built as an entity between 1220 and 1258, capped by the highest spire in England and flanked by the great green lawn of its close; Winchester with its 253-foot nave, its chantries and fourteenth-century choir – but the streets and buildings which spread out at their feet are also full of interest for those prepared to wander and investigate.

The Southern Cathedrals Festival lasts for four days (Thursday to Sunday afternoon) each late July, though at Winchester there are additional concerts on Wednesday evening and Thursday morning and afternoon. The regular pattern is as follows: Thursday – Evensong sung by one of the guest choirs, followed by an organ recital (in recent years the three distinguished host organists have stepped aside and left the stage to such visitors as Gillian Weir, Nicholas Danby, Peter Hurford, Noël Rawsthorne and Susan Landale) and a late-night fringe event (such as adaptations of *Pride and Prejudice* and *The Wind in the Willows*, both with music specially written by Richard Shepherd, or a Victorian Evening). Friday – Solemn Eucharist sung by the combined choirs, then a festival lunch and Evensong sung by the second guest choir and – in the evening – a concert of choral music by the combined choirs interspersed with readings on such themes as 'The Tree of Life' and 'Wisdom' (recent readers have included John Westbrook and the Bishop of Winchester). Saturday – a morning concert, lecture or discussion session, Evensong by the combined choirs and a final concert in which the choirs are joined by a visiting orchestra or instrumental ensemble. Sunday – services as usual sung by the 'home team'. In addition, there are meals, gardens open, exhibitions and a festival club.

The extra events at Winchester start with an eve of the festival concert in which the cathedral forces are joined by other local choirs (notably the Waynflete Singers and Reading Bach Choir), visiting orchestra and soloists to perform major choral works – in 1981, the Verdi *Te Deum* and Tippett's *A Child of Our Time* (with Jill Gomez, Elizabeth Stokes, William Kendall and David Thomas); in 1984, Holst's *Hymn of Jesus* and the exquisite Duruflé *Requiem* (with Catherine Wyn-Rogers and Stephen Varcoe). Then, on the Thursday, there is Sung Matins and an afternoon choral/organ recital – all with Winchester forces.

Visiting orchestras and ensembles that have played at Southern Cathedrals Festivals since 1978 include the London Symphony, Bournemouth Symphony and English Chamber Orchestras, the Bournemouth Sinfonietta, the Steinitz Bach Players and Albany Brass Ensemble. The range of music performed is wide, from Fayrfax and Byrd to the Wesleys and Elgar, from Victoria and Tallis to Messiaen and Britten, from Taverner to Tavener – with liberal helpings of Mozart and Schubert, Monteverdi and Bach in between. New music specially commissioned by the festival has, over the years, included major works by Bernstein (his *Chichester Psalms*), Mathias (*An Admonition to Rulers*), Tavener (*Little Requiem for Father Malachy Lynch*) and Maconchy (*And Death Shall Have No Dominion*), while more recently canticles and anthems have also come from Jonathan Harvey and Richard Shepherd. Important musical anniversaries are observed – as when in 1982 the Stravinsky centenary was marked with a performance of his Mass for Chorus and Wind Instruments and Herbert Howells's ninetieth birthday was honoured with his *Requiem* and Gloucester and *Collegium Regale* canticles. Three years later, the respective anniversaries of Tallis, Schütz, Domenico Scarlatti, J. S. Bach and Handel gave rise to a positive feast of their music.

STOUR – MUSIC IN EAST KENT

The waters of the Great Stour cut their way through the Kentish Downs from Ashford north towards Canterbury. It is a peaceful valley, sprinkled with charming villages and country houses – Chilham, with its seventeenth-century castle and a water-mill set amid hop-gardens and orchards; Wye and the Georgian manor of Olantigh; and Boughton Aluph whose pilgrim Church of All Saints, flanked by open

Stour Music – all the activities take place in or around the church at Boughton Aluph.

fields at the foot of the Downs, is the very heart of the Festival of Music in East Kent.

Stour Music was founded in 1963 by the celebrated countertenor Alfred Deller and his son, Mark, is still its artistic director. Their idea was to invite distinguished artists from many countries to come to perform principally Renaissance and Baroque music in the kind of setting for which it was originally composed. From the start, the performers were put up in private houses and fed in a marquee erected for the purpose in the Dellers' garden.

The first festival was a modest, one-day affair, with concerts by the Deller Consort, the Kalmar Chamber Orchestra and Jaye Consort of Viols in Chilham Castle and Church and at Olantigh. The following year, the music filled six days and now occupies two full weekends at the end of June. Since the late seventies, Boughton Aluph Church, noted for its roomy acoustic, has been the focus of activities. Though the festival repertoire has particularly favoured the sixteenth to eighteenth centuries, there is always a significant injection of modern music, and composers of the stature of Rubbra, Anthony Milner, Wilfred Mellers and Peter Racine Fricker have had new works commissioned.

The Stour pattern is, generally speaking, of two concerts each day – the first, at about 7.30 p.m., being an orchestral or choral concert featuring the festival's own ensembles (these include the Stour Baroque Soloists and the Stour Festival Choir and Orchestra), the second, a 10 p.m. 'late-night extra', relying on more modest forces (such as the Deller Consort or solo performers on lute or harp). Sunday concerts – usually large-scale occasions – take place mid-afternoon to avoid clashing with church services. Each festival includes a major choral work, sometimes Baroque or Classical (Handel's *Dixit Dominus* or *Samson*, the Monteverdi *Vespers of 1610*, a late Haydn mass), sometimes modern (Tippett's *A Child of Our Time* in 1980, Howells's *Hymnus Paradisi* two years later). Soloists at these and other concerts tend to be long-standing Deller associates – Lynne Dawson, Rogers Covey-Crump, Maurice Bevan, Paul Elliott, Alastair Thompson – with Mark Deller himself conducting.

Visiting musicians, over the years, have included Susi Jeans, Desmond Dupré, Gustav Leonhardt, Colin Tilney, Frans Brueggen, David Munrow, Julian Bream with his Consort, the English Consort, the Music Group of London, the Purcell Consort of Voices and the Allegri String Quartet. Most festivals at Stour have also included an evening of words and music featuring performers such as Richard Pasco, Barbara Leigh-Hunt, Julian Glover, Isla Blair, Dorothy Tutin, Derek Waring, Judi Dench and Michael Williams.

The keynote of Music in East Kent is the warmth and intimacy of the occasion, combined with music-making of an exceptionally high standard.

THREE CHOIRS

Herbert Howells used to tell the story of how, in 1910, his teacher Herbert Brewer casually remarked that some unknown young musician was bringing a strange new work to the Three Choirs Festival at Gloucester that year – 'something to do with Tallis'. And Vaughan Williams himself, the composer of that incomparable Fantasia, recalled a moment when, casting a glance to the back desk of the first violins in the course of conducting the first performance of his *Five Mystical Songs* at Worcester the following year, he saw the great Kreisler sitting there (actually he was playing in a new string) and wondered whether he was suffering 'delusions as well as terrors'. It is anecdotes like these that are the stuff of the Three Choirs – a festival whose name is inextricably linked with those of some of the outstanding British composers of two centuries – S. S. Wesley, Parry, Stanford, Wood, Bantock, Walford Davies, Ethel Smyth, Elgar (whose name appeared in the list of amateur violinists playing in the scratch orchestra recruited for the 1878 festival), Bliss, Holst, Ireland, Finzi, Berkeley, Tippett, Walton, Britten, Hoddinott, Milner, Crosse, as well as Vaughan Williams and Howells themselves.

Now well over two hundred and fifty years old* and Europe's longest-lived music festival, the Three Choirs is held in successive years in the ancient cathedral cities of Gloucester, Hereford and Worcester. Each festival presents a unique opportunity for the music-lover to enjoy a midsummer's week-long programme of choral and orchestral concerts, while soaking up the atmosphere of an historic city set in the breathtaking countryside of the border marches. The international stature of the

* Something of the early history of the Three Choirs will be found in the chapter on 'Origins', pages 15–21.

Herbert Howells (*left*), Ralph Vaughan Williams and Rutland Boughton – three composers at the 1937 Three Choirs Festival at Gloucester. Other members of the group are unknown.

The Narrators in the first performance of Ralph Vaughan Williams's *Hodie* at Worcester in 1954.

Three Choirs has long been established, and each year many overseas – particularly American – visitors mingle with regulars from all parts of Britain. In recent years the festivals have been noted for the wide spectrum of music offered – from favourite classics such as the *St Matthew Passion*, *Messiah*, the Mozart *Requiem*, the Brahms symphonies or the Elgar Violin Concerto, to lesser-known pieces and up to half a dozen first performances each year. Of course, the Three Choirs has always championed new works – Vaughan Williams's *Fantasia on Christmas Carols*, for instance, and *Hodie* (as well as the *Tallis Fantasia* and *Five Mystical Songs*), Finzi's Clarinet Concerto and *Intimations of Immortality*, Holst's *Choral Fantasia*, Howells's *Hymnus Paradisi* – and in recent years the flow has, if anything, increased. Malcolm Williamson's *Mass of Christ the King* was first heard at Gloucester (1977), as were Nicholas Maw's *Serenade* (1980) and both Elis Pehkonnen's Symphony and Paul Patterson's *Missa Maris* (1983); Worcester programmed Frank Martin's *Requiem* and Richard Rodney Bennett's *Spells* (both in 1975), Lennox Berkeley's *Judica Me* (1978), Jean Langlais' *Mass: Grant us Thy Peace* and no fewer than three works by Aulis Sallinen (1981) and Peter Racine Fricker's *Whispers at these Curtains* (1984); and Hereford was responsible in 1976 for major works by Geoffrey Burgon (his *Requiem*) and Graham Whettam (Trio for Violin, Horn and Piano), and three years later for John Joubert's *Herefordshire Canticles*.

The 'three choirs' were, in the early days of the festival, the cathedral choirs of the three cities, but today's festival chorus now consists of some 250 singers drawn mainly from the long-established choral societies of Gloucester, Hereford and Worcester. It is on this chorus that the main performing burden falls each year, assisted by visiting orchestras and soloists (in 1985, these included the Royal Philharmonic Orchestra, the City of Birmingham Symphony Orchestra, the English String Orchestra and the Orchestra da Camera, Margaret Cable, John Noble, Brian Rayner Cook, Neil Jenkins, Nigel Kennedy, Janet Price, Jill Gomez, Stephen Roberts and Penelope Walker). Each year the principal conductor is the cathedral organist of the host city, assisted by his two 'guest' colleagues and distinguished visitors from further afield (in 1985, Sir Charles Groves, William Boughton, Grayston Burgess).

By no means all Three Choirs programmes are made up of heavy-weight works performed by large forces. There are also solo recitals, chamber concerts, lectures, exhibitions, concerts given by the combined cathedral choirs and the pivotal services of Sung Eucharist and Choral Evensong. And though many of the events take place each year in the sublime setting of the host cathedral, festivities are being carried increasingly far and wide. Audiences make the journey from Hereford to Ledbury Parish Church or Leominster Priory to hear chamber music in sympathetic acoustics, the Gloucester festival uses the Abbeys of Prinknash and Tewkesbury as well as the Pittville Pump Room at Cheltenham, and Worcester migrates to Pershore Abbey or Hartlebury Castle for instrumental and vocal recitals.

The Three Choirs holds a very special place in the affections of music-lovers both in this country and abroad. It is not merely a question of history or tradition or associations. Edward Heath, writing in 1977, put it this way:

Massed choirs at Worcester in 1984.

I do not know of any other festival which combines at the same time such continuity of style with such variety of content. Even so, Three Choirs Festivals will always remain unique for one outstanding characteristic, for the atmosphere and surroundings, consolidated over more than two and a half centuries, in which they are held. It is because of this, almost above everything, that many come to the music meeting again and again, year by year. They know that there they will see their friends and acquaintances. There, for a short spell, they will be able to escape from the wear and tear of modern life and enjoy the leisurely pursuit of their own individual interests. There they will be able to relax over coffee in the morning, or tea in the afternoon, or a drink late at night and talk about the event of the day. In the intervals of listening they will be talking, always talking, about music and musicians and how these contribute to the enrichment of their daily lives. All this happens in the shadow of the Cathedral, an indissoluble part of English history, the embodiment of so much for which so many have laboured down the centuries, a centre of stability in our nerve-racked society, a haven of music when we meet together.

46

Geoffrey Burgon
A CHANCE TO SPREAD MY WINGS

Geoffrey Burgon is that relatively rare phenomenon – a living composer of serious music who has featured in the pop charts (thanks to the hauntingly beautiful *Nunc dimittis* he composed for the BBC TV series based on John le Carré's *Tinker, Tailor, Soldier, Spy*) and has achieved widespread popularity through his television scores – notably that for Granada's serialization of Evelyn Waugh's *Brideshead Revisited*.

Throughout his career as a composer – and earlier as a professional trumpet player – Burgon has had a wide experience of festivals: from the small-scale, like Farnham, Tilford or Little Missenden on the one hand, to the grand (the Three Choirs, Cheltenham and Edinburgh) on the other. He speaks with particular affection about Little Missenden and the three or four commissions it offered him early in his career. 'It was for me,' he recalls, 'a terrific opportunity, a chance to spread my wings' – and he emphasizes that even modest festivals can have a profound influence on a composer's development. Without them, he conjectures, our musical life would be seriously impoverished. Far less new music would be written, far fewer young composers would get the performances that so often act as springboard to their later careers.

Another benefit which festivals bestow is the chance for composers like Burgon to write for children. Outside the festival context there are not many opportunities to get young singers and players together for the length of time required to prepare and perform new music. 'I particularly enjoyed working on a piece of mine called *Songs of Night* (1970) with a choir of three hundred kids at a High Wycombe Festival some years back. It taught me a great deal about how to write for youngsters – recognizing the difficulties they might encounter and trying to forestall them without in any way changing the impact of what I wanted to say.' It also taught him something of the rigours of performance from the conductor's angle, as he remembers, somewhat ruefully. 'My piece was the last on the programme, and as I was waiting my turn to conduct, I could see that in the hot, cramped conditions they were performing in, the children were beginning to sag horribly. I dreaded what was going to happen to *Songs of Night*. But just before I got up to take my place on the podium, I had the idea of writing S M I L E in large, bold letters across the back of my programme. Just as we were about to begin, I held up the programme and signalled my message to the choir. Unfortunately, they went several better and burst into fits of uncontrollable laughter. But it saved their pitch and the piece was fine.'

Writing music for festivals can impose limitations on a composer, but Burgon is the first to admit that this is really no bad thing. He feels this to be particularly the case when he is writing a large-scale choral work, knowing that it is to be performed by mostly amateur singers. 'Under such circumstances it does not pay me to be "difficult". What is the point of my writing, shall we say, highly complex choral counterpoint if it takes all the choir's energy and enthusiasm just to get the notes right – let alone make the piece sound good? It turns what should be an enjoyable experience for them into a real worry.' It must, he feels, be highly frustrating for someone like Tippett that a masterpiece of the order of *The Vision of St Augustine* is so rarely performed because it is simply far too difficult for amateurs to sing. 'But then, they used to say that about the *Missa Solemnis!*'

Along with bearing in mind just what is or is not possible from the performers' point of view, Burgon enjoys the opportunities festival commissions present of writing music for particular buildings or settings. He found inspiration for the *Brideshead* music primarily in the Baroque splendour of Castle Howard, where the series was filmed; and he has made a point of studying the acoustics of the great cathedrals for which some of his most expansive scores have been written, working out carefully how particular effects can be achieved both orchestrally and vocally within the sound-box of the building in question.

Over the years, Burgon has gained a particular affection for the Three Choirs Festival, having had three pieces commissioned by its organizers to date. He recognizes that the festival has a rather traditional, middle-class image, but he is quick to point out that it has always encouraged new music and young composers, that there is a sense of complete commitment in any performance given there – no matter how avant-garde the music may be – and that there is a great charm in the way in which amateur and professional musicians work side by side to make what they can out of new music that can sometimes seem very mystifying. He recalls that the first piece of his to be given at a Three Choirs festival was *The Fire of Heaven*, actually suggested by the Cathedral Organists' Association and given in 1973 at Hereford. It went down well, by all accounts, with both performers and audience. On the strength of this success, when some time later he felt the urge to compose a requiem, he contacted the organizers and asked if they would care to commission it. Looking back, he admits it was a cheeky thing to do. But it worked – the committee was keen, the Arts Council came up with the funding and the *Requiem* (1976), among Burgon's most moving and magnificent scores, was born.

'The other good thing about festivals,' he maintains, 'is the contact that can be established between composers and the people who make up their audiences.' Particularly in the medium-sized or smaller festivals there is a great sense, he feels, of comradeship, of no-nonsense communication. Whether he meets people at specially arranged 'Talk to the Composer' sessions, or more casually in a bar or in the street, he very much values hearing what they think about his music. He likes to learn from them just how their ears have received what he has written, what sort of detail they have extracted, what sort of overall impression they have received. Can he see himself starting his own festival in the tiny Gloucestershire village in which he has recently bought a cottage? 'Well, not really. Much as I love festivals and value what they do, I'm just not the organizing sort – and the amount of careful organization that needs to go into even a small festival is quite hair-raising. There is also a danger with composer-oriented festivals that the individual personality takes over too completely. The whole thing *can* become one long ego-trip. It is to Britten's everlasting credit that he never allowed that to happen at Aldeburgh. He was always putting other composers' music into his programmes – Walton, Shostakovich, Lutoslawski, you name them – and that is one of the things that has made Aldeburgh a great institution.'

TILFORD BACH FESTIVAL

Tilford is a quiet, unspoiled village standing beside the River Wey three miles from Farnham, in the depths of Surrey. At its heart is a triangular cricket green of some antiquity, around which cluster pub, shop, school, cottages and the towerless, brick-built Church of All Saints.

It was Denys Darlow who, as organist of All Saints, in 1952 proposed Tilford as an ideal setting for an unsophisticated but professionally performed festival of the

Stephen Dodgson conducting a rehearsal of his Concerto for Chamber Orchestra commissioned by the Tilford Bach Festival.

music of his favourite composer, J. S. Bach. In spite of initial difficulties, he and a group of like-minded local enthusiasts got the venture off to a start the following year. The Tilford Bach Society came into being with the avowed aim 'to promote an annual festival of the music of J. S. Bach and his contemporaries, predecessors and successors in a manner most consistent with the style and demands of the period'. In order to achieve this aim, Darlow has, over the years, built up a number of outstanding professional groups to whom the bulk of the festival work is entrusted. These include the Tilford Bach Festival Orchestra, playing on modern instruments; the London Handel Orchestra (a group founded by Darlow for his Handel festivals at St George's, Hanover Square), playing on Baroque instruments; the London Festival Players, formed some years ago by members of the Tilford Bach Festival Orchestra; and the Tilford Bach Festival Choir, a wholly professional group which includes young singers who have already begun to make their mark as soloists.

Though the main festival events take place in Tilford itself during May, Members' Evening Concerts are also given at other times of the year at venues such as the

Great Hall of Farnham Castle and the Hunters Music Room at Frensham. In recent years, the festival has also expanded into London, the first of its 'Bach in London' weeks at St George's, Hanover Square, taking place in 1973.

Festival programmes are, of course, dominated by the music of Bach – including a ritual performance of the B Minor Mass on the final evening – but other composers are well served. In 1984, for example, the London Festival Players (who include such distinguished names as Trevor Williams and Frederick Riddle) gave a concert of Beethoven and Spohr, the London Handel Orchestra played Handel, and the cantata concert which featured Ian Partridge and Brian Kay as soloists ended with Rubbra's *Crucifixus Pro Nobis*. Contemporary music has, indeed, been regularly programmed, and from time to time the festival has commissioned new works. Notable in this field were *The Fall of Lucifer* by Geoffrey Burgon and the late Stephen Dodgson's Concerto for Chamber Orchestra.

———— TRURO – THREE SPIRES FESTIVAL ————

Inaugurated in 1980, this is a festival of music and the arts centred on Truro Cathedral. Indeed, it takes its name from the striking and unusual triple spires of John Loughborough Pearson's Victorian-Gothic building. Truro is administrative heart as well as cathedral city of Cornwall and is an important cultural centre for the duchy and a favourite tourist resort. Its popularity derives to a great extent from its sheltered estuary position on the Cornish Riviera, whose exceptionally mild climate encourages sub-tropical trees and plant-life to flourish, and from its elegant Georgian architecture.

The festival, which occupies ten days to a fortnight each June, is an important arts event for the South West of England, bringing performers and audiences from the region into contact with nationally and internationally known artists. As well as a full programme of musical events, there are also art exhibitions (the County Museum and Art Gallery already boasts a fine collection of paintings by Rubens, Lely, Kneller, Hogarth, Gainsborough, Romney, Constable and Millais), poetry recitals and celebrations of Cornish culture. The fringe festival brings performers from all over Cornwall to the streets of the city – morris-men, clog dancers, brass bands, street theatre – and there is a riot of poetry, storytelling and sea shanties in local pubs. In 1985, drama came to the Three Spires for the first time in the shape of a production, in the Cathedral, of T. S. Eliot's *Murder in the Cathedral*.

The musical events, under the direction of Richard Hickox, range from the grand to the intimate, from the Bournemouth Symphony Orchestra, London Symphony Chorus and Three Spires Festival Singers in Walton's *Belshazzar's Feast*, the Berlioz *Te Deum* or Geoffrey Burgon's recently composed *Revelations*, to Christodoulos Georgiades (piano) playing Schubert, Prokofiev and Liszt. Recent festival appearances have also been made by Benjamin Luxon (himself Cornish born and bred), the Marisa Robles Harp Ensemble and the Northern Sinfonia of England in concerts which also featured Dong-Suk Kang (violin) and Steven Isserlis (cello).

WANGFORD

The pleasant Suffolk village of Wangford lies on the northern rim of Aldeburgh country, just up the road from Blythburgh and Southwold, and possesses a stately, well-windowed church that dates from mediaeval times. This building, which causes more than a few passers-by to linger and gaze, is – for a week each July – the centre of activities for Wangford's own festival of music and the arts. The event started life in 1966 with the aim, like so many country music festivals, of promoting music in the area, encouraging local talent and setting standards by including in the programmes artists of national, and occasionally international, standing. For the past eleven years, however, Wangford has been developing another aspect of its activities – one shared by few even of the big-league festivals – namely an annual competition for young composers, for a work running anywhere between twenty and thirty minutes and suitable for school performance. Each year distinguished composers descend on the village to assist with the adjudication: in 1985, Phyllis Tate and Gordon Crosse had the task of choosing between a number of pieces written specially for the Wenhaston Boys' Choir, director Christopher Barnett. The winning entry is given pride of place in a festival concert in the church – in 1975, it was David Nevens's *Dr Concocter*, performed by Worlingham Middle School Choir and the Lowestoft Youth Orchestra.

1975 was also the centenary of the birth of Martin Shaw, who spent the closing years of his life in Southwold, and the Wangford organizers marked the event by giving his music special attention during the festival.

There is something for most tastes at Wangford – jazz and folk evenings at one or other of the village pubs, drama, art exhibitions, period music (an Elizabethan evening put on by the New Suffolk Singers, directed by Philip Thorby, perhaps, or a concert of Baroque music entitled 'Birds, Beasts and Battles'), concerts choral (the Choral Scholars of King's College, Cambridge, running the gamut from Tudor polyphony to negro spirituals and close-harmony arrangements in Blythburgh Church); orchestral (the Mozart Orchestra in Boieldieu, Mozart and Butterworth, the West Suffolk Youth Orchestra in a programme embracing works by Handel and Britten) and both choral and orchestral (the festival's own choir and orchestra, assisted by the South Suffolk Teachers' Choir, conducted by Brian Lincoln, in Bach, Handel and Fauré's *Requiem*).

While most of the festival takes place in Wangford Church itself, there are occasional excursions to neighbouring villages, to Heveningham Hall or even as far afield as Lowestoft.

—3—

The Pealing Organ

Many festivals take place, in part or whole, in churches or cathedrals, and most of them, not surprisingly, make use in their programming of the resident organ. What could be more festive than to rouse from his noble slumbers the king of instruments at Wells or York or St Paul's in London and have him speak his part in the Berlioz *Te Deum* or Walton's *Belshazzar's Feast*? Or show his paces in a concerto by Handel or Poulenc, or a solo piece by Bach or one of the French masters of the nineteenth century? Indeed, a good number of festivals that do not have the advantage of a church setting manage to incorporate organ recitals – perhaps on the revamped instrument in the Victorian town hall or the one in the city's spanking new concert hall, its space-age pipework dominating the auditorium.

It is scarcely surprising that a few music festivals have actually grown up around the organ and its repertoire. At Bath, the Abbey is the home (for two weeks in early October) of an event whose aim is to promote the organ both in its solo role and also in ensemble with other instruments and with voices. This West of England Organ Festival – like its counterparts in Dunfermline, Manchester and St Albans – spices its programme of concerts and recitals with an organ-playing competition.

A recent arrival on the scene is the Oundle International Organ Week (mid-July) which exists for the specific encouragement of young organists and to establish an international forum for organists, teachers, organ builders and the interested public. It includes both a competition and a number of seminars by performers of international standing, and is centred on Oundle School.

DUNFERMLINE ABBEY

Dunfermline, for six centuries the capital of Scotland, boasts one of the finest ecclesiastical buildings north of the border. The great Abbey Church – part twelfth century, part nineteenth – with its commanding view over the Firth of Forth, is the last resting place of a number of Scottish monarchs, among them St Margaret and Robert the Bruce. It is also the home of a music festival which has taken place during the last week of June each year since 1981.

Dunfermline Abbey from the west.

The festival has at its centre an organ-playing competition for performers under the age of twenty-five, and each morning the Abbey resounds to the music of Bach or Howells or Vierne as competitors battle their way through preliminaries, semi-finals and finals. The winner gives a closing recital at noon on the last day. Dunfermline has attracted guest adjudicators of the highest order since its inception – among them Francis Jackson, Nicholas Danby, Susi Jeans and Jacques Marichal – who have delighted festival audiences with their own guest recitals and concert appearances. As well as the organ competition, there have also been competitions in anthem and hymn writing, and choir training workshops.

Each evening there is a concert (usually in the Abbey, though the Music Pavilion in the town's lovely Pittencrieff Park is used for lighter entertainments – such as Bill McCue or Ian Wallace in concert); sometimes this is choral and orchestral (the Duruflé *Requiem* coupled with the Berlioz *Te Deum*, or the Verdi *Requiem*, or Bach's

B Minor Mass, or a double-bill of the Mozart and Fauré *Requiems*), sometimes instrumental (Francis Jackson giving the first performance of his own Concerto for Organ, Strings and Percussion, the Scottish Baroque Ensemble, the Band of HM Royal Marines, or the London Gabrieli Brass Ensemble playing Boyce, Grieg, Gabrieli, Bartók and Paul Patterson. Regular performers are the Fife Youth Choir and Orchestra under Richard Galloway and the Abbey Choir and Festival Orchestra under Andrew Armstrong, the festival's director. This latter group is responsible for the music at the inaugural service which takes place on the opening Sunday afternoon and always includes a major musical offering – the Bach *Magnificat*, perhaps, Mozart's *Missa Brevis* K192 or Haydn's *Nelson Mass*. Alongside the musical events there are also art and historical exhibitions, drama and an important flower festival.

MANCHESTER

The September festival, which now takes place annually, started in 1978 as an organ jamboree, concerned with instruments of all kinds – classical, theatre and fairground. Indeed, an international organ competition still takes up a large share of festival interest, the Hradetsky instrument at the Royal Northern College of Music being the scene of contest for twenty-five top-flight young organists from all over the world. The competition is supported by a number of celebrity recitals – in 1984, John Scott played Baroque and modern pieces on the college organ, Ronald Frost gave a concert of Franck, Messiaen and Guilmant at St Ann's Church and Gordon Stewart gave a performance of Messiaen's *La Nativité du Seigneur* in Manchester Cathedral. On the lighter side, Brian Sharp and Hector Olivera gave recitals of music for theatre and electronic organs in the Free Trade Hall, there was a series of lunchtime 'Concerts at the Mighty Wurlitzer' and St Ann's Church was the setting for a 'Battle of the Organs' dual recital by Ronald Frost and Simon Lindley. Out of doors, Heaton Park at Prestwich, to the north of the city, played host to a fairground-organ rally, featuring more than forty different instruments.

But the Manchester Festival is no longer all organs. It now features jazz, classical music, drama and dance, exhibitions, light music, family events, films, visits and open-air entertainments, combining the contributions of nationally known professionals with the best that Manchester's talented amateurs have to offer. On the musical front, recent attractions have included a Viennese evening with the Hallé Orchestra conducted by Bryden Thomson, a popular concert by the Manchester Youth Orchestra under Victor Fox, and a variety of chamber recitals – Tang Yun (violin) and Christopher Cox (piano) playing Beethoven, Chausson and Paganini, the Alpha Duo in a programme of guitar duets from J. S. Bach to Bartók, and an instrumental and vocal concert of early English music featuring Paul Hillier (baritone).

Most musical events take place in central Manchester, at the Free Trade Hall, the Royal Exchange Theatre or the Royal Northern College of Music. However, the festival also provides the opportunity for audiences to experience music-making in a number of interesting, mostly historical, settings outside the city. In 1984, the Music Room at Heaton Hall, a fine Georgian stately home dating from 1772, was the setting for a celebrity organ recital by the festival's artistic director, Geraint Jones, who played music by Gabrieli, Pasquini, Krebs, Bach, Haydn, Wesley, Scarlatti and a number of eighteenth-century Portuguese composers. Also appearing at Heaton Hall were the singer Penelope Walker, Nicholas Daniel (oboe) and Julius Drake (piano) in a programme entitled 'The Menagerie', concerned with cataloguing some of the creatures that have found their way into the work of composers from Purcell to Poulenc, Schubert to Fats Waller, and followed by a five-course banquet. Adlington Hall, a half-timbered, black and white Cheshire manor house near Macclesfield was the scene of organ recitals by Gordon Stewart and Keith Elcombe, while less expected settings were provided by the Jodrell Bank Observatory (for a chamber concert by the Hartley Trio) and the narrow boat 'Castlefield', sailing the Manchester waterways to the accompaniment of Steven Smith's guitar.

Back in the city, the festival usually presents a number of exciting dance theatre programmes, involving such groups as the Manchester Youth Dance Theatre and the Northern Ballet Theatre.

As this survey suggests, to get the most out of the Manchester Festival, the classical music-lover still needs to be an organ enthusiast. But times are changing, and maybe the next few years will see the much needed introduction of more enterprising orchestral and choral concerts, some opera – however small-scale – and a wider encouragement of young composers and performers.

ST ALBANS
INTERNATIONAL ORGAN FESTIVAL

Few festivals anywhere in the world can take place in so magnificent a setting as St Albans Abbey. Its great square tower, built by the Normans during the eleventh century with red bricks plundered from the old Roman settlement of Verulamium, dominates the city. Its interior amazes the eye with its enormous length and spaciousness, and with the exceptional mediaeval wall-paintings – Annunciation, Crucifixion, likenesses of the saints – that line the nave. It is in the massive, echoing nave that most of the festival's major concerts – both choral and orchestral – take place.

The St Albans International Organ Festival, first held in 1963, was the brainchild of Peter Hurford, at that time Master of Music at the Abbey. His idea was for an ambitious blend of concerts, competitions and lectures which, while focusing on the king of instruments and the music written for it, also embraced the choral, orchestral and chamber repertoire. Above all, Hurford had two objectives – to set up a prestigious competition which would help to launch young organists on an international career, and to prove to the world that the organ has a part to play outside its familiar liturgical context. His philosophy of 'blowing away some of the dust from the image of the organ, its music and its performers' is one that continues to be cherished at St Albans today.

For the organ specialist, the festival offers a particularly interesting schedule, including exhibitions and demonstrations of chamber organs by some of the leading British makers, lectures on aspects of organ building, master-classes on the art of improvisation, and recitals by distinguished British and foreign organ virtuosi. Then there are the two highly regarded competitions – the Interpretation Competition and the Tournemire Prize – which attract gifted young players from all over the world.

For the general music-lover, the festival's eight early July days are crowded with delights: a major choral work given by a visiting orchestra and soloists with local choirs (in 1985, Verdi's *Requiem* brought the Royal Liverpool Philharmonic conducted by Walter Weller, with Suzanne Murphey, Sarah Walker, Arthur Davies and Kenneth Collins); a gala orchestral concert to round off the festival (in 1985, the Bournemouth Symphony under Vernon Handley played Elgar, Sibelius and Malcolm Williamson's Organ Concerto, in which Gillian Weir was soloist); a 'Three Choirs' concert in which the Abbey choir is joined by those of two other cathedrals or colleges in the Midlands or South of England (recent visitors have come from Guildford, Lichfield, Canterbury and New College, Oxford); a staged work (Britten's *Noye's Fludde* in which John Lubbock directed St Albans schoolchildren in 1983, Stravinsky's *The Soldier's Tale* with Timothy West and Aquarius conducted by Nicholas Cleobury two years later); children's concerts (Richard Baker, Alexander Baillie, the Albion Ensemble); chamber concerts (the English Concert under Trevor Pinnock, the Nash Ensemble with Norman Del Mar, the Orchestra of St John's, Smith Square, directed by John Lubbock, the Belgrade Strings directed by Alexander Pavlovic); and – in the festival club – local jazz, folk and cabaret groups. Regular contributions to the festival are also made by the locally based Hatfield Philharmonic Orchestra.

The organ is, of course, St Albans' most important unifying element, but efforts are made to bring a pattern to each year's programme by highlighting a particular theme. In 1985, the centenaries of J. S. Bach, Handel, Schütz, Tallis and Butterworth were all observed. New music is also a regular feature, recent commissions including a choral work by Judith Weir, a piece for chamber organ and small ensemble by John Casken and an organ work by Giles Swayne.

Events take place at St Albans from early in the morning until quite late into the evening. Festival visitors find themselves scrambling through breakfast in order to make the nine o'clock start of one of the competition elimination sessions in the Abbey. Then off to a lunchtime lecture at the Abbey Theatre, maybe, or an organ recital in St Michael's Church. The energetic might take in an afternoon concert, or explore the Roman remains at Verulamium or the fourteenth-century houses in French Row; lovers of church music will doubtless repair to Choral Evensong at five o'clock before snatching a meal and hurrying back to the Abbey for the evening concert. And – as if all this were not quite enough for one day – by ten o'clock, jazz or cabaret in the festival club are only just getting under way! The International Organ Festival is an exhilarating mixture, a marvellously hectic eight days in a splendid and accessible setting.

—4—
Some English Music Festivals

Festivals are thicker on the ground in England than in any other part of Britain. This is not a new phenomenon: Leeds, Norwich and Norfolk, the Three Choirs were all going strong long before Edinburgh or Cardiff were even thought of. And the post-war surge that has added tens of festivals to the musical landscape of Scotland and Wales has added hundreds to that of England. They have sprung up in tiny villages, in city suburbs, in the precincts of ancient cathedrals, in tourist-conscious seaside towns, in factories, in colleges and schools. They flourish in churches – especially churches – on summer lawns, in faded town halls, in faceless leisure centres, in hotels and restaurants, even in private houses – everywhere striving, be it by great and affluent means or small, to bring beauty and refreshment, challenge and enrichment to the daily lives of the communities they serve, whether, as at Stogumber, those communities are made up of a few hundred souls living in a sequestered nook of Somerset, or, like Aldeburgh, they reach out to embrace the entire musical world.

—ALDEBURGH—

Say 'festival' to music-lovers world wide, and many will reply 'Aldeburgh'; say 'Aldeburgh', and their unanimous response will be 'Britten'. Both the town, bright and bustling with its motley architectural styles, and its festival have become synonymous with the humanity and genius of one of the great figures of British music.

Yet the Aldeburgh Festival has never been a one-man show. Right from the start its direction was a co-operative venture – Britten joining with Eric Crozier and Peter Pears in overcoming the myriad financial and technical difficulties that stood in the way of a successful launch in 1948. By 1985, the number of artistic directors had risen to nine – Pears, Philip Ledger, Colin Graham, Steuart Bedford, Mstislav Rostropovich, Murray Perahia, Simon Rattle, John Shirley-Quirk and Oliver Knussen – all of them associated with the highest standards of performance and with the encouragement and development of the best in new music.

The origins of Aldeburgh were vividly described by Eric Crozier in the programme book for the very first festival. The previous year, he, Britten and Pears had been

---

Above: Aldeburgh; *Below:* The English Chamber Orchestra conducted by Jeffrey Tate playing at St Mary's Church, Bury St Edmunds, in 1984.

involved in the fatiguing, costly and time-consuming business of touring *Albert Herring* and *The Rape of Lucretia* through Europe, and it had struck them that there was something distinctly absurd in the fact that British operas had to be taken abroad to get an airing, performances in this country being both unheard of and impossible. It was Pears who had come up with the notion of starting their own festival – a modest one 'with a few concerts given by friends' – at which British music could be heard on home ground. On their return to Suffolk, they had set about selling the idea to the people of Aldeburgh and solving some of the problems that had inevitably suggested themselves – could they ask people to pay to attend concerts in church? was there enough room in the town to accommodate festival visitors? what was the best time of year to launch the venture? The townspeople, as things turned out, were hugely enthusiastic, a fact that encouraged the organizers to think beyond that first year, to 'a series of annual Festivals, to Aldeburgh as the centre of arts in East Suffolk, with its own hall for the annual visit of its Festival artists'.

The opening Aldeburgh season – squeezed into the parish church, the Baptist chapel, the Jubilee Hall and the cinema – contained ingredients typical of what was to come in succeeding years: new music by Britten (the *St Nicholas Cantata*) and other British composers (Martin Shaw's choral setting of *God's Grandeur*, Arthur Oldham's *Variations on a Carol Tune* for string orchestra), opera (*Albert Herring*, with a cast including Pears, Joan Cross, Margaret Ritchie, Nancy Evans, Otakar Kraus, Denis Dowling), chamber music (the Zorian Quartet), recitals (Clifford Curzon, Lennox Berkeley, Pears accompanied by Britten), lectures (E. M. Forster, William Plomer, Kenneth Clark) and exhibitions (Constable and contemporary East Anglian artists). Then, as now, the festival drew as much on amateur performers from all over Suffolk as on professionals.

As the years passed, houses, halls and churches in towns and villages around Aldeburgh also began to be pressed into concert service. The area is especially rich in fine churches – Blythburgh, just up the coast to the north, Framlingham inland to the west, Orford (scene of the first performances of *Noye's Fludde*, 1958, and the three Church Parables, 1964–8) to the south. But one of the festival's most important landmarks was reached in 1967 when the twentieth season opened at the newly converted Maltings concert hall at Snape. These spacious Victorian storehouses, set amid the bird-haunted marshes and flat grasslands that stretch either side of the River Alde, made a splendid, warm-sounding auditorium, capable of seating over eight hundred people and adaptable for both concert use and opera. The destruction of this building by fire in 1969 was a great blow, but it did nothing to deter the festival's continuity and growth. A restored Maltings was ready for opening in 1970.

A glance at what is happening in the eighties reveals further developments in Aldeburgh's organization and programming. For one thing, there is the participation of students from the Britten-Pears School, which since 1979 has been providing year-round practical and academic courses for young musicians on the threshold of a professional career. 1986 sees the start of a Mozart Festival in which Murray Perahia will be directing a production of *Così fan Tutte* with singers from the school.

Then there is the system by which a distinguished composer is invited each year to be the festival's composer-in-residence (Takemitsu in 1984, Dutilleux the following year). Film now also makes an important contribution each season, René Clair being the featured director in 1985. The natural beauty of the Aldeburgh area and the historical interest of some of its buildings are recognized in organized visits to places like Thorpeness and Framlingham. But the original emphases are also still present: British premières of works by Ligeti, Colin Matthews, Takemitsu (his *Rain Spell, A Flock Descends into the Pentagonal Garden* and *Toward the Sea II*), Holst, Robin Holloway, William Alwyn, George Perle, Stephen Paulus and Britten himself (*Tema SACHER* for solo cello); opera (*Owen Wingrave* and Handel's *Rodelinda*) and a wide range of choral, orchestral and chamber music.

Sadly, Peter Pears died as this book was going to press, but the dedication of all those at Aldeburgh to the legacy of Britten and Pears inspires confidence that the dream to which they gave life and reality will continue to attract the affection and support of audiences from all over the world.

——ALDEBURGH – ROSTROPOVICH FESTIVAL——

'Slava and Galya offer this Festival to Ben and Peter with love.' So ran the inscription on the first page of the programme book for the first Rostropovich Festival at Aldeburgh in August 1983. Mstislav Rostropovich and his wife, the singer Galina Vishnevskaya, first came to Aldeburgh, to the festival, in the mid-sixties. They were immediately captivated by the intimacy of the music-making and the warm friendly welcome they received from Britten and Pears. In return, Britten's admiration for the cellist's virtuosity and deep instinctive musicianship was evident from the flood of pieces he wrote especially for him – the Cello Sonata, the three cello suites and the Symphony for Cello and Orchestra. The Rostropoviches' love for Aldeburgh was, if anything, intensified after 1978 when they were deprived of Soviet citizenship – Aldeburgh and Britten being, by their own confession, 'the most precious things' in their lives.

Their festival was given annually from 1983 to 1985, but from 1987 is to become a biennial event, the Mozart celebration (see page 60) taking its place in August 1986. The idea for a Rostropovich Festival actually sprang from a conflict of loyalties. His appointment as one of the Aldeburgh Festival's artistic directors happened to coincide with his acceptance of the post of musical director of the National Symphony Orchestra of Washington, whose summer season clashes with Aldeburgh. Determined not to be just a figurehead, a name to appear on the official stationery, he decided to launch his own festival, lasting four days in high summer. Programmes bear the strong stamp of the Rostropovich personality – master-classes both in cello and Russian song, song recitals by Vishnevskaya with her husband at the piano (the 1984 festival included a feast of Rachmaninov, Mussorgsky and Tchaikovsky, plus Britten's Opus 76 cycle to words by Pushkin, *The Poet's Echo*), cello recitals (Bach unaccompanied suites in Blythburgh Church in 1985) and informal 'Russian Tea'

Right: Sir Peter Pears in the restored Snape Maltings concert hall.

Below: Anne-Sophie Mutter (violin), Rostropovich (cello) and Bruno Guiranna (viola) in 1985.

at which visitors have the chance to meet the Rostropoviches and raise funds for the Britten-Pears School. The Britten-Pears Orchestra makes frequent appearances, usually under the baton of Rostropovich, in programmes both popular (the *Classical Symphony* and *Peter and the Wolf* of Prokofiev, the latter with Peter Pears as narrator) and not so popular (Bach cantatas and concertos, with Heather Harper and Anne-Sophie Mutter as soloists). There is also always a chamber recital and usually some opera. This might come in film form (1984 featured Russian films of Tchaikovsky's *The Queen of Spades* and *Eugene Onegin*) or in concert performance, as when the opening festival included Tchaikovsky's one-act lyric opera *Iolanta*, with Vishnev-skaya, Nicolai Gedda and Dimiter Petkov.

Nor is the Rostropovich Festival – for all its brevity – lacking in great occasions: in 1983 Krzystof Penderecki conducted the Philharmonia Orchestra in the Sibelius Second Symphony and the British première of his own Cello Concerto No. 2, with Rostropovich as eloquent soloist. In 1985, cellist turned conductor to give the first performance of Britten's unfinished last work, the cantata *Praise We Great Men*, with Philharmonia forces and Heather Harper. The Rostropovich Festival may be short, so very short, but it is indeed marvellously sweet.

ARUNDEL

The Arundel Festival, which came into being in 1977, has traditionally revolved around the presentation of a Shakespeare play by the New Shakespeare Company (from Regent's Park Open Air Theatre in London) in the unequalled setting of the Tilting Yard of Arundel Castle.

But the Bard has never had it quite all his own way, and alongside *As You Like It* (1983) or *The Merry Wives of Windsor* (1984) there has been a host of other activities with which to crowd ten late-August days – carnivals, art exhibitions, poetry workshops, cabaret, sporting events, cinema (in 1985, the focus was on films with strong musical connections, from Losey's version of Mozart's *Don Giovanni* to Visconti's *Death in Venice* with its Mahlerian soundtrack), revue, musicals (*Half a Sixpence* 1983, *Two by Two* 1984, *A Little Night Music* 1985), more drama and an increasing quantity of music, from rock to the classics. Indeed, in 1985, Shakespeare stood aside and left the Tilting Yard stage to the world première of Iain Hamilton's opera *Lancelot*, with a cast including Mary King, Tom McDonnell, Michael Rippon and Jeremy Munro and the Orchestra of St John's, Smith Square, conducted by Christopher Nance. A large-scale musical undertaking of this sort, however, is something of a rarity at Arundel. Concerts tend to be on a more intimate scale and are presented in the more appropriate, though scarcely less striking, settings of the Parish Church of St Nicholas, the Roman Catholic Cathedral or the Great Drawing Room or Private Chapel of the Castle.

Notable visitors to the festival since 1982 have included the Endellion, Medici and Coull string quartets, Ian and Jennifer Partridge, Janusc Stechley (in idiomatic Chopin), Ruth Faber (harp), the Albany Brass Ensemble, the Carlos Bonell Ensemble, Nigel Kennedy, Julian Lloyd Webber, the BBC Singers under John Lubbock, José Feghali (piano), Ann Mackay (soprano) and the Guildhall String Ensemble. Organ recitals – by Richard Coulson, Andrew Newberry or Andrew Dean – have also been a regular feature and local contributions have come from the Chichester City Band, the Arun Choral Society (which in 1984 performed Elgar's *The Apostles* accompanied by the English Symphony Orchestra under John Atkins, with a fine line-up of soloists – Alison Pearce, Catherine Wyn-Rogers, Maldwyn Davies, Brian Rayner Cook, John Noble and Christopher Keyte), and Downland Opera, which delighted a cushion-clutching cathedral audience with its presentation of Mozart's *The Marriage of Figaro*.

Simon Standage
INSPIRING YOUR BEST EFFORTS

Simon Standage (*left*) and other members of the Salomon Quartet –
(*left to right*) Mica Comberti, Trevor Jones and Jenny Ward-Clarke.

As a violinist, Simon Standage takes part in a wide variety of musical
activities. He is leader of the City of London Sinfonia, plays – mainly as
soloist – with the English Concert and is a member of the Salomon Quartet.
In each of these roles he has experienced both the pleasures and the frus-
trations of festival work. 'Ideally,' he explains, 'a festival should be an occasion
for inspiring your best efforts. Of course, players tend to breeze in and out
of festivals during the season, and they are – before all else – a job of work.
But there is in a good festival concert a strong interaction between audience
and performers – greater, perhaps, than under other circumstances.' He
looks back with affection to the ten or so years when he played with the
English Chamber Orchestra: 'Going up to Aldeburgh was an annual event
and it was always exciting to be working on new music, not only by Britten.
but by other composers as well. The Snape Maltings is a very fine, a very
rewarding hall to perform in, and there always seemed to be a special
atmosphere at the concerts we gave there.'

It became a family tradition to combine the festival with an extended
holiday, but Standage is not at all sure that the arrangement really worked.
'You see, there is this conflict: holidays are about relaxing and unwinding
completely, whereas performing important works – often for the first time –
requires you to be keyed up, on your toes. You need to get the adrenalin

going not only in the concerts but also in the rehearsals, which – in the Aldeburgh case – were very much occasions in themselves.' At the same time, he is quick to recognize the value of festival engagements which entail his being in one place for several days on end. Nothing is worse, to his way of thinking, than a whistle-stop tour made up of one-night stands. The strain it places on a musician is immense, and sometimes makes it very difficult for him to give of his best. Besides, a lot of festival centres are, like Aldeburgh, pleasant to be in. Two or three days in a place which has its own interest and beauty can be a good way of recharging batteries.

'Of course,' he points out, 'one's response to a place or a situation can very much depend on one's company. It can be very lonely going to a strange place as a solo musician, even though festival organizers – especially those working on a smallish scale – are well known for their hospitality. And playing a concerto is in any case more of a strain than orchestral or ensemble work. On the other hand, if you are travelling as member of an orchestra, the benefits of company can quite easily be offset by the fact that you are sometimes forced to live in one another's pockets.' Almost all travelling orchestras and ensembles have experienced the tedious long coach journeys, the overcrowded and often draughty changing facilities or the problem of having to make do with platform seating and lighting arrangements which are far from ideal.

But Standage is not seriously worried about such problems if the occasion or the atmosphere of the festival can give him the necessary lift. He recalls his considerable disappointment with a concert he was engaged to play in as part of a festival in the London area. 'It really was a scrappy affair. It was labelled "festival" but it was far from festive in any way whatsoever. They were trying to make something out of nothing, and it just did not come off.' Nor, he believes, are grand or beautiful buildings enough in themselves to add the festive spice if they are lacking acoustically or fall short in other respects. It is all very well programming Purcell in Oxford's Sheldonian Theatre – an early Wren masterpiece – but it is very offputting to a player to have his performance punctuated, if not drowned, by traffic noise from the street outside. The acoustics of a building, he has found, tend to be all the more critical when the players are using old instruments. Some of the worst results have been in ultra-modern university lecture halls.

While he feels there is room for improvement in some departments of festival organization, Simon Standage is far from critical of festivals in general. He would like, one day perhaps, to settle down in a secluded spot and start his own. 'It's an attractive thought, but I'm very vague about the details at present. At all events, I hope I won't have to wait until retirement before doing something about it.' And he certainly has some firm ideas.

ASHBURTON

A ten-day event in this pleasant Devon town (early July).

ASHINGTON

An ambitious undertaking providing nearly a hundred events (a judicious mixture of the imported and the homegrown) for the inhabitants of the Wansbeck district of Northumberland (biennial, mid-May).

BADDESLEY CLINTON

A Sunday afternoon dance display and evening concerts at one of the National Trust's most popular Midlands properties (mid-June).

BANSTEAD

Music is just one of the attractions at this multi-media festival in the Surrey heartlands (two weeks or so in early May).

BATH

When, in 1984, Sir William Glock retired as artistic director of the Bath Festival (his distinguished predecessors having included Sir Yehudi Menuhin and Sir Michael Tippett), he suggested that a number of factors contributed to its huge success. In the first place, Bath is a striking town and one which grows more vivid and beautiful when thronged with visitors at festival time; second, its ideal size – population about 80000 – ensures that the festival does not get swallowed up, as sometimes happens in larger cities; and third, its attractive and well-appointed buildings are exactly suited in style and proportion to the performance of chamber music, which is the festival's main speciality. Although the 1984 festival actually employed no fewer than sixteen venues, it is on five in particular that the main burden falls – the Assembly Rooms and Guildhall for solo recitals and small ensembles, the newly restored Theatre Royal for opera and occasional ballet, and Bath Abbey and Wells Cathedral for choral concerts.

Bath Festival programmes offer seventeenth- and eighteenth-century music in plenty, to some extent suggested by the town's fine Georgian architecture, but the nineteenth-century repertoire is by no means elbowed out, at least so far as chamber music is concerned – though there are no purely orchestral feasts of Tchaikovsky or Brahms. Infinite care is taken over the concert planning – performers are asked for specific programmes and works rather than invited to bring what they have already in their repertoire. During the last ten years or so, there has been a steady increase in the number of contemporary works heard at Bath. In 1984, out of three

The Albany Brass Ensemble in the Guildhall at the 1985 Bath Festival.

hundred pieces included in festival concerts and recitals, sixty-seven were modern, and twenty-seven by living composers. Among living composers featured recently are Colin Matthews, John Tavener, Geoffrey Burgon, Edward Lambert, Roger Reynolds, Wolfgang Rihm, Harrison Birtwistle, Nicholas Maw, Simon Holt and – notable as resident composers during the 1984 season – James Dillon and György Kurtág.

Bath's great strength lies in its concentration into sixteen or so days in late May and early June of performances and programmes of a standard and interest that would be difficult to match anywhere else, even on London's South Bank. During recent festivals, for instance, visitors have been able to hear recitals by Benjamin Luxon, André Tchaikovsky, Nicholas Danby and Cécile Ousset, by the Brodsky, Chilingirian, Endellion and Medici Quartets, the Stuttgart Piano Trio and the Beaux Arts Trio of New York. In 1981, Julian Bream gave a guitar recital ranging from Bach to Gerhard and including Hans Werner Henze's *Royal Winter Music I*, Stephen Pruslin gave the first performance of Peter Maxwell Davies's Piano Sonata, Noël Lee played Stravinsky piano music and Laurence Allix juxtaposed works by Schumann and Messiaen. The same season, the Theatre Royal witnessed the first English performance of Maxwell Davies's *The Lighthouse* and a particularly fascinating programme was offered by Rohan de Saram and John Mayer who brought together pieces by Bach, Xenakis and Mayer himself with a display of traditional drumming from Ceylon. Contrasting choral concerts were given by the Tallis Scholars (directed by Peter Phillips) who sang Palestrina, Allegri and Byrd, and the John Alldis Choir who ran the gamut from Gabrieli to Birtwistle (the first performance of his *On the Sheer Threshold of the Night*).

It is in the area of choral concerts that Bath allows itself greatest flexibility. The Abbey – with its tricky acoustic and no-clapping rule – can take performances on a modest scale, such as the Hickox Singers and Orchestra in Haydn and Schubert masses or the London Sinfonietta and Chorus in a post-Romantic programme of Wagner, Messiaen and Robin Holloway (his *Evening with Angels*). One notch up, as it were, comes Wells Cathedral catering for more expanded forces – the Monteverdi Choir and Orchestra under John Eliot Gardiner, for instance, in the Mozart C Minor Mass and *Requiem*. But grandest of all are the occasional concerts put on in Bristol's Colston Hall, as when the then New Philharmonia Orchestra and Chorus with assorted soloists performed Beethoven's *Missa Solemnis* under Sir Charles Mackerras.

A *Times* columnist remarked recently that 'Bath is every British tourist attraction with a plus – Chester-with-a-view, York-with-good-food, Edinburgh-with-charm, Brighton-with-class.' In purely festival terms, of course, such comparisons are inappropriate, though tourism and festivals are frequent bedfellows. Perhaps it is enough to say that with the Bath Festival you know just where you are and what to expect – at the very highest level.

BATTLE

This festival, which recently notched up its quarter century, presents music in the town's historic parish church and other local venues, plus a spicing of art and literary and dramatic events (the second half of May).

BRACKNELL

South Hill Park Arts Centre has for some years been the focus of a range of summer festivities – mostly musical – catering for audiences both from the new town of Bracknell and also from further afield. Taking place between mid-June and mid-July, they each provide a weekend of specialist activity – dance, jazz, folk and – until recently – English music. 'Until recently' because in 1984 the festival, which for six years had been crowding choral and orchestral, chamber and solo, popular and esoteric, venerably old and precociously new music with a pronounced English accent into its crazily tight timetable, changed its name and became the Wilde Festival of Music. It did so for two reasons: first, because South Hill Park acquired a splendid new purpose-built auditorium in the shape of the Wilde Theatre to complement the facilities already available in the main house itself (South Hill Park is a handsome, if heavily Victorianized, mansion dating from 1760), and second, it was decided that the festival fare should no longer be exclusively English but should bring in music of other lands for purposes of context and comparison.

Though the Wilde Festival has a definite leaning towards new music, visitors do not have to be devotees of minimalism in order to find a great deal of enjoyment in its various activities. Festival commissions and other first performances jostle happily with more standard repertoire, to say nothing of the many informal recitals and light entertainments, from morris-men to Edwardian music-hall songs, that abound.

'Saturation' is – or perhaps should be – the Wilde motto. Every conceivable performing space is utilized: the theatre, suitable rooms in the main house – the Tall Hall, Cellar Bar, Gallery, Recital Room – and even a large marquee pitched for the occasion in the grounds. And virtually every minute is occupied. In 1985, Saturday started at 11 a.m. with a talk by Symon Clarke and Daryl Runswick about pieces they had written for that year's festival. At 1 p.m., the Albernis played Britten's First String Quartet in the context of a talk about the composer's quartet output. From 2 o'clock until 8 o'clock audiences had to choose – Wimbledon fashion – between rival attractions: was it to be Julian Lloyd Webber playing Britten, Bridge and Rachmaninov or Andrew Ball playing Tippett's First and Third Piano Sonatas? – Daryl Runswick's new work (played by the Contemporary Chamber Orchestra conducted by Odaline de la Martinez) or new pieces for clarinet and piano by Hugh Wood and Eric Maudat (played by Nicholas Cox and Vanessa Latarche)? – more Lloyd Webber (though in a different programme) or another cellist, Rohan de Saram, with his clarinet trio, in a programme of Beethoven, Kenneth Leighton (*Variations on an American Hymn Tune* Opus 70) and Simon Bainbridge (a festival commission)? – a second appearance of the Alberni Quartet playing Tippett (No. 2) and Britten (No. 3) or a divertissement entitled 'Royalty and the Muse' consisting of compositions by the families of Queen Victoria and Prince Albert played on nineteenth-century instruments? – a Bernard Roberts piano recital (Brahms and Bach) or an a capella choral concert of music from the fifteenth and sixteenth centuries? – Andrew Ball playing the Second and Fourth Tippett Piano Sonatas or the Bournemouth Sinfonietta in a middle-of-the-road programme of Boyce, Mozart, Rodrigo (the *Concierto de Aranjuez* with Guillermo Fierens) and Copland? And if the making of such choices was not enough, Philip Astle and Paul Williams played mediaeval and Renaissance music in the Tall Hall throughout the afternoon, while the cinema gave continuous screenings of a film about the life and work of Elizabeth Maconchy. And those who were not entirely exhausted by the day's activities could retire to the Cellar Bar to hear the Parlour Quartet in a late-night cabaret of Victorian ballads.

And all this was crowded into just one day. Other highlights of the 1985 festival included visits by the Orchestra of the Menuhin School (more Tippett as well as Barber, Mozart and Tchaikovsky), the London Gabrieli Brass, Aquarius (under Nicholas Cleobury), Collage and the Auriol String Quartet (playing Tippett and Hoddinott). Further new works making their first or second appearances were *Music for Strings* by Anthony Powers, Ron McAllister's songs to words by Adrian Henri, and Paul Patterson's *Mean Time*.

The Wilde Festival is a busy, joyous affair which fills its allotted time and space to overflowing and succeeds admirably in its aim of providing something for everyone.

BRIGHTON

Since its beginning in 1966, the Brighton Festival has both expanded – its season now lasts three full weeks each May – and undergone some changes in emphasis. Alongside local performers it has always featured world-famous artists (Olivier, Menuhin, Walton, Barenboim, Baker, Haitink, Abbado, Count Basey, Ella Fitzgerald, Rubinstein, the Amadeus Quartet, Ashkenazy, Arrau, Segovia, Previn, Zukerman, Brendel, Rostropovich, Ormandy, Perlman, Sutherland, Söderström, Cream, The Who) and it has always striven to illuminate the arts with its never heavy-handed thematic approach to programming (as when, in 1983, it focused on '1791 – the Last Year of Mozart's Life', with music of all sorts written by Mozart and his contemporaries, a double-bill of Pushkin's *Mozart and Salieri* read by Bernard Miles and Rimsky-Korsakov's opera of the same name, and an 'Inquest' into the circumstances of Mozart's death conducted by Francis Carr and Horace Fitzpatrick – all culminating in a performance of the *Requiem* given by Ann Mackay (soprano), Catherine Denley (contralto), Laurence Dale (tenor) and Henry Herford (baritone) with the Brighton Festival Chorus and the Royal Philharmonic Orchestra directed by Yehudi Menuhin.

With the appointment of Gavin Henderson as artistic director in 1984, however, the focus shifted somewhat. In the first place, Henderson set out to involve the local community in festival activities to a far greater extent than had been the case in the past, and to this end he encouraged the setting up of satellite festivals in outlying areas of the town – in Moulsecoomb, for instance, which now boasts marching bands, jugglers, magic, street theatre, dog displays, pony rides and its own Moulsecoomb Olympics, as well as in Kemp Town, Queen's Park and Saltdean. Henderson's other main aim was to strengthen the international content at Brighton, and this he has brought about by introducing twin themes each year, one of which relates to the artistic achievements of a particular foreign country: in 1984, 'Brighton's Heritage' went hand in hand with Poland (and visits from Warsaw Opera and Chamber Opera, the Cracow Radio Symphony Orchestra, the Warsaw Sinfonietta conducted by Tomasz Bugaj and Krzystof Penderecki, who directed performances of a number of his own works); in 1985, 'Clowns, Clowning and the *Commedia dell'Arte*' was matched with a look – quite appropriately – at the arts of France and Italy; in 1986, 'The Four Elements' is linked with Germany (the Dresden Philharmonic Orchestra joins with the Brighton Festival Chorus in Britten's *War Requiem*); and 1987 sees things through Scandinavian eyes, with visits from the Drottingholm Opera Company and Finnish National Radio Orchestra.

Just how well the thematic scheme works at Brighton, without becoming tedious or over-contrived, can be seen from a glance at some of the performers and events of the 1985 festival. Clowns and clowning were represented in many areas – in an

Above: Harlequin entertaining the crowds at the opening ceremony in 1985 when the festival theme was 'Clowns, Clowning and the *Commedia dell'Arte*'.

Below: Norman Del Mar conducting Mahler's *Symphony of a Thousand* in the Dome in 1985.

exhibition at the Gardner Centre entitled 'Behind the Auguste Mask' and in a workshop exploring the identities of 'Harlequin, Punch and Pierrot in England' at the Brighton Museum. They appeared too in the Ballet Rambert's production of Schoenberg's *Pierrot Lunaire* and in performances by Lindsay Kemp's Mime Company, the clown Dimitri and the solo mime artist, David Glass. On the musical front, Regency Opera conducted by Simon Gray put on Leoncavallo's *I Pagliacci*, the Consort of Musicke directed by Anthony Rooley performed Renaissance music-theatre, including works by Marenzio and Monteverdi rooted in the *commedia dell'arte* tradition, in the idyllic setting of Glyndebourne, The Fires of London gave Peter Maxwell Davies's *Le Jongleur de Notre Dame*, Michael Finnissy's *Mr Punch* and another version of *Pierrot Lunaire*, Yuri Temirkanov conducted the Royal Philharmonic Orchestra in music from Prokofiev's *The Love of Three Oranges* and – in another concert – Stravinsky's *Petrushka*, and new works by Harrison Birtwistle, Chris Dench, Justin Connolly, George Nicholson and Philip Grange on the festival theme were premièred at lunchtime concerts in the Unitarian Church. The clown motif was pursued further both in performances by Gerry Cottle's Circus and in several plays staged by British and Italian companies.

The Franco-Italian theme was both woven into this pattern of events and also stated independently: New Sussex Opera, directed by Bryan Balkwill, staged Berlioz's rarely seen *Benvenuto Cellini* (with a cast which included Neil Jenkins, Louisa Kennedy and Denis Wicks) and the BBC Symphony Orchestra under Lorin Maazel gave an all-French concert of Berlioz, Debussy (*La Mer*) and Ravel (the complete *Daphnis et Chloé*), while Poulenc's Organ Concerto was coupled with the Duruflé *Requiem* in a concert given by the combined choirs and orchestras of several Brighton schools, the Brighton Orpheus Choir and Orchestra performed Puccini's *Messa di Gloria* (in a concert which also featured Parry's *The Pied Piper of Hamelin*) and there were visits from Carlo Maria Giulini, Bireli Lagrene and Jacques Loussier. Brighton's themes are, however, seldom done to death, and distinctly unclownish music came in the form of Giulini's performance, in the Dome, of Beethoven's *Missa Solemnis* (with Philharmonia forces and soloists Anne Evans, Anne Gjevany, Siegfried Jerusalem and Robert Lloyd) and Norman Del Mar's account of Mahler's *Symphony of a Thousand*, in which distinguished soloists, including Teresa Cahill, Linda Esther Gray, Anne Howells, Helen Watts, John Mitchinson and Stafford Dean, were joined by the Brighton Festival and London Symphony Choruses and the Bournemouth Symphony Orchestra and Sinfonietta.

In 1909, when efforts were being made – in vain, as it turned out – to establish a music festival in Brighton, a writer in the *Daily Telegraph* had this to say: 'Brighton is nothing if not queenly. Is she not the queen of watering places? Now, bent on extending her sway, she is seeking to oust sundry inland cities from their high estate as queens of festival, and I am not at all certain that the day is far off when she will succeed in an effort which, begun today, is fraught with magnificent possibilities.' It is perhaps not too fanciful to suggest that, in the 1980s, the predicted success has come and the magnificent possibilities have been realized.

─────────────── BROADSTAIRS ───────────────

Not so much a festival as a series of concerts and recitals promoted by Broadstairs Music Club at intervals during February, May and June. Ballet usually starts the ball rolling and there are solo and chamber recitals.

─────────────── BROMSGROVE ───────────────

A well-established event in which ten to twelve concerts and recitals take place over the space of two weeks. The emphasis is on the classical repertoire, though there are also evenings of jazz and the occasional recital of words and music (April/May).

─────────────── BURY ST EDMUNDS ───────────────

The annual Bury St Edmunds (or St Edmundsbury) Festival takes place in the middle of May. It started in 1981 as a weekend event at the town's Theatre Royal, and has grown – under the watchful eye of the borough council – into a full fortnight of 'words and music', designed to appeal to townsfolk and tourists alike. The county town of West Suffolk, Bury St Edmunds has many fine and fascinating heritage buildings – the late eighteenth-century Athenaeum assembly rooms, the Angel Hotel with its Pickwickian associations, the ancient Cathedral noted both as the burial place of St Edmund and as the birthplace of Magna Charta – which provide appropriate backdrops for festival events.

Concert and recital programmes by well-known British and foreign musicians tend to be on the safe side. Peter Katin comes to play the *Moonlight Sonata*, *Clair de Lune* and Chopin's A flat Polonaise; Sir Charles Groves leads the Royal Philharmonic Orchestra in the Beethoven *Pastoral* and Sibelius Second Symphonies; and when the English Sinfonia visits the town, it is to give performances of Bach's Third Orchestral Suite and B Minor Harpsichord Concerto together with Vivaldi's *The Four Seasons*. Other recent festival appearances have been made by the Pipes and Drums of the 1st Battalion Scots Guards, Fritz Spiegl, Kenny Ball and his Jazzmen, the London Mozart Players, Martino Tirimo, Robert Cohen and the ubiquitous Carlos Bonell. Local talent gets a look in in the form of brass band concerts in the Abbey Garden cloisters, organ recitals (often on the fine instrument in the United Reformed Church) and choral concerts such as that given in 1983 when the St Edmundsbury Bach Choir and Orchestra under Harrison Oxley turned their attention to the English scene with Oxley's own *In all things the Lord*, Vaughan Williams's *The Lark Ascending*, Howells's *Hymnus Paradisi* and Gerald Finzi's beautiful *For St Cecilia*.

Other events during the fortnight include film (a complete mini-season of Olivier Shakespeare in 1985), lectures (such as Benny Green's account of the social and literary links between Wilde and Shaw) and entertainments of the order of *Don Juan in Love* (with Barbara Leigh-Hunt and Gary Bond) and *In the Eye of the Sun* (with

John Clegg as Rudyard Kipling). One of the highlights of each year's festival is a literary dinner at the Angel Hotel, with guest speakers who have in the past included Ludovic Kennedy, Alan Whicker, John Mortimer and the Earl of Lichfield.

BUXTON

The idea of comparing Buxton with Bath in a survey of music festivals may seem a little odd – at first, and indeed second, sight they appear to have little in common. But compare the two towns – their Roman origins, their popularity as eighteenth-century watering-places, their many fine buildings (Buxton's Crescent was built in direct rivalry to the Royal Crescent in Bath), their more recent development as year-round tourist and cultural centres – and things begin to fall more logically into place.

Buxton, capital of the Peak District, is very close to the sky, being one of the highest towns in England. The air is clear and heady, and the surrounding countryside – with its alternation of great craggy ridges and lush valleys – is breathtakingly beautiful. Architecturally it combines elegance with solidity, and contains many attractive and noteworthy buildings – from the Devonshire Royal Hospital (which boasts the widest dome in the world) to the well-gardened Pavilion and the Opera House. The festival was inaugurated in the late 1970s as a thematic arts event, occupying anything from two to almost four weeks each July and August. The original idea was to take a literary character – Sir Walter Scott, William Shakespeare, David Garrick – and explore his influence in the arts. But, in 1982, attention was turned to celebrating the centenary of the Hungarian composer Zoltán Kodály, and since then the themes have been less closely tied to individual personalities. The core of each festival is its operatic productions, supported by concerts, recitals, films, lectures, art exhibitions and a children's opera – all of which reflect the central theme – plus jazz, revues and other events on the fringes.

An idea of how this works in practice, and how tightly knit the music programming manages to be, can be given by looking at Buxton in two consecutive years. In 1984, the theme – chosen with National Heritage Year and the two hundredth anniversary of the opening of Buxton's neo-classical Crescent in mind – was 'The Greek Revival', the rediscovery of ancient Greek architecture and design in the second half of the eighteenth century, which had a profound influence on European thought and culture. The operas selected were Cherubini's *Medea* (with Rosalind Plowright in the title role) and Cavalli's *Jason* (in its British professional première) – both of which are based on the myth of Jason and the Argonauts. Anthony Hose – the festival's musical director – conducted, with the Buxton Festival Chorus and Manchester Camerata. Cherubini also figured largely in other concerts of the season: the Lindsay String Quartet gave a lecture-recital in which they explored his influence on Beethoven, while individual works (the *Anacréon* Overture and D Major Symphony) formed part of programmes offered by the Royal Liverpool Philharmonic Orchestra under Günther Herbig (with Anne Queffélec playing the second of Beethoven's piano concertos) and the Manchester Camerata. The latter concert was firmly rooted in the classics, with arias (sung by Caroline Green) from Gluck's

Iphigénie en Aulide and *Orfeo ed Euridice* and Mozart's *La Clemenza di Tito*, together with the *Idomeneo* Overture and *Jupiter* Symphony. Another Camerata concert, conducted by James Lockhart, struck a more modern note by including the Five Greek Dances by Skalkottas. All this was supported by lectures and exhibitions, a production of Racine's *Andromache* and a most enterprising programme of films, including Pasolini's *Medea*, with Maria Callas.

The following year saw a complete thematic contrast, with its focus on the legacy of the *commedia dell'arte* and its revivals of Piccinni's opera *La Buona Figliola* (based on Samuel Richardson's *Pamela* and last staged professionally in this country in 1810) and Galuppi's *Il Filosofo di Campagna* (last seen in England during the eighteenth century). Concerts included a programme of Vivaldi, Rossini and Tchaikovsky (the thoughtfully chosen *Souvenir de Florence*) by the Goldberg Ensemble directed by Malcolm Layfield and the London Barbican Ensemble playing Vivaldi, Salieri, Pachelbel and Bach on eighteenth-century Italian instruments. The Lindsay String Quartet gave a lecture-recital entitled 'Wit and Improvisation in the String Quartet' – an exploration of the development of the scherzo – and Peter and Raphael Wallfisch discussed the influence of Italy and the Italian Comedy on music for cello and piano in 'Il Violoncello Italiano'.

Much of what happens at Buxton is distinctly *not* run-of-the-mill; thoughtfully planned programmes illuminate the central theme in a way which combines entertainment with education. Buxton may not be the easiest place in the country to get to, but it is definitely worth the effort.

CAMBRIDGE

Cambridge has claims to being – after London – the most popular tourist resort in England. During the three months of June to August, its narrow streets and broad walks are thronged with visitors – long-stay holiday-makers, weekenders and day-trippers alike. Add to these the many language school students, the members of the university who do not disappear with the first hurrahs of the long vacation, the influx of professional men and women attending summer conferences at one or other of the colleges – not to mention the patient locals themselves – and you have one, at least, of the prime conditions for a successful festival: an almost captive audience.

The Cambridge Festival – nowadays a large-scale celebration embracing theatre, architecture, film, a self-contained folk festival and such special events as a festival half-marathon and carnival fair – started life as a purely musical event. Concerts and recitals, especially those given by the Cambridge Philharmonic and other local performers, had long been a feature of the summer months. In 1964, it was decided to try to concentrate some of these into a single 'festival' week, as a way of focusing attention on what was going on in the city and of attracting greater support from tourists and residents alike. Within a couple of years, the festival had developed beyond all expectations: performers started to come from outside the Cambridge area, non-musical events took root and flourished, a variety of fringe activities sprang up in schoolrooms and church halls throughout the city. The single week soon had to be stretched to two.

The Cambridge Festival is in no way an elitist event. The city council has, by means of its funding policy, encouraged it to play an important community role. This, together with the fact that Cambridge attracts by way of financial support from Eastern Arts rather less than half of the sum given to its near neighbour at King's Lynn, has led to the devising of concert programmes with a frankly popular appeal. The Mendelssohn Violin Concerto and Dvořák's *New World Symphony* may not get the critics up from London, but under conditions where high box-office returns are vital, they do at least pay their way.

Another of the problems festival music has to contend with in Cambridge is the lack of a modern, purpose-built concert hall with good acoustics and reasonable seating capacity. Ely Cathedral, sixteen miles away, is used for some large-scale performances, as is King's College Chapel, but the majestic settings they provide are not always enough to compensate for awkward seating arrangements and cavernous sound. Some orchestral concerts have been housed in a vast marquee in the grounds of Cherry Hinton Hall – as happened recently with an appearance by the Royal Philharmonic – but to no great advantage. The cramped and scruffy Guildhall also has to be pressed into service for a number of events each year. However, the problem should be effectively overcome by 1987 when it is hoped that conversion of the city's Corn Exchange into a 1500-seat auditorium will be complete. The college chapels come into their own as settings for chamber concerts, and one of the delights of any Cambridge Festival must be the opportunity to hear King's College Choir on its home ground. In recent years, a midday music series in St Edward's Church and daily organ recitals in one or other of the college chapels have been welcome additions to the festival programme.

Opera does not get much of a look-in, though productions which bring together professional and amateur singers under the umbrella of Cambridge Opera are put on in the Cambridgeshire College of Arts and Technology's tiny Mumford Theatre with some success. An interesting double-bill was provided in 1985 by Robin Orr's *Full Circle* and Ethel Smyth's *The Boatswain's Mate*.

Amid the profusion of events that make up the Cambridge Festival, music continues to play an important part – from the unofficial street musicians who set up their stands in quieter corners of the city centre, to international performers such as Vladimir Ashkenazy, Cécile Ousset and Andrew Davis, shipped in for prestige events. Though it is sometimes difficult to see much in the way of an overall scheme in the various activities, there is certainly plenty for the average music-lover to explore and enjoy. A typical recent season included the Verdi *Requiem* (with soloists Nelly Miriacou, Penelope Walker, Keith Lewis and Matthew Best), the BBC Philharmonic Orchestra in an all-French programme under Maurice Handford, Bach cantatas from the London Bach Society and Steinitz Bach Players, *Messiah* from King's College Choir and the English Chamber Orchestra, programmes by the Endellion and Lindsay Quartets and guest recitals by John Bingham (piano) and

Madrigals on the river with King's College Chapel in the background.

Robert Cohen (cello). Plus Gilbert and Sullivan, Stanley Black, the San Francisco Girls' Chorus and an Ernest Read children's concert in a hangar at Duxford Airfield.

CANTERBURY

The Canterbury Festival is a very new venture, having started life – under the direction of Mark Deller – in 1984, with the twin aims of 'providing pleasure and enrichment for local inhabitants and visitors alike, and presenting annually a unique combination of events which cannot be enjoyed elsewhere'. Taking as its starting point the fact that for many centuries people have travelled from all over Europe – and beyond – to visit Canterbury, it is essentially a festival of European art. Each year focuses mainly on the arts of a single country. In 1984, it was Britain; in 1985, Italy. Canterbury is splendidly endowed to host such a festival: the Cathedral and the new Marlowe Theatre – named after the city's most famous son – provide the settings for choral and orchestral concerts, opera and plays; the Shirley and Westgate Halls house chamber concerts and recitals; and the Poor Priests' Hospital and Old Synagogue are used for lectures and demonstrations. Most of the auditoriums are within comfortable walking distance of each other inside the ancient city walls.

The Canterbury Festival lasts for three weeks in late September and early October, weeks when there is still an autumn loveliness upon the city, and a sense of repose. Each day has anything up to half a dozen major events, with guided tours, workshops and illustrated talks starting at mid-morning and large-scale concerts providing a suitable climax just as night is closing in. As well as the main festival, there is a wide-ranging and lively fringe, catering for all ages and tastes, which brings activities very much into the city streets. There are also special Youth Days, on which performances and events are given both for and by young people, forming a vital thread throughout the three weeks. The first festival, in 1984, included performances of Adrian Cruft's opera *Dr Syn*, commissioned by Kent Opera and designed for presentation by schools.

1984 also saw Kent Opera's productions of Tippett's *King Priam* (conducted by Roger Norrington) and Mozart's *The Seraglio* (under Ivan Fischer). The Tippett was supported by an introductory talk by the composer, special workshop programmes for schools and adults, and Alan Howard in Christopher Logue's *War Music* (an adaptation of part of Homer's *Iliad*). There were orchestral concerts by the Kent Opera Orchestra (with Jill Gomez singing Britten's *Les Illuminations*), the English Concert (in a programme of Purcell, Handel, Telemann and Bach) and the Philharmonia Orchestra (Sir Charles Groves conducting Vaughan Williams, Walton and Elgar's Violin Concerto, with Nigel Kennedy as soloist). Other musical events included concerts and recitals by the Cathedral Choir (in Britten's *Rejoice in the Lamb*, the Howells *Requiem* and pieces by Walton, Berkeley, Tippett, Parry and Stanford), the Medici and Chilingirian Quartets, Peter Katin, the Julian Bream Consort, Alan Wicks (in an organ recital of music by British composers – including the first performance of a piece by Alan Ridout), the Deller Consort, the Stour Music Baroque Soloists under Mark Deller (in Purcell's *King Arthur*) and the Canterbury Choral Society (with Richard Cooke conducting *Belshazzar's Feast* and Vaughan Williams's *Five Mystical Songs*, David Wilson-Johnson soloist). Then there were jazz from George Melly, two separate Ballet Rambert programmes and the National Theatre Company in Giles Block's production of Goldsmith's *She Stoops to Conquer*.

If anything, the 1985 festival – on an Italian theme – was even more crowded. Kent Opera gave Handel's Italian opera *Agrippina* (with Felicity Palmer, Ulrik Cold and Meryl Drower) and Verdi's *La Traviata*, Theatre Project put on a Dario Fo/ Franca Rame double-bill, and there was a grand festival of Italian film. Andrew Parrott's Taverner Consort and Players performed Monteverdi and Gabrieli in the candlelit choir of the Cathedral, there was a Cloisters Prom concert given by the Chelsea Opera Group Orchestra (Rossini, Puccini, Respighi and Britten), and the festival came to a blazing climax with the Verdi *Requiem* (the Canterbury Choral Society, with Rosemary Hardy, Linda Finnie, William Kendall and Robert Hayward). There were lectures on violin-making, Italian opera, pasta-making, Leonardo da Vinci, St Francis, Bugatti and his cars, and the wines of the Veneto; there were excursions to Italian gardens at Penshurst Place and Hever Castle; there were displays of Italian *haute couture* and folksong and dance from Sardinia; there were masquerades and torchlit processions, a spectacular pageant entitled *Excelsior* given by the marionettes of the Teatro Carlo Colla e Figli, and a final *Grande Spettacolo* with fireworks, brass band and parachutes. Kent Opera's encouragement of music for young people continued with performances of Alan Ridout's opera *Angelo* and there were concerts of Italian music of all periods from the European Baroque

Orchestra (under Ivan Fischer), Malcolm Binns (piano), Alan Wicks (organ), the Jaye Consort of Viols, the London Early Music Group (conducted by James Tyler), L'École d'Orphée, the Deller Consort, the Songmakers' Almanac, the City of London Sinfonia (conducted by Richard Hickox), the Grimethorpe Colliery Band (under Elgar Howarth) and the Divertimenti Ensemble (with Sarah Walker).

A wonderfully imaginative, colourful enterprise, with bags of potential and very intelligent direction.

CHARLECOTE PARK

A short series of concerts given in the hall of another National Trust property, this time a mainly Victorian building not far from Stratford-upon-Avon (late July).

CHARNWOOD

A number of arts events involving residents in the area, with a special focus on young people, cluster around a small professional core. There are workshops as well as performances (late May).

CHESTER

The old Chester Festival expired in 1973 and its successor was born five years later, thanks to the patience and hard work – which perforce ran to fund-raising in all sorts of unlikely ways and catering on a gargantuan scale – of a small band of young devotees. Now firmly established as a major cultural event in the North-West, the festival runs for a week at the end of each July and aims to provide, in the words of its founding artistic director Martin Merry, 'something for everyone'. Concerts and recitals usually take place in the Gateway Theatre, St Mary's Centre – in the shadow of Chester Castle – and the fine Norman Cathedral, and fills slots at lunchtime, during the afternoon and early evening, and late at night, as well as the more usual concertizing hour of 8 p.m.

Main attractions each season are the choral and orchestral concerts in the Cathedral, with orchestras such as the London Mozart Players (conducted by Martin Merry himself), the Hallé (under Stanislaw Skrowaczewski), the Royal Liverpool Philharmonic, the Academy of St Martin-in-the-Fields (directed on different occasions by Iona Brown and Sir Neville Marriner), the BBC Philharmonic (conducted by Günther Herbig), the London Sinfonietta (Oliver Knussen) and the Royal Philharmonic (under Louis Frémaux) drawing appreciative audiences. A number of specialist choirs have also been guests of the festival, among them Oxford's Schola Cantorum and the National Youth Choir of New Zealand, but the main choral burden each season now falls on Chester's own 130-strong Festival Chorus, which performs works as widely different in mood and idiom as Fauré's *Pavane*, Mendelssohn's *Elijah*, Walton's *Belshazzar's Feast*, Vaughan Williams's *A Sea Symphony* and Handel's *Solomon* and Coronation Anthems.

Though many of Chester's programmes are fairly mainstream, new music gets more than a token nod. Each season now includes a festival commission (*Cantos de Amor* by Odaline de la Martinez in 1985) while Richard Rodney Bennett was composer-in-residence in 1984. Two years earlier there was a positive McCabe explosion, with the composer playing Haydn and Clementi piano music, and his own Third Symphony (*Hommages*), Third String Quartet and choral music appearing in programmes by different groups.

Chamber music is generally well represented at Chester: the 1985 festival opened with the Stuttgart Piano Trio (Haydn, Ravel, Schubert), went on to the Salomon Quartet with clarinettist Alan Hacker (Mozart and Beethoven) and drew to a close with the piano quartet Domus in a programme of Mozart, Fauré and de la Martinez. Recitalists that year included Susan Milan (flute), John Harle (saxophone), Nicholas Kyneston (organ), Malcolm Messiter (oboe) and Pascal Rogé (piano). Rogé was also responsible for the festival's second master-class, the first having been given the previous year by Erich Gruenberg. For the specialist music-lover there were the Barbican Percussion Ensemble – playing Salzedo, Takemitsu, Bartók and Reich – Les Saqueboutiers de Toulouse in a programme of Renaissance music, the Albany Brass Ensemble (music from Praetorius to Peter Racine Fricker) and the Amaryllis Consort. And, on the lighter side, there were appearances by the Pasadena Roof Orchestra, Mike Westbrook and Harvey and the Wallbangers.

The Chester Summer Music Festival is very much alive and well, in spite of recent financial stringency on the part of the Arts Council. It provides for the residents of an old and lovely city the opportunity to hear internationally famous artists (Ousset, Sarbu, Cohen and Baker in recent seasons) in a broad repertoire, without having to travel to Liverpool or Manchester or London for the privilege.

CHICHESTER

It was in 1975 that the people of Chichester saw fit to commemorate the nine hundredth anniversary of the event which first put their city on the map. Their '900 Festivities' were an acknowledgement of the fact that, had it not been for Bishop Stigard's decision to transfer his see from Selsea to what, during the early years of the Norman Conquest, was little more than an obscure inland settlement, their city, with its gem of a Cathedral, might never have become what it is today. And the gratitude continues, for the festival has now become an annual fixture, the 1985 event being billed as 'Chichester 910 Festivities'.

The Norman Cathedral, modest in size but exquisitely proportioned and lovingly maintained, is the principal venue for festival music. Its nave thunders to the sound of a symphony orchestra and massed choirs in full cry, or answers more subtly to the tones of solo cello, harpsichord or string quartet. The familiar – the so-English sounds of cathedral choristers in concert – alternate with the unfamiliar – perhaps an evening of jazz or close harmony or the colourful rhythms of the flamenco guitar.

There is music elsewhere in Chichester too – a piano recital in one of the public buildings, a brass band playing outdoors near the Market Cross.

The 1985 festival provided audiences with a typically satisfying mixture of music for all tastes. The Cathedral heard concerts by the English Chamber Orchestra (in a Baroque/Classical programme directed by Philip Ledger), the Bournemouth Symphony Orchestra (a gala evening in which Richard Armstrong conducted Schubert, Wagner and Brahms and Rosalind Plowright gave a moving account of Strauss's *Four Last Songs*) and the more local Southern Chamber Orchestra. The Cathedral Choir and the Consort of Twelve presented music written for the Chapel Royal and there were recitals from Peter Donohoe (a well-received all-Chopin programme) and Kyung-Wha Chung. Premières of festival commissions figured in programmes by the Academy of St Martin-in-the-Fields (Carl Davis's *Fantasy for Flute, Harpsichord and Strings (Diana and Actaeon)*) and in the performance by Frances Kelly (harp), Ann Mackay (soprano) and Susan Milan (flute) of a new piece by Robert Walker. The Chichester area's own St Richard Singers performed Magnificats by Whyte, Schütz, Pergolesi, Stanford and Leighton at Boxgrove Priory, while visitors from further afield included the Morriston Orpheus Choir (accompanied by the Royal Artillery Band), the Schola Cantorum of Oxford and the Yorkshire Bach Choir and Baroque Soloists.

As for the non-musical – there were lectures, exhibitions, children's activities and entertainments, sporting events, film programmes and late-night happenings. A thoroughly warm-hearted July fortnight which succeeds in setting the whole of Chichester aglow.

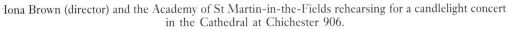

Iona Brown (director) and the Academy of St Martin-in-the-Fields rehearsing for a candlelight concert in the Cathedral at Chichester 906.

CHIDDINGLY

Amateur meets professional in an annual four-day celebration, a little off the beaten track near Lewes in East Sussex (early October).

CHURCH STRETTON
AND SOUTH SHROPSHIRE

Church Stretton – the red-roofed market town on which Mary Webb's 'Shepwardine' is said to be based – snuggles in a fleece of trees at the foot of the imposing Long Mynd ridge. To the north-east rises Caer Caradoc, where Caractacus made his last stand against the Roman legions, while to the west – beyond Bishop's Castle – lies the Welsh border.

The festival here started life in 1967 as a small one-off celebration with music and other events, featuring students from the Royal College and Royal Academy of Music, complemented by local amateur organizations. Its success prompted a repeat festival in 1968 and it has since developed into an annual two-week fixture, held at midsummer, and covering as wide a range of the arts as possible. Concurrently with the fortnight of concerts and recitals, there is an exhibition of art, photography and crafts, mainly by local people, some of whom demonstrate their skills in action.

Over the years, Church Stretton has progressed from a student-plus-amateur format to a mainly professional series of high-quality events, the aim of the organizers being to bring the best in artistic endeavour to a part of rural Shropshire remote from the larger centres of culture. The festival now also proves something of an attraction for holiday-makers from other parts of the country.

Things are planned on an intimate, friendly scale. Church Stretton has a population of around 3500 and the surrounding countryside is not densely peopled. The largest venue for events is the town's school hall, holding a maximum audience of three hundred, though use is also made of churches and halls in other South Shropshire towns and villages – including places as far-flung as Clun and Bishop's Castle.

Not surprisingly, musical events are largely on a chamber scale and tend to employ young performers just starting out on a professional career: the Taskin Trio, the Meridian Chamber Choir, the Roth and Caradoc Quartets, Serenata, the Camille Ensemble and Cantabile. The Shropshire Schools' Symphony Orchestra and Desford Colliery Band (under the direction of Howard Snell) have made music on a somewhat grander scale over the last five years, while solo performers have included national award winners Anna Markland (piano) and Richard May (cello). Most years see intimate opera productions by Pavilion Opera (*Don Pasquale* in 1983, *The Marriage of Figaro* in 1984, *La Traviata* in 1985) and touring ballet companies also make appearances. The 1985 season featured a celebrity piano recital by the festival's president, Frank Wibaut.

CLEVELAND

Cleveland is a festival in the making: the seeds were sown in February/March 1985, when some 1200 musicians from all parts of the county were joined by about 150 visiting professionals in three weeks of music-making. If sufficient support is forthcoming, it is hoped that the Cleveland Festival will become a biennial event, starting in 1987. The major aim of the 1985 venture was to provide a platform for as many musicians from the region as possible, concerts of rock, pop, folk, jazz, music from the shows, contemporary dance, choral, orchestral and brass band music being arranged in centres as widely spread as Stockton, Redcar, Middlesbrough, Guisborough, Hartlepool, Saltburn and Norton.

Highspots were the opening concert given by the specially formed Festival Choir and Orchestra under David Whittington, in which the main work was the Berlioz *Te Deum* (soloist Robin Leggate), a visit by the Berlin State Symphony Orchestra conducted by Otmar Suitner in a programme of Beethoven and Brahms, a Northern Sinfonia concert (conductors Sir Michael Tippett and Richard Hickox) in which three Tippett works (*Songs for Ariel*, *Songs for Dov* – both featuring William Kendall – and the *Fantasia Concertante on a Theme of Corelli*) were spaced between pieces by Handel and Stravinsky, and a grand finale in the shape of a performance of Bach's B Minor Mass (the Cleveland Philharmonic Choir and Northern Sinfonia Orchestra directed by Owain Arwel Hughes, with soloists Rita Cullis, Gillian Knight, John Graham-Hall and Peter Knapp).

If the overall programme benefited from a good stiffening by professional ensembles, local choirs and orchestras certainly played a significant part in the festival's success. The Teesside Polytechnic Orchestra, under Graeme Rudd, played Brahms and Gordon Jacob at its Middlesbrough base and the Guisborough Choral Society and Orchestra gave Haydn's *Creation* on their home territory; the Cleveland Philharmonic Orchestra, conducted by Edwin Raymond, played Arnold, Mahler (the First Symphony) and Mozart (Jack Brymer was guest soloist in the Clarinet Concerto) in Middlesbrough Town Hall and the Teesside Symphony Orchestra, also under Edwin Raymond, took the Dance Episodes from Copland's *Rodeo*, Dvořák's *New World* Symphony and the Bruch First Violin Concerto (with Katherine Loynes) to Hartlepool. The Michaelmas Singers wove a tapestry of English church music for the benefit of audiences in Hartlepool and Stockton, while the Middleton Festival Choir appeared in Saltburn. Youth was well represented, not least at the Schools' Prom presented by Hartlepool Youth Choir, Hartlepool Senior Wind Quartet, Langbaurgh Youth Choir and Cleveland Youth Orchestra, all under the baton of Peter Haughton. Cleveland is clearly fertile soil for a festival, and it is to be hoped that 1985's pilot venture will lead to something permanent in the future.

CORBY

A rich mixture of events from symphony concerts to country-and-western music, plus exhibitions of arts and crafts and late-night films. A special feature is the travelling drama group which plays in outlying towns and villages during the daytime (dates vary – provisionally October in 1986).

CROSBY

Plenty of encouragement for community participation for twelve days or so in early October, but the festival also includes professional events in a variety of areas of the arts.

DAWLISH

A Devonshire festival which provides a platform for groups and individual artists from the immediate South-West (June–July).

DISLEY

Lyme Hall, a stately home set in 1300 acres not far from Stockport, is the setting for this *Augustfest* of craft, folk music and country pursuits, capped with a range of evening concerts.

DOLTON AND DOWLAND

Only about 500 people live in these two North Devon parishes, but the festival they hold each summer attracts visitors from a wide radius. Concerts, exhibitions and village events are the order of the day (May–June).

DURHAM

Devoted entirely to presenting all kinds of classical music in such pleasing and appropriate settings as the grey-towered Cathedral (for major choral and orchestral contributions), the Great Hall of the Castle (for mediaeval and other early music) and the various halls and theatres of the University (for chamber concerts and lecture recitals), the Durham Festival ambles its way through four genial October weeks. A wholly professional affair, it offers music-lovers in the North-East the chance to hear well-known performers from home and abroad (Radu Lupu, Manoug Parikian, Malcolm Binns, Tamás Vásáry, Rohan and Druvi de Saram, Gina Bachauer, the Vienna Boys' Choir and the Gabrieli and Hungarian Quartets) as well as young musicians at the start of their career. The Newcastle-based Northern Sinfonia takes the lion's share of orchestral work, while among smaller ensembles the Praetorius Consort and Collegium Musicum St Martin of Bremen have made welcome visits. Festival programmes cover generously the range of music from the 1500s to the present day, a single season being as likely to offer works by Dowland and Skalkottas as it is major works by Schubert and Brahms.

The Durham Festival is a co-operative venture sponsored by church, university and city council; its smooth running and high standards show what can be achieved by the pooling of resources and the sharing of responsibilities.

EXETER

Exeter's two weeks of festival merrymaking in May and June come to a boisterous conclusion with an open-air square dance in the High Street, a torchlight parade and fireworks in the gardens where Rougemont Castle once stood. For a decade, this festival 'by the people and for the people' of the capital of the South-West has been encouraging a staggering range of popular interests from beer-tasting to pavement artistry, from five-a-side football to model railways, from city walking to clowning. Indeed, throughout the festival fortnight, Exeter seems to explode in a riot of activity, with nine or ten major events taking place in a single day. Music and ballet, theatre and the visual arts all have a major part to play, the emphasis being decidedly on entertaining rather than educating the audiences.

The majestic twin-towered Cathedral is the centre for most major musical activities, though there are also regular concerts at other venues close by, such as St Stephen's Church, the Barnfield Theatre and the Exeter School of Music. St George's Hall is used for pop concerts and the Northcott Theatre, on the university campus to the north of the city, caters for drama and ballet.

Performances by talented local groups are sandwiched between those by guest professionals from outside: in 1984, the Cathedral was the setting for concerts by, on the one hand, the Devon County Choir and Orchestra (Vaughan Williams's *A Sea Symphony* coupled with Janyce Pringle's *They that go down to the sea*, conducted by Sir David Willcocks), Exeter Cathedral Choir (by candlelight, with Marisa Robles), Devon County Chamber Orchestra (under Antony le Fleming, with Julian Lloyd Webber as guest soloist), and on the other, the Band of the Grenadier Guards, the Chieftains, Bernard d'Ascoli (playing a popular selection of Chopin, Debussy, Schumann and Ravel), the University of Missouri Singers and the City of Birmingham Symphony Orchestra conducted by Simon Rattle (the centrepiece being the *Eroica* Symphony of Beethoven). Further encouragement of local talent was in evidence in concerts by the Devon Sinfonia, the Exeter Children's Orchestra (both at the Barnfield Theatre) and the Exeter School of Music Singers, and in a plethora of lunchtime organ, guitar and vocal recitals at churches around the city. At the Northcott Theatre, home-based productions of *As You Like It* and Martin Sherman's disturbing play, *Bent*, eventually gave way to exciting programmes from the Ballet Rambert, employing music from Monteverdi to Janáček.

Exeter fills itself with festival in these two early summer weeks, the sense of occasion being enhanced by the closeness to the Cathedral and the city centre of most of the churches and halls used for the staging of events. If the annual musical recipe looks, from a distance, a little unenterprising – to a major choral work add a couple of orchestral concerts and recitals to (popular) taste, season with local talent and stir – at least it makes for a diet of which a large number of Exonians approve and on which they seem to be thriving. And that, at the end of the day, is what matters.

FAKENHAM

Well-known professionals join with local enthusiasts in this well-established Norfolk event, which started in the mid-sixties as a single thanksgiving concert to celebrate the recently completed renovation of the parish church. Music ranges from heavy pop to light classics and there are drama productions, exhibitions and lectures. It is held biennially in May.

GILLINGHAM

Funded by the local borough council, Gillingham Arts Festival in North Kent looks to interest individuals and groups of all ages and organizes events in suitable venues throughout the area (April–May).

GLOUCESTERSHIRE AND WORCESTERSHIRE PHILOMUSICA FESTIVALS

The Philomusica of Gloucestershire and Worcestershire is a society of dedicated amateur musicians – some seventy-five orchestral players and one hundred and forty choristers – who are joined by professional instrumentalists and singers in festival music-making in and around the 'Three Choirs' counties of Gloucestershire, Herefordshire and Worcestershire. Though their main activities now focus on the music of Elgar and the performance of seventeenth- and eighteenth-century repertoire in the Baroque splendour of Great Witley Church, their first festival was a one-off Vaughan Williams celebration held in the composer's birthplace, Down Ampney, in 1972.

The first Elgar Festival was held in Tewkesbury in 1978. The Philomusica forces were augmented for the occasion by the Avon Schools' Orchestra, the Birmingham Philharmonic Orchestra and the Choir of Sir Thomas Rich's School, Gloucester. The Abbey was the setting for all the concerts and recitals, while the Roses Theatre was used for a number of talks (including one by Dame Isobel Baillie on her life and memories of Elgar). The works performed were the Imperial March, the anthem 'Great is the Lord', the Cello Concerto (with Roger Lewis as soloist), the oratorios *The Light of Life, The Kingdom, The Apostles* and *The Dream of Gerontius, Sea Pictures* and a number of other songs, the First Symphony and *Cockaigne Overture*, the *Coronation Ode* and *The Spirit of England*, the G Major Organ Sonata (played by Roy Massey), the Serenade for Strings, *The Music Makers*, the *Enigma Variations* and several lighter pieces. And all this was accomplished in the space of two weeks in late May.

The Herefordshire festival, held two years later, was equally ambitious, though a number of works were repeated from the Tewkesbury programmes. To these were added the cantata *Caractacus*, the *Froissart Overture*, *Falstaff*, the Violin Concerto (with Ralph Holmes), several part-songs, the Civic Fanfare, *The Starlight Express* and the Piano Quintet (given by the Richey Quartet with Dorothy Maxwell Geddes).

The biennial pattern of Elgar festivals was continued with a Gloucestershire season in 1982 and one in Worcestershire in 1984. The latter was notable for performances of *King Olaf*, *The Banner of St George*, *Gerontius* and *The Spirit of England* given in St George's Catholic Church, Sansome Place, Worcester, where Elgar served as organist and choirmaster from 1885 to 1888 and for whose choir he composed several of his early choral works. During the autumn of 1984, the society also mounted a parallel Gloucestershire festival, repeating a number of the Worcester concerts in churches throughout the county.

The Great Witley Festival started as a fund-raising event – in support of the restoration of the church – in early summer 1985. Handel was the central focus of the concerts, though music by his contemporaries, J. S. Bach and Vivaldi, also featured in the programmes. The works performed included the oratorios *Samson*, *Judas Maccabaeus* and *Messiah*, together with a number of solo arias and anthems. The great financial success of the venture led to the planning of a Haydn-Mozart Festival for 1986.

GLYNDEBOURNE

What is Glyndebourne? A very English institution. A place of pleasant lawns and wooded walks, nestling under the Sussex Downs not far from Lewes. A fine, though

Supper in the garden during the long interval at Glyndebourne.

not gaudy, country house which had the good fortune to fall into the hands of a wealthy music-lover and his singer wife and which – under their direction – acquired its very own opera house. A nursery for promising young opera singers from all parts of the world. The London Philharmonic Orchestra's home-from-home for the summer. A kind of legend. A name synonymous with the highest standards of operatic performance, brought about by half a century of association with the genius of men such as Jani Strasser, Fritz Busch, Carl Ebert, Rudolf Bing, Vittorio Gui, John Pritchard, Peter Hall and Bernard Haitink. Motoring or taking the train down from Victoria on a bright June afternoon, in time for a leisurely cream-tea and a wander round the Organ Room before the five o'clock performance. Rubbing shoulders (well, almost) with the rich and famous – the Thatchers bustling to their place just in time for curtain-up, the Foots and Silkins taking a turn round the walled garden during the long interval – assorted lords, critics, faces from television, musicians – Bernard Levin here, there and everywhere. Black ties and gowns that were once elegant. Corners of the lawns stacked with picnic chairs and hampers and rugs in readiness for *dîner sur l'herbe*. Midges. Unexpected light drizzle. And incomparable productions: pre-purist Monteverdi (*L'Incoronazione di Poppeia* realized and directed by Raymond Leppard, with Richard Lewis on the top of his form as Nero), Jean-Pierre Ponnelle's genial, bustling production of Verdi's *Falstaff*, rarities such as Strauss's *Die Schweigsame Frau* or Janáček's *The Cunning Little Vixen*, Mozart favourites (*Die Zauberflöte*, with David Hockney's splashy designs, *Così fan Tutte* and a magical *Le Nozze di Figaro*) and new works like the recent Oliver Knussen/Maurice Sendak collaborations *Where the Wild Things Are* and *Higglety, Pigglety, Pop!* No really big names on the cast-lists, but fresh young voices – Linda Esther Gray, Felicity Lott, Elizabeth Gale, Teresa Cahill, Norma Burrowes, Thomas Allen and John Tomlinson during the seventies – on their way to bigger things. Glyndebourne is all this and more.

Perhaps it is not strictly a festival – its season of five productions (two new and three revivals each year) runs all the way from late May to mid-August – it is, none the less, music-making under the most glitteringly festive of circumstances. It may be elitist, but it is by no means selfish – during the late forties its productions were regularly trundled up to Edinburgh at a time when that festival's operatic traditions were still at the formative stage; forty years on, one of the highlights of the Promenade Concert season in London is a semi-staged performance of one of the operas currently in the Glyndebourne repertoire; and – most important of all – there is the touring company which each autumn does the rounds of a number of English and Welsh cities. It may be costly, but then four fifths of its financing comes from box-office receipts, the other fifth from private sponsorship and donations. And tickets may be difficult to come by, unless you are a member of the Glyndebourne Festival Society or get your application in months before the season opens.

What is Glyndebourne? Entire books have been devoted to its glorious history and achievements. Simply say that it is one of a kind. Festival opera at its brightest and best. Under no circumstances to be missed.

Linda Esther Gray
BALLOONS AS WELL AS MUSIC

The name of Linda Esther Gray – winner in 1973 of the coveted Kathleen Ferrier Scholarship – is chiefly associated today with the international opera stage and particularly with the performance of Wagner. But festivals have played a significant part in her development as a singer and she still makes as many festival appearances as her busy schedule will allow.

Linda Esther Gray's career got off to an uncertain start at the Greenock Festival – a competitive event held in the Scottish town where she was born. She tells amusingly of how round about the age of five to seven she was repeatedly entered for the singing competition, and repeatedly came last on account of forgetting the words or the tune or both! Undeterred, she turned to the instrumental section, and actually did rather well as a pianist. It was singing, however, that after a spell at music college took her – on the wings of a John Christie Award – to Glyndebourne and the real beginnings of her career.

Looking back on her six years with the Festival Opera – from 1971 to 1976 – Linda Esther Gray recalls particularly the high standard of training which young singers received. Hours were long and financial rewards were very small, but the rehearsals, the music calls, the in-house 'showings' where young aspirants could take part in performances watched by an audience of their fellow singers – all came together to produce the high ensemble standard recognized throughout the opera world. Working at weekends, and especially on Sundays, was a bit of a shock at first, but this was offset by the sense of comradeship (Elizabeth Gale and John Tomlinson were close contemporaries who remain good friends) and the special atmosphere of Glyndebourne.

'Atmosphere' for members of the company was not perhaps what it was for the audiences. Not for them the alfresco suppers, the evening dress, the interval strolls through the dusk-filled gardens. Their atmosphere, she recalls, was more to do with the sense of joy at working hard at great music, the sense of elation at a good performance. Performers were kept well away from the front of house once the audiences began to gather, and they sometimes responded with glee at the sight of picnickers hitching up their dresses and sprinting for cover during one of those not infrequent Sussex showers. If the weather was sometimes a let-down, however, the same was unlikely to be true of the performance. 'People who go to Glyndebourne,' she remarks, 'do not go to hear great singers or big stars. That's not what it is all about. They go to hear well-drilled, carefully rehearsed performances. You will never hear a dull performance at the festival, but equally you will probably never hear a great one.' She speaks with some regret of the fact that the singers themselves – for all the care that goes into their preparation – are treated very much as members of a team – 'no more individual than the people who work in the cutting room' – and that they are not encouraged to develop their own musical personalities. To do that, they have to go elsewhere.

After opera, the concert platform comes next in Linda Esther Gray's affections. She enjoys working on oratorios and cantatas with large choruses and orchestras because doing so is, for her, the nearest thing to opera. She recently took part in the opening concert of an Edinburgh Festival – one of the first Scottish singers to achieve this distinction – performing the Beethoven *Choral Symphony*. 'The only thing that bothered me was the sneaking feeling – which I don't get with opera – that there was probably someone up there behind me in the chorus who could do the job just as well as me.' For her, the Edinburgh Festival is all that a festival should be. The city itself plays a large part in the creation of the right atmosphere, as does the time of year. But she also likes the fact that it is not just a music festival and that – as someone taking part – she can spend free time seeing a play or visiting an art exhibition. There is also that – for her – all-important sense of joy. 'Festivals,' she insists, 'should be balloons as well as music.' The festival atmosphere – or lack of it – can actually affect the standard of performance a musician gives. A keen, vibrant audience, sharing what for them may be a very rare musical experience, can 'lift' the singer and make him or her rise to new heights of interpretation in a way that some routine occasions can seldom do. 'When I sense that the audience is exhilarated by the occasion, it actually helps me to make my music to a higher standard and I know from the start that I'm going to have a good time.' It is too bad, she reflects, that some festivals do not have this feeling at all, that they stay essentially earthbound, with the result that the performances suffer.

Another aspect of festival performances that enthralls Linda Esther Gray is the sense of place that they often provide. There is a real thrill for her in singing in a fine setting – Britten's *War Requiem* in Coventry Cathedral was especially moving. But the power of a great building can sometimes be offset by its difficult acoustics. Trying to tune the 'Agnus Dei' of the Verdi *Requiem* in a place full of echoes can be agony. 'And, you know, you work at it hard and long during the afternoon rehearsal only to find when the time comes for the performance that they have put the front row of the audience only a couple of feet away from you, so that there are people staring up your nostrils, or maybe they have shifted your chair so that you cannot see the conductor properly.' Amateur organization can certainly be a problem. Linda Esther Gray remembers giving a recital at a small festival where the tuner had been called to practise surgery on an appalling piano at the very time that she and her accompanist were scheduled to be using it for rehearsal.

But such experiences are never likely to dampen her love for and appreciation of festivals, so long as they can keep their special sense of joy and universal involvement – and, of course, their balloons!

GRASSINGTON

The town of Grassington is set in the Dales of North Yorkshire and musicians – both professional and amateur – from the area take a major part in its two-week-long festival, founded in 1981. There are also lectures on some aspect of Dales life, as well as drama and poetry (June–July).

GREAT COMP

The seventeenth-century house of Great Comp (the name means 'open space' or 'field') lies down a narrow lane, amid Kentish oasthouses and orchards, not far from Sevenoaks. Set in seven acres of gardens which have been described as the best in private ownership in the country and which attract some 2000 visitors each year, its imposing brick and stone structure dates from the early 1600s. The gardens, their spacious lawns overlooked by groups of stately conifers, their paved walks flanked by vividly coloured heatherbeds, are a consuming passion of the owners, Joy and Roderick Cameron.

Another of the Camerons' passions is music and the festival which takes place each July and September in converted stables adjoining their house takes its special character from their close involvement. It all started in 1972 when a group of singers descended on Great Comp to help launch a display of antique prints that had been set up inside the house. As no room in the main house really lent itself to music-making, the Camerons offered the use of their stables. Assorted lumber and cobwebs were cleared away, the stall partitions were removed and makeshift seating (orange

The house and garden at Great Comp.

boxes and packing cases) was installed. The concert itself proved an outstanding success, not least because of the stables' naturally fine acoustic, and, on the strength of it, the Camerons decided to launch their own twice-yearly Great Comp Festival. They set about refurbishing the stable interior, building a small gallery and replacing the packing cases with cinema seating bought from a redundant Granada. Much of the work they did themselves with the sort of dedication they also apply to their gardens. The result was a comfortable, well-proportioned auditorium, with an audience capacity of about eighty.

Not surprisingly, and quite rightly, the owners' tastes have been closely reflected in the choice of performers and programmes for their concerts. Their great love is chamber music of the Classical and Romantic periods, and each season sees visits from distinguished quartets such as the Bochman, the Chilingirian and the Coull, playing the repertoire from Haydn to Dvořák. Roderick Cameron admits to something of an aversion to both French and contemporary music, and neither consequently features very largely at Great Comp. The piano, on the other hand, sounds well in the stable acoustic, and the instrument that normally resides in the drawing-room of the main house is frequently trundled across the courtyard, retuned and pressed into service. There are also occasional injections of more popular music – from Kentucky Blue Grass to Scottish songs and pipe-music – while most years there is also an intersprinkling of lectures on subjects ranging from Florentine art to English horticulture.

Great Comp has been described as 'the Glyndebourne of chamber music', and there is no doubt that a good slice of the festival's appeal comes from the house and its gardens, which are floodlit on September evenings and available for picnics. Much, too, is owed to the Camerons' meticulous attention to detail and unobtrusive stage-management, Joy being involved with catering arrangements, Roderick with front of house business.

In 1985, organization of the festival was placed in the hands of a committee, and a number of changes seem inevitable. It is to be hoped, however, that whatever the future holds in store, Great Comp's uniquely intimate music-making will continue to attract full houses.

GUITING

If you take one of the side-roads that leads off the main Stow-on-the-Wold to Gloucester highway, it will bring you to Guiting Power – a quintessential Gloucester-shire village of some three hundred souls, complete with village green, stone cross and sturdy Cotswold cottages. And if you make the detour towards the end of July, you will – as like as not – encounter the Guiting Festival, which for eight successive days offers intimate music-making in the comfortably equipped surroundings of the village hall. This building, which holds about 150 people at a pinch, has a true, faithful acoustic and is particularly well suited to the performance of chamber music.

The festival – founded and, until 1984, directed by the pianist Russell Brandon – has as its motto 'Off the Beaten Track', a reference not so much to its out-of-the-way setting as to its twin artistic aims of providing a platform for the growing number of talented professional musicians resident in the area and programming unperformed or unfamiliar works by living composers, both British (especially local) and East European. Typical was the piano recital which opened the tenth anniversary season in 1980, when Cheltenham-based Colin Sherratt sandwiched pieces by Pál Kadosa and David Harries between generous slices of Bach, Mendelssohn and Schumann. That same year, the Highnam Court Chamber Orchestra (which hails from the former home of Sir Hubert Parry near Gloucester and is directed by Roger Smith) introduced Kanullo Lendvay's *Kifejezesek for Strings* in a programme which also included Vaughan Williams's *Dives and Lazarus* and works by Grieg, Bach and Mozart. Another local group, the Berkeley Wind Ensemble, combined music by Rosetti and Ibert with a new piece by Mary Chandler (her *Masquerade*) and works by the Hungarian composers Istvan Láng, Gyula Dávid and Ferenc Farkas. On other evenings, audiences were treated to widely contrasted programmes by the Brass

Ensemble of the BBC Welsh Symphony Orchestra, pianist Alexander Kligerman, the Cardinal Singers (from Oxford) and Russell Brandon himself, who rounded off the festival with what was arguably the first complete performance in a single evening of Bach's *Well-Tempered Clavier*.

Distinguished visitors over the years have included cellist Alexander Kok, April Cantelo, David Stone, the Budapest and Esterházy Trios, and Graham Whettam was for two seasons composer-in-residence. Occasionally, concerts migrate to Guiting's Norman church or to the chapel of nearby Sudeley Castle, though this is no way affects the intimacy of the music-making. Each year there is also an exhibition of work by local artists which can be both viewed and purchased.

HARPENDEN

For a week in late June, outstanding musicians come to play in the concert hall of the Williams School of Church Music. The fare is mostly chamber scale, though in 1985 the final evening was devoted to a concert of music for string orchestra.

HARROGATE

People have found excuses for visiting Harrogate for well over two hundred years. As a spa town, with iron and sulphur springs, it attracted fashionable society during the eighteenth and nineteenth centuries. The Victorians planted it with solid, comfortable residences, and sowed the seeds of its burgeoning as Britain's foremost floral town, in midsummer brilliant with crowded flower banks yet at the same time leafily cool with its abundance of trees. Harrogate is a spacious garden town, with The Stray – open grassland two hundred acres in extent – pushing into its very heart. Since the Second World War, it has become important as a conference and tourist centre – the Yorkshire Dales stretch to north and south of the town – and since 1966 the first two weeks of August have seen the steady growth of its international festival 'of the arts and sciences'.

Over the years, Harrogate has taken a pride in providing a platform for aspiring young musicians, new dance and theatre companies, new music and emerging composers, as well as featuring internationally established artists from all sections of the arts world. The 'science' aspect is not developed every year – rather when suitable topics and connections present themselves, as when in 1974 there was an exhibition concerned with 'The Physics of Music', supported by lectures by Professor Charles Taylor (Cardiff) and Dr Keith Barker (Sheffield). There is, however, strong and regular emphasis on involving, not just entertaining, young people: as when the Sadler's Wells Opera Workshop introduced nine to thirteen year olds to some of the mysteries of staging an opera.

The Harrogate day generally begins at about eleven o'clock in the morning: children's events, solo recitals and the International Young Musicians series regularly fill this slot. In 1984, Ton Koopman (harpsichord) and Jukka Savijoki (guitar) gave

Right: Tom Yang in *Vesalii Icones* by Peter Maxwell Davies.

recitals in the friendly acoustic of Christ Church, while Julian Reynolds (piano), Nicholas Daniel and Julian Drake (oboe and piano), and Vovka Ashkenazy (piano) appeared in a seven-concert 'young musicians' series.

Evening concerts bring out the larger forces, though some chamber music is also scheduled for 7.30. In 1984, the Conference Centre played host to the Bournemouth Symphony Orchestra under Rudolf Barshai in an interestingly balanced programme of Mussorgsky, Britten (the Piano Concerto with Michael Roll as soloist) and Shostakovich (his Tenth Symphony). Russian and British composers were indeed the festival's theme that year and if the closing concert, given by the Scottish National Orchestra conducted by Neeme Järvi, seemed to err on the side of the Slavs (with Glazunov, Shostakovich and Tchaikovsky – the Violin Concerto with Boris Belkin), the concert given by the Philharmonia Orchestra under Paavo Berglund did something to restore matters with a good dose of Elgar (including the *Cockaigne Overture* and the Cello Concerto with Raphael Wallfisch). There was also a heavy emphasis that year on new music by British composers: The Fires of London gave the first performance in the North of Maxwell Davies's *The No. 11 Bus* as well as his now celebrated *Vesalii Icones* (with Tom Yang); Roger Steptoe's new piece for string quartet, oboe and clarinet (a festival commission) formed part of a Christ Church concert by the Bochman Quartet with Robin Canter and David Campbell; the BBC Northern Singers sang John McCabe's *Maugan Triptych* (another Harrogate commission); and Jane Manning's recital included not only the first performance of Jonathan Harvey's *Work for Voice, Piano and Tape* but also UK premières of pieces by Hallgrimsson, Machover, Rasmussen and Norgaard. At other concerts, the Moscow Virtuosi under Vladimir Spivakov represented the Russians, while Neville Marriner's Academy of St Martin-in-the-Fields took care of British interests. On two occasions, audiences were lured ten miles out of town to Ripon Cathedral to hear the Locke Brass Consort (whose programme included, on the one hand, Mussorgsky and Tchaikovsky, and on the other, George Lloyd and Bliss) and Carlo Curley. Then there were the Kasubka Cossacks and the Harehills Youth Dance Theatre, the Gesualdo Consort and the National Youth Brass Band of Great Britain, and Ivo Pogorelich and Cleo Laine. Something, indeed, for everyone, but presented in a balanced and well-thought-out manner.

HELMSLEY

The *Musical Times* has described the Helmsley Festival as 'a model of what a small festival should be'. For nine days or so in July, this modest market town in the North Riding of Yorkshire is the scene for professional music-making of a high standard – with opera complementing the more usual orchestral and chamber concerts in a variety of pleasing settings (including Duncombe Park). Little-known works by established composers and new, though not avant-garde, pieces specially commissioned feature every year.

——————HENLEY——————

The Henley Festival is not only a feast for the ear, it is also very much one for the stomach. Taking over the beautiful waterside setting of the Steward's Enclosure, with all its trappings of grandstands and marquees, for several days immediately following the Henley Royal Regatta, it sets out to create an atmosphere of Englishness and smart society fun.

Beginning each evening around 6.30 p.m. and going on until midnight (3 a.m. on the final Saturday), it is perhaps more reminiscent of a varsity May Ball than a conventional festival. Several of the lavishly decorated marquees are converted into out-of-town extensions of some of London's leading restaurants (the festival's sponsors include Wheeler's, Maxim's, Mario and Franco and the Café des Amis), and English, French and Italian cuisine is served to appropriate musical accompaniment. Thus, the English Pavilion features cabaret and songs from Noël Coward, Ivor Novello and Gilbert and Sullivan; the French Pavement Café has an accordionist and mime artists; and the Italian Piazza resounds to the youthful voices of the Spaghetti Opera Company in a selection from grand opera. Other marquees are given over to exhibitions (paintings, drawings and sculpture by Philip Gore in 1983, work by Andrew and Richard Logan in 1984, and recent work by John Piper in 1985) and to recitals by young musicians (Aquarius, conducted by Nicholas Cleobury, in Walton's *Façade* with Prunella Scales and Simon Butteriss; or The Menagerie – oboe, piano and Penelope Walker, contralto; or Cantabile; or Richard Mapp playing Bach, Chopin, Debussy, Ravel and Saint-Saëns). There is a bandstand, a punt loaded with madrigalists, a puppet barge, a sculpture lawn, close-harmony groups, wandering magicians and pierrots. It is part of the festival's policy to encourage young and locally based performers.

The central feature of the festival, however, is a series of concerts – mainly popular in flavour – given at the riverside (the audience is accommodated in the covered grandstand with the performers, subtly amplified, on a large floating pontoon in the river). These start at 8.30 p.m. and have, in the past, been given by such orchestras as the City of London Sinfonia (in an English programme, directed by Richard Hickox, which ended with *Music for the Royal Fireworks* accompanied by one of the most spectacular displays of pyrotechnics mounted since the War), the Wren, Philharmonia and Royal Philharmonic Orchestras and the Band of the Coldstream Guards with artists and conductors that included Jill Gomez, Yan-Pascal Tortelier, Lionel Friend, Carl Davis, Pauline Tinsley and Nigel Kennedy.

Each festival follows a particular theme, which is reflected in the choice of music, exhibitions, fringe events and overall décor. Recent themes – sensibly dictated by the setting – have included 'Water' and 'Pastoral'.

The final evening sees a rather grander presentation at the riverside auditorium – usually a double-bill. In 1984, the Lumière & Son Theatre Company's *Vulture Culture* (a blend of original music, choreography and black humour) was followed by a concert by the Band of the Coldstream Guards; in 1985, Timedance presented

Henley Tuesday Singers performing on the Madrigal Punt.

a specially commissioned adaptation of one of the great court masques of the seventeenth century, *The Marriage of Terpsichore and Thames* by Francis Beaumont and Giovanni Coperario, with original costumes, music and dancing.

Henley is concentrated festivity. Wherever you turn, there is something to see, hear, do or eat, from early evening until the witching hour. Happy, elegant (the dress code includes black ties or blazers for men, evening gowns for women), vivacious. And not too intellectually demanding!

HOUGHTON FEAST

This ancient event, a combination of celebratory feasting and merrymaking, has been the way in which the inhabitants of the Durham town of Houghton-le-Spring have marked the patronal festival of their Parish Church of St Michael since early mediaeval times. Today the emphasis is on local organizations entertaining the general public in a range of events and activities, many of them involving children. The church itself is the focus for concerts by visiting musicians – such as the Northern Sinfonia – and local performers alike (first two weeks in October).

KEELE

The Keele British Music Week has a distinguished pedigree. It started life in March 1982 when Philip Jones, Lecturer in Music at the University of Keele, organized a Delius festival in the tradition of those held in London under Sir Thomas Beecham's direction in 1929 and 1946 and in Bradford under the guidance of Eric Fenby in 1962. Jones's aim on that occasion was to present the music of Delius in a cosmopolitan context: his opening concert, given by the Birmingham-based Orchestra da Camera with pianist Allan Schiller, set the Fantasy Overture *Over the Hills and Far Away* (1897) beside works by Grieg and Dvořák written a decade or so earlier. Delius's French connection was highlighted in a concert by the Lindsay String Quartet in which his quartet was sandwiched between those of Debussy and Ravel. This concert was the first of two in a single evening: the second, which started at 10.30 p.m., was devoted to Delius part-songs, performed by the Stoke-on-Trent Bedford Singers. These pieces, like the Violin Concerto (played later in the week by Ralph Holmes with the Royal Liverpool Philharmonic Orchestra under Norman Del Mar in a programme which also included Elgar's Second Symphony), had also featured in the Beecham and Fenby festivals. The closing concert consisted of a performance of *A Mass of Life* with the (then) BBC Northern Symphony Orchestra and soloists Felicity Lott, Helen Watts, Kenneth Bowen and Thomas Hemsley. Perhaps the most interesting feature of this Fourth Delius Festival, however, was the first performance in this country of the political satire *Folkeraadet* by the Norwegian playwright Gunnar Heiberg, complete with Delius's incidental music played by the Keele University Orchestra conducted by George Pratt. The orchestral concerts in this 1982 season were given in the Victoria Hall, Hanley, with the chamber recitals, choral concerts and a number of highly relevant lectures being housed in various parts of the Keele University campus.

A similar overall pattern was adopted in 1984, when the first British Music Week was held, with its main focus on the fiftieth anniversary of the deaths of Elgar, Holst and Delius, and of the births of Peter Maxwell Davies and Peter Dickinson, who is Professor of Music at Keele. Elgar was represented by his Second Symphony, Cello Concerto (with Fiona Treherne), *The Dream of Gerontius* (with massed local choirs, the Royal Liverpool Philharmonic Orchestra, Helen Watts, Kenneth Bowen and Willard White, conducted by Philip Jones) and some songs; Holst, somewhat disappointingly, by just one part-song and the *Perfect Fool* ballet music; Delius by *Brigg Fair* (played in the opening concert by the BBC Philharmonic Orchestra under Nicholas Braithwaite) plus songs; Maxwell Davies by his String Quartet (part of an enterprising programme by the Alberni String Quartet, which also included works by Walton and Britten); and Dickinson – self-effacingly – by two part-songs, 'The Fall' and 'Wood Path', given as part of a wide-ranging and beautifully executed programme by Stephen Wilkinson's BBC Northern Singers. Other British composers represented in the festival were Havergal Brian, Vaughan Williams (the *Wasps Overture* and Fifth Symphony), Sullivan, Butterworth, Finzi, William Denis Browne, Ernest Farrar, Gurney, Howells, Maw, Lennox Berkeley, Maconchy, Parry and Stanford. At their late-night recital to commemorate the seventieth anniversary of the First World War, John Potter (tenor) and Stephen Banfield (piano) gave the first performance of Graham Garton's 'Remembrance Day'. Other festival events included a recital by Simon Preston in the university chapel of organ music from

Gibbons to Kenneth Leighton, a concert by the Royal Doulton Band illustrating the British band tradition, and jazz from the Stan Tracey Sextet.

It is intended that this extremely valuable and well-balanced Week, employing the best of Keele's excellent local resources as well as artists from other parts of the North West of England in a celebration of British composers, be repeated every two years. 1987 takes a look at what happened to British music in the nineteenth century.

KING'S LYNN

The King's Lynn Festival owes its existence in large measure to the efforts of one woman – Ruth, Lady Fermoy, a distinguished concert pianist and wife of the town's one-time Member of Parliament and Lord Mayor. It was she who, in 1951, had the idea of launching a major arts event to mark the opening of the newly restored Guildhall of St George (the largest ancient guildhall in England – dating from the early 1400s – not to have suffered war damage) and as a contribution to the nationwide Festival of Britain. She remained the festival's artistic director until 1975, when she was succeeded by another professional musician, Christopher Hogwood. The present incumbent is Alan Wilkinson.

The Guildhall, now a fully-fledged theatre complete with orchestra pit, naturally plays an important part in King's Lynn festivities, but the town is fortunate in having a number of other worthy venues near at hand – notably the St Nicholas Chapel, whose ample proportions can accommodate large orchestras and major symphonic works. Visitors at recent festivals have included the English Chamber, London Symphony, Hallé, Royal Philharmonic and Royal Liverpool Philharmonic Orchestras and the spirited Academy of St Martin-in-the-Fields. Works played have ranged from standard Classical and Romantic repertoire to first performances of pieces by living composers – Lennox Berkeley, Elizabeth Maconchy, Nicholas Maw. In 1985, Maw was appointed the festival's composer-in-residence and presided over a week of rehearsals, workshops and pre-concert talks. A number of his recent and not-so-recent works were given, including the Sonata for Two Horns and Strings (played by the Peterborough String Orchestra conducted by Adrian Leaper, with Beth Randall and Kevin Pritchard), which shared an evening with Fauré's Nocturne for Strings. Another Maw composition, his *Spring Music*, fitted neatly alongside further Gallic pieces (by Dukas, Franck and Berlioz – the *Nuits d'Été* sung by Janet Baker) in the Philharmonia Orchestra's concert under Esa-Pekka Salonen. Indeed, the French connection was very much in the air in 1985, another notable event being an exhibition of rarely seen drawings by Boucher, Claude, Fragonard, Poussin and their contemporaries.

Art shows have always been a special feature of this festival – indeed the once derelict warehouses which run down to the Great Ouse river behind the Guildhall have in part been turned into the Fermoy Art Gallery. Paintings by Sidney Nolan, works by Whistler and Osbert Lancaster, Renaissance treasures from Tuscany, icons and silverware from King's Lynn itself have all attracted knowledgeable and

King's Lynn Festival – (*left to right*) Nicholas Maw, composer-in-residence; Viscount Norwich, honorary festival adviser; General Sir Harry Tuzo, chairman of the Fermoy Centre Foundation; Alan Wilkinson, director of the festival; David Rutherford of Martini and Rossi, the sponsors; and Ruth Lady Fermoy, the founder president.

enthusiastic crowds. Other non-musical events have included mime shows, literary lunches, film, theatre, revue, local visits, while back in the concert halls and recital rooms there have been madrigals (Peter Pears directing the Wilbye Consort), lecture recitals, mediaeval music (the Praetorius Consort), solo recitals (Rafael Orozco showing the way from Mozart to Prokofiev) and chamber concerts – not to mention jazz and the music and dance of other lands.

King's Lynn runs for about nine days in late July. A sunny, friendly, lively event.

LAKE DISTRICT

A well-established event which operates in a variety of settings in this lovely part of England. It is mostly devoted to music – the balance is generally in favour of chamber recitals, though choral and orchestral concerts sometimes feature – and film and literary events also put in an appearance. The performers are mostly professional, and in the past have included such names as Walter Klien, Ralph Kirkpatrick, the Haydn Trio of Vienna, the Allegri String Quartet and the Geraint Jones Orchestra (early September).

LEASOWES BANK

About ten miles to the south of Shrewsbury is an area of high moorland interspersed with rocky outcrops commanding wild but magnificent views. Most dramatic of all these outcrops are the Stiperstones, rising to 1700 feet and supposed, according to local legend, to be the place where, on Midsummer Night, the devils gather to choose their leader. A few miles to the east is the Long Mynd, a ten-mile ridge of bleak heath, dotted with ancient barrows and earthworks. And midway between the two, in a spot which is said to suffer some of the cruellest winter weather but to enjoy seemingly endless sunny days in summer, is Leasowes Bank, formerly an isolated hill-farm, half a mile from any other habitation.

In 1980, Leasowes Bank was acquired by John and Frances Williams, who saw it as an ideal spot to start a small-scale music festival, catering for all tastes. At first, their summer concerts were held in their living-room in the farmhouse, but in 1982 they set about converting a sturdy stone barn into a concert hall capable of accommodating about 80 people.

Each festival consists of five concerts – one a week – in the course of July and August. John Williams is a jazz saxophonist of note and his appearance as soloist or as member of his own octet is a regular feature of the Leasowes season. Other jazz performers in recent years have been Barbara Thompson with the Martin Blackwell Trio, John Surman and Karin Krog, and the Don Rendell Quartet. On the classical side, there have been visits from Charles Brett and Robert Spencer; the Perry String Quartet (playing Elgar, Howells, Haydn and – with John Williams himself – the first

Barbara Thompson and the Martin Blackwell Trio at Leasowes Bank in 1983.

performance of another work written specially for Leasowes, Herman Wilson's Quintet for Baritone Saxophone and String Quartet); the harpist Ruth Faber – both by herself and with her trio; Images, a flute and guitar duo whose repertoire ranges from Bach, Fauré and Vivaldi to traditional Brazilian music; and – perhaps inevitably – the celebrated London Saxophone Quartet. A particularly happy occasion took place in 1985, when Ian and Jennifer Partridge gave the first performance of Trevor Hold's specially commissioned song cycle of poems by Mary Webb, *When the Thorn Blows*, as part of a recital of Romantic and modern song.

Leasowes has many attractions – its informality, its setting, its isolation, its musical range and interesting programming. But it owes most, without question, to the vision and personality of its founders.

LEEDS

It was in 1858 that Queen Victoria, trusting herself to the mercy of the railways, travelled north to Leeds, to open the recently erected neo-Gothic Town Hall. Such an occasion, the city fathers decided, warranted celebration in the grand style – nothing less than a music festival would do, complete with its own specially trained chorus to sing aloud and make a suitably joyful noise to greet Her Majesty. So it came about that the Leeds Triennial Festival and the Leeds Festival Chorus were born: and they have been together, through thick and thin, ever since.

Among the more heady days must be counted the period when Sir Arthur Sullivan was both artistic director and principal conductor (another distinguished composer, Alexander Goehr, took the helm in 1974, succeeding that doyen of arts administrators, Lord Harewood) and a veritable flood of new choral commissions came from the pens of such composers as Raff, Dvořák, Massenet, Humperdinck, Parry, Stanford, Elgar and Sullivan himself. More 'fat years' came in the nineteen-twenties and thirties: one of the best loved and most frequently performed choral works of this century was first heard at Leeds – *Belshazzar's Feast* (1931) by the precocious young William Walton – as was Holst's more reflective *Choral Symphony*. It was during this era that the conductors John Barbirolli and Malcolm Sargent became closely associated with the festival, continuing – with a pause for the hostilities of the Second World War – into the forties.

But 'lean years' were just around the corner, and during the 1950s both chorus and festival faltered, it being found impossible to raise and train a chorus in 1953 or to hold a festival at all three years later.

It took another royal visit – this time by Queen Elizabeth II on the occasion of the festival's centenary in 1958 – to get things moving again. That year saw the Leeds spirit revive, with much interesting music – Beethoven's *Missa Solemnis*, the first performances of Britten's Nocturne (with Peter Pears as soloist) and Peter Racine Fricker's *A Vision of Judgment* – and appearances by Annie Fischer, Yehudi and Hephzibah Menuhin, Teresa Berganza, Joan Sutherland and Jon Vickers. Then, during the sixties, Carlo Maria Giulini and John Pritchard made their respective marks

– the former in amazing performances of the Verdi *Requiem*, *Les Noces* (Stravinsky) and Rossini's *Stabat Mater*, the latter directing Britten's *War Requiem*, Henze's *Novae de Infinito Laudes* and the first performance of Alexander Goehr's *Sutter's Gold*.

In 1970, two new developments took place: the festival became a biennial event and the chorus, which up to then had been disbanded after each festival and reformed for the next, was put on a permanent footing. In recent years, the chorus has also slimmed down to a membership of about 120 so that, when really large forces are required for festival concerts, the Leeds Philharmonic Chorus has to be engaged to lend support.

The festival has also started to adopt a thematic approach to programming of late – in 1981, the theme was 'Music in Britain' and works by Britten, Gordon Jacob, Wilfred Mellers (the first performance of his *Glorificamus* given by the Yorkshire Imperial Band), Parry, Elgar, Finzi, Moeran, Patrick Hadley, Ireland, Balfour Gardiner, Purcell, Tallis, Handel, Holst, Byrd, Giles Swayne (the première of *Count-Down*), Warlock, Goehr, David Blake, Sullivan, Samuel Wesley, Tippett, Lambert, Delius, Wilfred Josephs (the first hearing of his Sonata for Double Bass) and others filled the sixteen days of programmes. Other highlights of the 1981 season included a visit by the Concertgebouw Orchestra with Bernard Haitink playing Bruckner's Eighth Symphony, Handel's *Solomon* conducted by Roger Norrington with soloists Helen Watts, Sheila Armstrong, Elizabeth Gale, Philip Langridge and Stephen Roberts, Nigel Kennedy playing the Elgar Violin Concerto, and the Bruckner *Te Deum* and Beethoven *Choral Symphony* from Linda Esther Gray, Anne Wilkens, Robin Leggate, John Tomlinson, the Festival Chorus, Sheffield Bach Choir and the City of Birmingham Symphony Orchestra, all directed by Erich Schmid.

In 1983, the then artistic director, John Warrack, took as his theme 'Painting and Music', and set out to explore the relationship between auditory and visual imagery in a number of fascinating ways. One of these was to commission a new work from composer and artist Edward Cowie – his *Choral Symphony* on paintings by Turner, given by David Wilson-Johnson with the Festival Chorus and the Royal Liverpool Philharmonic Orchestra under Howard Williams. Then there were the piano and orchestral versions of Mussorgsky's *Pictures from an Exhibition* (the programme book containing reproductions of many of Hartmann's paintings), the former being given in a recital by Martin Roscoe, the latter in a concert by the English Northern Philharmonia under David Lloyd-Jones, the programme also including Scriabin's *Prometheus* with accompanying light-play.

1985 saw the festival shrink to a mere nine days' duration – but nine days packed with musical activity of all kinds. Choral music dominated: the Festival Chorus took part in four of the concerts, giving performances of Beethoven's *Missa Solemnis* (with the London Symphony Orchestra and Leeds Philharmonic Chorus under Sir Charles Mackerras and soloists Edda Moser, Bernadette Greevy, Keith Lewis and Robert Lloyd), Berlioz's *Roméo et Juliette*, Bruckner's Mass No. 2 in E Minor and a new *Benedicite* by Arthur Wills; other concerts were given by an ensemble directed by Graham Treacher (for the première of Anthony Powers's *Venexia* and a feast of

Monteverdi), Leeds Girls' High School Choir, the Choirs of Leeds Parish Church and Ripon and Wakefield Cathedrals, the Chorus of Opera North, that of Chetham's School in Manchester, and – in a more relaxed vein – the Light Blues. There were also visits by the Philharmonia Orchestra conducted by Geoffrey Simon, the Allegri String Quartet (playing Haydn, Beethoven and Tippett), Dame Janet Baker, the Lute Group with Tessa Bonner, Simon Preston (in an organ recital of music by Liszt, Vierne and Dupré) and the City of Leeds College of Music Jazz Ensemble.

The Leeds Festival is now held in early November.

LEOMINSTER

This is a fairly recent newcomer to the festival scene, having been founded in 1980 and held biennially ever since. The main focus for musical events – of which there are plenty – is the ancient priory church (occasionally used for Three Choirs performances as well). The range is from the classics of all periods to jazz and a special focus is placed on providing entertainment for young people. Art, crafts and drama are also included (June).

LINCOLN

A May festival (running for two weeks at the beginning of the month) and one which seeks to recapture the vigour and freshness of traditional Maytide celebrations. It does so with music (choral and orchestral, jazz and folk), dance, theatre, mime, film and the visual arts. Mainly professional in emphasis.

LUDLOW

The slow, dark waters of the Teme make scarcely a sound as they pass beneath the massive sandstone walls of Ludlow's eleventh-century castle. It was behind these now derelict battlements that generations of Englishmen fortified themselves against the marauding Welsh; here that the first Earl of Bridgewater celebrated his inauguration as Lord President of the Welsh Marches in 1634 with a masque, *Comus*, specially written for the occasion by the celebrated composer, Henry Lawes, and the comparatively unknown young poet, John Milton. It was, indeed, a series of gala performances of *Comus* within the castle precincts to raise money for the restoration of St Laurence's, the town's parish church, that in 1960 sparked off the festival as we have it today. Its centrepiece was, and remains, the performance of a Shakespeare play by a group of professional actors. Nineteen different plays were put on during the festival's first quarter century. But Ludlow is not solely concerned with theatre – it also embraces film, art, lectures on a wide variety of topics (in 1984 these included detective fiction, portrait miniatures, the town's architectural history and the raising of the *Mary Rose*) and music of all kinds.

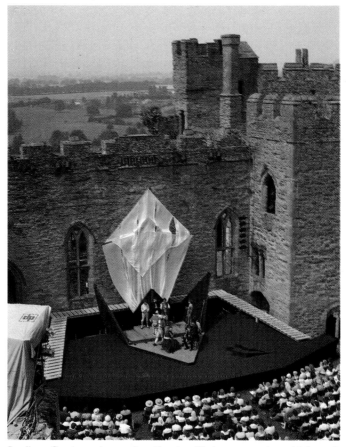

Ludlow Castle – the setting for the Shakespeare play which each year forms the centrepiece of the festival. This was Ludlow's production of *The Tempest* in 1985.

Orchestral concerts sound particularly well in the resonant acoustic of St Laurence's and visiting orchestras have included the City of Birmingham Symphony, the Royal Liverpool Philharmonic, the Hallé, the Northern Sinfonia and the London Bach Orchestra under such distinguished conductors as Hugo Rignold, Sir Charles Groves, Jane Glover, Richard Hickox and George Malcolm. In 1984, English Festival Brass gave a concert which featured two specially commissioned works, Christopher Gibbs's *Ludlow Festival Overture* and Stuart Johnson's *Triple Concerto*.

The countryside around Ludlow contains many fine houses in which the festival organizes smaller-scale concerts with buffet supper. There have been memorable occasions – guitarist John Williams and poet R. S. Thomas in recital at Ashford Hall, Osian Ellis with C. Day Lewis and Jill Balcon at Oakly Park, Gerald Moore at Mawley Hall. Chamber and solo recitals also take place in Ludlow itself, as do concerts of light music and jazz (Terry Lightfoot, the Dankworths and Humphrey Lyttelton have all attracted full houses) and special programmes for children.

Ludlow Festival faithful are able to look back on some outstanding musical moments: Oleg Prokofiev narrating his father's *Peter and the Wolf* from the pulpit in St Laurence's (accompanied by the Orchestra of St John's, Smith Square), Sir Arthur Bliss directing his own works in the 1960s, Campoli accompanied by Katin, the Smetana Quartet in a programme of Mozart and Dvořák.

Indeed, Ludlow's two midsummer weeks regularly provide a feast for culture-vultures of all ages. If the lack of any kind of clear theme each year is in some ways a drawback, the general excellence of the performances and the beauty and variety of the settings are unmistakable bonuses.

MALVERN

A late-spring Sunday afternoon in Malvern. Grey skies with occasional spots of rain, but warm enough, even verging on the oppressive. After-lunch strollers wander through the Abbey grounds or heave themselves up the narrow streets at the top of the town. Others make more purposefully in the direction of the faded but bunting-decked Winter Gardens, for the last fortnight in May is festival time in Malvern,

Malvern with the nine-mile range of the Malvern Hills behind.

and residents and visitors alike can be pretty certain that there will be something special to see and hear.

It is not perhaps unfair to suggest that Malvern itself has seen better days. Nestling a little smugly under the huge bulk of the hills to which it has given a name, it was at its most fashionable as a Victorian and Edwardian spa town. Its first festival took place as long ago as 1929 and was dedicated to productions of the plays of Bernard Shaw and – to a lesser extent – J. M. Barrie. After a number of ups and downs, it was given a new lease of life in 1977 with the decision to add a musical element, focusing particularly on the works of Elgar, that great lover of the Malverns who made his home in the town for some years. The seats in the Winter Gardens may not be over-comfortable and seeing the platform from more than halfway back may be a bit of a struggle, but there is nevertheless something very special about performances of Elgar in Malvern, even today. Where visiting orchestras may give rather world-weary accounts of, say, the *Eroica* or *Pastoral* Symphonies, they seem to find new inspiration when confronted with *Cockaigne* or the *Enigma Variations* or the Introduction and Allegro for Strings. Indeed, not just Elgar but British music in general seems to blossom in this climate, and regular visitors to the festival have long memories for fine performances of Holst and Ireland, Bliss and Vaughan Williams.

Sir Michael Tippett conducting the English String Orchestra
at the 1985 festival which was a celebration of his eightieth birthday.

The 1985 festival was a particular landmark in that it celebrated the eightieth birthday of Sir Michael Tippett, who came to Malvern to meet people and talk about composing and to conduct and listen to a number of his works. The BBC Philharmonic Orchestra's concert included a performance of his Triple Concerto (with Gyorgy Pauk, Rivka Golani and Ralph Kirshbaum), local conductor Neil Page presided over *A Child of Our Time* (with Jo Ann Pickens, Catherine Wyn-Rogers, Martyn Hill, Stephen Varcoe, the Malvern Festival Chorus and Hallé Orchestra) and the Leicestershire Schools' Symphony Orchestra under Nicholas Cleobury included his *Praeludium* for Brass, Bells and Percussion and *Shire Suite* in their mostly English concert. William Boughton, the festival's artistic director, conducted his English String Orchestra in performances of the *Little Music* for Strings and the ever-popular Concerto for Double String Orchestra, and Tippett himself rounded off the same orchestra's Italian Baroque/English Romantic programme with his *Fantasia Concertante on a Theme of Corelli*. The final concert of the festival was given by the Bournemouth Symphony Orchestra under Richard Armstrong, and had as its centrepiece the *Ritual Dances* from the opera *The Midsummer Marriage*.

But Malvern is not devoted solely to large-scale orchestral concerts – indeed in the late seventies it tended if anything towards the chamber repertoire – and the 1985 festival saw works by Tippett included in Neil Smith's guitar recital, a joint concert given in the Big School of Malvern College by the Aldwyn Consort of Voices and the Michael Thompson Horn Quartet, Andrew Ball's piano recital (the Third Piano Sonata, in this case) and a recital by the Lindsay String Quartet (the Third Quartet).

And in addition to this great feast of Tippett – albeit Tippett at his most accessible – there was a concert of Bach and Handel given by a local orchestra and school choirs directed by Yan-Pascal Tortelier, as well as appearances by John Ogdon (playing Shostakovich), violinist Ernst Kovacic (in the Beethoven concerto) and Edward Downes. Programmes included hefty helpings of Beethoven and Elgar along with the music of English composers from Dunstable to Britten.

Not a festival to nibble at, but one to relax over and savour – and Malvern has plenty of hotels and guesthouses, with spectacular views, to make this possible.

MANANAN

Port Erin is a charming fishing village and holiday resort at the southern tip of the Isle of Man. In 1971, the former Methodist chapel in the village's Victoria Square was on the point of being taken over by a local garage as a home for its hire cars, when a group of farsighted individuals joined forces to rescue it and turn it instead into the Erin Arts Centre. Facilities were somewhat primitive to begin with, but the availability of the Centre inspired John Bethell – spurred on by Raymond Leppard and Sir John Betjeman – to use it as the focus for a brand new festival designed to encourage local talent and to attract to the island artists of international standing.

The first Mananan Festival (the name is that of the old Manx sea-god) duly came into being in 1974. Initially it was on a modest scale, occupying only a few days, but in the past decade it has grown and become well established. It now covers ten to twelve days each June/July and draws audiences made up not only of Manxmen but also of summer visitors from the Adjacent Island, as the British mainland is sometimes called.

Mananan has always embraced music of all kinds – including opera and ballet – as well as film, lectures, light entertainments, children's events and exhibitions of arts, crafts and photography. Local groups, such as the Manx Festival Chorus, Manx Folk Dance Society, Manx Girls' Choir and Manx Youth Orchestra, played an important role right from the start, while the work of Manx artists has benefited enormously from the recently inaugurated exhibition facilities provided by the island's Travelling Gallery – a converted double-decker bus. The list of musicians who have come to Port Erin during the last ten years includes some distinguished names: the Amadeus and Brodsky Quartets, pianists Malcolm Binns, Iris Loveridge and Clive Lythgoe, violinists Alfredo Campoli, Hugh Maguire and Nigel Kennedy, the Northern Brass Ensemble, the King's Singers and the Grimethorpe Colliery Band.

A typical recent festival opened with a harp recital by Sioned Williams given in the chapel of King William's College with a programme ranging from Krumpholz and Bach to Hindemith and Jean-Michel Damase. Then followed three nights of Mananan Opera Group's production of *Don Pasquale* with piano accompaniment, at the Arts Centre (opera now makes an appearance every other year, alternating with a major drama production). Other musical events included a lecture recital by Brian Kay entitled 'But what do you do for a living?', a piano recital by Clive Lythgoe (Liszt, Gottschalk, Debussy, Malcolm Williamson and George Gershwin) and a chamber concert by the Lindsay String Quartet playing works by Haydn, Schubert, Dvořák and John Casken. An out-of-town interlude was provided by Andrew Shaw's recital on the organ of the eighteenth-century St Mark's Church, followed by a 'Manx Tay' of bonnag, potato cake and soda scones at the local school. The final concert of the festival, given in King William's College, was a piano recital by Sequiera Costa, who played Schumann's *Waldscenen*, Debussy's *Suite Bergamasque*, Ravel's Sonatine and some Rachmaninov transcriptions.

Mananan is strong in its encouragement of young performers. As well as a series of concerts focusing on the talents of the island's schoolchildren, there was a recital shared by Emma Johnson (BBC Television's Young Musician of 1984) and Jonathan Kneale (Young Musician of Man for the previous year). In addition, the festival regularly hosts music workshops and competitions, including the Lionel Tertis International Viola Competition, usually held in late August.

Mananan is an enterprising festival which mounts small and medium-sized events very capably, but which has not yet gone into the business of attracting symphony orchestras or professional opera companies to the island. However, it has developed hugely in the course of its ten or so years of existence, so there is no saying what undreamed-of delights it may have on offer in the future.

MANSFIELD

Established a little over eighteen years ago, this Nottinghamshire festival seeks to present professional performances in a wide spectrum of the arts to as large an audience as possible. Artists are both homegrown and international imports (two weeks in early October).

MILDENHALL

This started life as the Forest and Fen Festival and was based mainly in schools and directed at children. In the intervening eight years, it has widened its scope enormously to involve both amateurs and professionals in a full programme of music, dance, drama, workshops, art and crafts, and is now known as the Forest Heath Arts Festival (two weeks in June).

MINEHEAD AND EXMOOR

West Somerset, with its combination of sea, moor, thatched cottages and fine churches, provides a festival setting of striking natural beauty. From the heights of Dunkery Beacon, over the Lorna Doone country to the cliffs, bays and seaside villages along the Bristol Channel, the region offers a grand, uncrowded landscape. The festival which radiates from Minehead to such towns and villages as Porlock, Luccombe, Dunster and Dulverton was inaugurated in 1963 by Tim Reynish (now of the Royal Northern College of Music). Each summer, he would invite friends from Cambridge, Oxford and the National Youth Orchestra to spend a week by the sea studying, rehearsing and performing. In more recent years, the festival has grown into a two-week event, the first week being devoted to concerts and recitals by a variety of individual soloists and groups, while the second is dominated by programmes given by the Festival Orchestra, a fifty-strong ensemble drawn from all over the country.

The first week's activities are launched by a Festival Service in St Michael's Church, Minehead, which is regularly followed by a 'Young Artist' concert at which the stage is given to an up-and-coming local performer on the threshold of his or her musical career (in 1985, Philip Scriven was organ soloist). Successive evenings are then given over to the festival play (an adaptation of *Lark Rise to Candleford* was the most recent offering), solo recitals, a folk evening and chamber concerts (as, for instance, that by the Taunton Sinfonietta with Gonzala Acosta, violin, in which Bach, Handel and Telemann rubbed shoulders with Ysaye and Nielsen).

During the second week, performances by the Festival Orchestra (conducted by Richard Dickins) provide the only opportunity each year for West Somerset to hear live orchestral music. Rehearsals start on the Sunday and three separate programmes are put together for performance during the ensuing six days. In 1985, these were largely popular in appeal, though with some interesting pairings: Stravinsky's Octet with Bach's E Major Violin Concerto (soloist Alison Kelly), the Mozart Clarinet Concerto (with Mark van de Weil) and Tchaikovsky's Fifth, and – in the final 'Summer Serenade', complete with wine and cheese – Copland's *Rodeo* with the Letter Scene from *Eugene Onegin* (soloist Melanie Armistead).

1985 saw the start of David Yates's reign as festival director, the arrival of an expanded fringe (the Exmoor Ensemble, Exmoor Wind Group, poetry reading and a flute and guitar recital) and arts exhibition, and – for the first time in several years – financial solvency. Minehead and Exmoor is clearly going places and its twenty-fifth anniversary in 1987 promises to be rather spectacular.

NETHER WALLOP
——INTERNATIONAL ARTS FESTIVAL 1984——

It all came about because of a throwaway remark columnist Stephen Pile made in the *Sunday Times* about the increasing unmanageability of the Edinburgh Festival and the fact that many of its enormous number of events seem to go on at one and the same time. Why, he wanted to know, should Edinburgh enjoy this absurd *embarras de richesse* when other parts of the country were crying out for the merest crumb of culture? 'Why not,' he asked, 'have a simultaneous festival in, oh, say, Nether Wallop?'

Within a matter of days, a letter arrived on his desk from the Parochial Church Council of this tiny (population about 500) Hampshire village, informing him that, at a specially convened meeting, they had appointed him (*in absentia*) the artistic director of the first Nether Wallop International Arts Festival. A suitably tongue-in-cheek response to a tongue-in-cheek remark – and there things might have rested had it not been for Jane Tewson and Charity Projects. It was a chance meeting between Tewson and Pile in a London wine-bar and their realization that a well-publicized spoof festival might raise a lot of money for worthy causes as well as being huge fun, that led to the idea being taken much more seriously than anyone had ever intended.

That was all in 1982. The festival actually took place on a warm autumn weekend two years later, after a great deal of planning, of string-pulling and of entreaty – a great deal, in other words, of what is involved before *any* festival can get off the ground. Advice was solicited from the most exalted quarters: Joan Littlewood was strong on the need for the festival to have a theme, John Drummond – who had been managing affairs at Edinburgh for a number of years – offered little more than a warning of the pressures under which festival directors are expected to operate in the 1980s. It was not long before Pile was in a position to enunciate his festival policy – one shared with 90 per cent of festivals up and down the country – namely to spice performances by talented locals with appearances by world-class artists. Or, to put it another way (his), 'to combine . . . the vicar's conjuring act, Miss Daphne Gill's fine voice and Mrs P. Brown's show-stopping monologue on how to make a silk purse out of a sow's ear with the best of international megastars, ideally Pavarotti, the Rolling Stones, Boy George, etc.'

In the event, though these particular names were unfortunately not available – just as well, perhaps, for the sanity of rural Hampshire – Nether Wallop's two days of high festivity more than lived up to his ideals, even if some of the guest artists appeared in somewhat unfamiliar roles – dancer Wayne Sleep making his rather breathless operatic début in an aria from *La Traviata*, Rolling Stone Bill Wyman scripting and taking part in his own comedy sketch, Jenny Agutter turning conjuror's assistant and Jessye Norman turning the pianist's pages at the concert organized by the village choir-mistress. Among the apocryphal tales that have grown up round the festival is the one that, when Miss Norman indicated her willingness to sing an unaccompanied spiritual at the end of the concert, her offer was politely declined as time was pressing and next on the agenda was the much-anticipated organ recital by Colonel Mew.

Wayne Sleep did, in fact, dance as well as sing. He joined members of the local Brownie group in a ballet specially composed by Michael Berkeley and choreographed by Lynn Seymour on the subject of the life of the mayfly. The festival was, however, by no means an exclusively musical affair. Another grand spectacle was provided by the festival pageant in which Sir Michael Hordern, Jenny Agutter, the Wallop Scouts and children from Wallop Primary School were directed by the Royal Shakespeare Company's Trevor Nunn. On a quieter note, writers Gore Vidal and Ned Sherrin signed copies of recent books in the village store, and Bamber Gascoigne presided over a quiz in which the villagers managed to beat a team of the World's Greatest Philosophers (led by Professor A. J. Ayer) by one point. Another competition – this time on the village pitch – took the form of a football match between Nether Wallop and neighbouring Over Wallop, refereed by professional players Simon Stainrod and Gary O'Reilly. The visual arts were represented by Ralph Steadman and Humphrey Ocean, the theatre by Maria Aitken (reciting 'Songs of Wallop', a collection of poems by a former vicar of Wallop) and Judi Dench (giving a rare public reading of the history of the village's church). Other visitors included poets Brian Patten and Roger McGough, composer Andrew Lloyd-Webber, comedians Billy Connolly, Rowan Atkinson, Mel Smith, Peter Cook and John Wells – in his Denis Thatcher guise – and jazz-singer Marian Montgomery, who survived having to change in the cricket pavilion lavatory to render 'What's a Girl Like Me Doing in a Joint Like This?' with great feeling.

All of which was crowded into two brief days (oh Edinburgh!) and a number of suitably cramped venues – the school hall, the tythe barn, the corrugated-iron village hall and a specially erected marquee – within the village. Looking back on the venture after the dust had settled, Pile confessed to seeing it as 'a bit of a blur', but publicity and television royalties raised money both for the church roof fund and for Jane Tewson's Charity Projects – which was, after all, the main point of the exercise.

NEWBURY

When you enter Newbury on a Spring Festival evening, after – as like as not – an exhilarating drive across the wide-horizoned Berkshire Downs, you might, quite honestly, be in any plain but prosperous market town in the country. The streets have a shut-up look and there are few people about. There is remarkably little to tell you that an important and well-regarded festival is in full swing. But wander round by the Kennet, through the churchyard heavy with yew and flowering cherry, and into the airy grandeur of St Nicholas's Church and you will discover that things are not quite what they at first seemed. You will find the hard wooden pews and the large number of extra chairs brought in for the occasion crammed with music-lovers of all ages, raptly attentive while the building resounds to the Royal Philharmonic Orchestra in Beethoven's *Pastoral* Symphony or the LSO playing Elgar and Brahms.

The two-week Spring Festival first opened for business in 1979, with the aim of bringing to Newbury and its surrounding villages in West Berkshire and North Hampshire 'concerts and recitals of excellence given by orchestras, conductors and soloists of international reputation' and coupling this with a visual arts programme featuring exhibitions by distinguished artists. There is little, if anything, in the way of a local input – whether amateur or professional – no festival choir, no coming together of schools' orchestras, though the exhibitions do sometimes reflect home-grown talent and 1985 saw the inclusion of the Bayer UK Competition for Young Musicians. The festival also coincides, conveniently, with another event calculated to bring visitors to the area – the Newbury Spring Race Meeting.

While the larger-scale concerts take place in Newbury itself, other events have artists travelling to a wide scattering of nearby towns and villages: in 1985, for instance, the Alberni Quartet performed in the Long Gallery at Englefield House (Theak); Guillermo Fierens (guitar) and the Llanelli Male Choir appeared in Hungerford; the Faber Trio in Shaw-cum-Donnington; Sharon Gould (harpsichord) in Wantage; George Chisholm and his Band charted '100 years of Dixieland Jazz' for the benefit of the inhabitants of Thatcham; the Burlington Trio played Haydn, Mendelssohn and Ravel in Kintbury's beautiful church; and Maria de la Pau captivated the audience at Highclere Castle. Then there were recitals, concerts and even opera (Arne's *The Cooper* with Antony Hopkins's *Hands across the Sky*) in such places as Cold Ash, Compton and Woodhay. All of which perhaps accounts for the lack of much to suggest that a festival is in progress in the streets of Newbury itself. This is a far-flung event requiring regular supporters to organize their own transport or master the mysteries of the local bus network.

At the same time, Newbury is a thoughtful festival. Out-of-town concerts frequently include some kind of refreshment in the ticket-price, while concert-goers at St Nicholas should have no trouble in parking and will find a warm welcome at the local pubs both before the performance and during the extended interval.

Newbury does not set out to explore particular themes in its musical programmes,

Members of the London Baroque in the churchyard at East Woodhay, one of the outlying villages drawn in to the Newbury Festival.

but to give of the best available in a number of departments. There are regular organ recitals, for example, guest performers having included Christopher Herrick, Thomas Trotter and James Lancelot. There are chamber recitals by such celebrated groups as the Amadeus, Chilingirian and Aeolian Quartets and specialist concerts by visitors from other festivals – the Dolmetsch Ensemble and the Tilford Bach Festival Choir and Orchestra. Regular appearances since the festival's foundation have been made by Christopher Hogwood and his Academy of Ancient Music, giving authentic performances of Bach, Mozart, Haydn or Handel (their 1985 offering was something of a rarity – Handel's oratorio *La Resurrezione*). For full symphony concerts, the LSO has trundled over from the capital, as have the Royal Philharmonic Orchestra and the Philharmonia; the BBC Philharmonic has found its way from Manchester and the BBC Welsh Symphony Orchestra has braved the M4 from Cardiff. Great names there have been in abundance – Lill, Weller, Gimpel, Tortelier, Brymer, Tilson Thomas, Masur, Perahia, Menuhin, Baker, Frankl, Vásáry – all providing Newbury's patrons with good standard fare, reliably (often inspiringly) presented and conveniently packaged.

NEWCASTLE

For seven years after its inception in 1969, the Newcastle Festival devoted its energies to bringing ballet, opera, choral and orchestral concerts, lieder and instrumental recitals – as well as goodly helpings of drama, lectures and exhibitions – to England's industrial North-East. The change to a more popular emphasis in 1976 added to the established ingredients liberal quantities of jazz and folk music, film and a first-day parade with all the trappings of decorated floats and clowns. There is still music in plenty, from City Hall concerts by the locally based Northern Sinfonia to Larry Adler and from Steeleye Span to the Philip Jones Brass Ensemble in a programme of ceremonial music of all periods.

NORFOLK AND NORWICH

The festival that takes place every third year in East Anglia's ancient provincial capital is a rare survivor. Originally founded towards the end of the eighteenth century to raise funds for the hospital from which it takes its name, it was re-established in 1824 and has put in an appearance more or less regularly ever since.

Usually held over ten days in mid-October, before chill easterlies begin to wheeze across the Broads and the open fens, it gives pride of place, on the musical front, to amateur choirs (from all parts of the region as well as from the city itself) who join together to perform with visiting orchestras – such as the Royal Philharmonic – choral works of a scale normally well beyond the capacity of individual groups. They make a thrilling sight and sound. Even in the age of the train, Norfolk remains a notoriously isolated part of England, and those who live there maintain a strong tradition of cultural self-sufficiency. Singers come to join the special Festival Choir from colleges, schools, parish churches and choral societies, in order to share the splendour of performing – to a crowded Cathedral or, more recently, Sir Andrew's Hall – classics of the repertoire such as Beethoven's *Missa Solemnis* (with soloists of the calibre of Mary Wells, Helen Watts, Alexander Young and Ian Comboy) and modern masterpieces like Walton's *Belshazzar's Feast*. There was a particularly moving occasion, some five festivals ago, when four hundred Norwich schoolchildren took part in a staging of Britten's *Noye's Fludde*. Several noted choral conductors have been associated with Norfolk and Norwich over the years, and the tradition remains in safe hands with Vernon Handley as the festival's current artistic director.

Recent festivals have demonstrated the high standards maintained at Norwich with performances of such demanding rarities as Delius's *A Mass of Life* (1979, with the Philharmonia Orchestra and soloists conducted by the then reigning artistic director, Norman Del Mar), the Szymanowski *Stabat Mater* (the Royal Philharmonic Orchestra, with Eiddwen Harrhey, Margaret Cable and Brian Rayner Cook, under Vernon Handley) and Holst's *Choral Symphony* (1985). In 1982, the festival's joint celebration of Tippett and Berlioz had as its choral buttresses the latter's *Grande Messe des Morts* and *Te Deum*, while works specially written for young people came, in successive festivals, from John Paynter (his *Voyage of St Brendan*), Douglas Coombes and Raymond Warren. Indeed, Norfolk and Norwich has a proud record of special commissions, including works by Alexander Goehr (*Kafka Fragments*), Wilfred Josephs (*Circadian Rhythms*), David Blake (*Seasonal Variants*), Stephen Oliver (*Seven Words*) and Nicholas Maw (*Morning Music for Orchestra*).

Alongside the major choral performances, there are orchestral concerts, organ recitals, chamber recitals and liberal doses of jazz and folk music. Visiting artists have included Alfred Brendel, Cécile Ousset, Amaryllis Fleming, Manoug Parikian, John Lill, Gillian Weir, Jill Gomez, and the Allegri and Chilingirian String Quartets. Other arts now featured in the festivities are drama, film and painting.

NOTTINGHAM

Nottingham is nothing if not a people's festival, catering for a staggering range of interests in two broad areas: the arts and sport. It has taken place yearly since 1969 – with one unfortunate lapse in 1973 – and has sought to encourage the active participation of local groups and individuals as well as bringing in nationally and internationally known performers. Events cover some sixteen days in late May and early June. The city is well provided with suitable venues for all kinds of activity and a number of events take place in the suburbs and in outlying towns.

For large-scale musical events, the splendid new Royal Concert Hall is the principal focus, though policy over the planning of the festival programmes put on there is a little unclear. In 1984, almost all the orchestral concerts were decidedly popular in appeal – the Hallé Orchestra was conducted by Bryden Thompson in a Spanish evening (*España*, *Capriccio Espagnol*, *Boléro*, the *Concierto de Aranjuez* with Carlos Bonell), by Nicholas Cleobury in a Viennese pot-pourri of Léhar, Suppé and the Strauss family, by Jacek Kasprzyk in a programme of over-familiar Tchaikovsky, Rachmaninov and Mussorgsky and by Owain Arwel Hughes in Nottingham's own 'Last Night of the Proms', *Pomp and Circumstance*, *Jerusalem*, *Sea Song Fantasia* and all. Even the Philharmonia Orchestra under Vladimir Ashkenazy settled for popular pieces by Weber and Dvořák, though there was something a little more challenging in Boris Belkin's account of Shostakovich's First Violin Concerto.

By way of contrast, the following year's festival opened with John Lubbock conducting the Orchestra of St John's, Smith Square, (with Katia and Marielle Labeque the dazzling soloists) in an all-Mozart programme which steered clear of the obvious, went on to Giuseppe Sinopoli with the Philharmonia in Bruckner's Seventh Symphony (preceded by Martha Argerich playing the Beethoven Second Piano Concerto) and ended with the Northern Sinfonia under Richard Hickox in a classically scaled programme of Haydn, Mozart (the K503 Piano Concerto with Radu Lupu) and Beethoven. More obviously popular offerings that year came from the Hallé under Owain Arwel Hughes (Walton, Vaughan Williams – the *Greensleeves Fantasia* – Elgar's *Enigma Variations* and Tchaikovsky) and James Loughran (Berlioz, Mendelssohn's Violin Concerto with Zdenek Broz and, again, Tchaikovsky).

Nottingham Festival – school steel band concert at the Victoria Leisure Centre.

The lack of choral input in the Royal Hall concerts is offset elsewhere in the festival – by the Cantamus Girls' Choir in a programme of 'Songs for a Spring Evening', for instance, or by the Newstead Abbey Singers (performing in the Salon at Newstead), the Carlton Male Voice Choir, the St Peter's Singers (in a programme both secular and sacred, including Puccini's *Messa di Gloria*) or the Nottingham Boys' Choir. A specially welcome festival feature is the series of liturgical performances of settings of the Mass given each Sunday by the English Sinfonia Chorale conducted by Andrew Burnham at different churches in the area: one Sunday it will be Byrd's Mass for Five Voices at the Roman Catholic Cathedral, the next Bruckner's Mass in E Minor at St Stephen's Church, Sneinton, or Mozart's *Coronation Mass* at St John's Church, Carrington. There are also organ recitals (Gillian Weir, Carlo Curley, John Keys), chamber concerts (the Endellion Quartet playing Mozart, Beethoven's Opus 131 and Bartók's Third Quartet; the Baroque Virtuosi; Philip Astle and Paul Williamson in their programme 'The Art of Minstralsye'; Margaret Fingerhut at the piano), brass and military bands, jazz (Chris Barber, Monty Sunshine, George Melly), steel bands, evenings of classical Indian music and dance, folk music, gospel and plenty of pop (Chris Rea, Barbara Dickson, Ultravox, Bucks Fizz).

Theatre is also well served by the festival, as are poetry and cabaret, while films – both popular and esoteric – seem to run almost continuously. On the sporting side, the main activities are rowing, sailing, boxing, wrestling, cricket and of course – since this is Nottingham – archery. The festival also boasts a lively fringe.

———PETWORTH———

Petworth House in West Sussex is a striking setting for a mostly music festival, especially one that concentrates its attention on the English repertoire. Artistic directors Robert Walker and Donald Fraser see to it that their festival's single week in mid-June is crammed with lunchtime and evening concerts and that there are plenty of non-musical features (art exhibitions, craft displays, morris-dancers and – in 1985 – a kite-flying competition in the grounds of the house) to interest their enthusiastic audiences.

———PORTSMOUTH———

The Portsmouth Festival takes place two years out of every three, the third being devoted to the city's Triennial International String Quartet Competition. It started in 1970 with certain clear-cut objectives: first and foremost, it was to be relevant, reflecting the special character of the city, seeking to stimulate local interest and participation rather than simply buying in a string of star entertainers (though big names have always appeared on festival programmes). Next, it aimed to be not just an isolated two-week jamboree, but a trigger for year-round cultural activity in the area. Third, it saw itself as a means of breaking down social and artistic barriers and bringing to the people of Portsmouth a real community awareness. It was – and still is – a multi-media festival in which music plays a central part, but with important contributions from dance, theatre, poetry, film and the visual arts.

Since 1970, increase in local support and interest has led to an expanding of the festival's boundaries, with events taking place in Southsea, Portsea, Waterlooville and on Hayling Island, as well as in Portsmouth itself. On the other hand, there has in the eighties been a reduction in the number of guest orchestras and soloists invited to come to the city from other parts of Britain and abroad. In the early years, these included the London Philharmonic, Royal Philharmonic, Utah Symphony and Bournemouth Symphony Orchestras, whereas in 1983 and 1984 the lion's share of concert work went to the Bournemouth Symphony and its sister Sinfonietta, with a little help from the home-based Hampshire Pro Musica. Local representation has always been strong on the choral front, the Portsmouth Festival Choir in particular making regular and popular appearances throughout the seasons.

Right from the start there was a carefully judged thematic approach to programming. The 1983 festival, for instance, celebrated the meeting of East and West with liberal injections of Russian and American music, visits from conductors Thomas Bugaj and Harold Farberman, and a grand 'contact concert' with Elgar Howarth and Cristina Ortiz. The same year welcomed guitarists John Williams (with friends), Carlos Bonell (with Mara) and Robert Brightmore (in a concert which featured Rodrigo's much-loved *Concierto de Aranjuez* alongside British premières of two others of his works, the *Wedding Cantata* and *Ode to Salamanca*). Jazz was represented by Kenny Baker and Stan Tracey, opera by a Kent Opera 'insight' into *Le Nozze di Figaro* and a concert performance of *Porgy and Bess*.

The following year, the theme was a composite one, focusing both on 'War' (1984 saw the fortieth anniversary of D-Day and the seventieth of the outbreak of the First World War) and the English heritage in music, with special emphasis on Delius, Holst and Elgar. The opening concert brought everything together in a shattering performance in the Guildhall of Britten's *War Requiem* under Richard Hickox. Other concerts of English music, featuring the Bournemouth orchestra, were conducted by Norman Del Mar and James Loughran, while Stanley Black was in charge of a flag-waving D-Day celebration entitled 'Salute to the Services'. On a more intimate scale, the Medici Quartet and members of the Royal Shakespeare Company came together to perform 'Wood Magic', Michael Kennedy's evocation of Elgar's life in nearby Sussex during the years of the First World War; and Eric Fenby enthralled the audience in the Central Library with his reminiscences of Delius.

This particularly successful and close-knit festival also included regular lunchtime organ recitals, concerts by young musicians and appearances by the Phoenix Dance Company and London City Ballet. Poets Gavin Ewart and Vernon Scannell relived their wartime experiences, as well as those of millions of others, through the poetry written by men fighting in the armed forces during the forties, while films of the period and special exhibitions evoked memories of the way we lived then. In almost every respect, 1984 saw the Portsmouth Festival fulfilling its self-imposed aims in programmes that were as thought-provoking as they were entertaining.

PROMS IN THE REGIONS

A number of regional centres organize spring or summer promenade series, loosely based on the BBC Henry Wood model in London. The seasons vary in length from a few days to three or four weeks, but they mostly share the common objective of attracting young and family audiences with low ticket-prices and popular programming. In some cases, a local orchestra takes responsibility for all the concerts in the series, and there is often an opportunity for performers and audiences to let their hair down – Kensington style – in last-night merrymaking.

Centre	Time of Year and Duration of Season	Principal Orchestra
Aberdeen	7 concerts in mid-May	Scottish National
Birmingham	12 concerts in three weeks (June/July)	City of Birmingham Symphony
Bristol (Colston Hall)	8 days in early May	
Dundee (Caird Hall)	3 concerts in mid-May	Scottish National
Edinburgh (Usher Hall)	7 concerts in early June	Scottish National
Glasgow (Kelvin Hall)	15 concerts in two weeks (late June)	Scottish National
Leicester (de Montfort Hall)	3 concerts in mid-June	
Manchester	20 concerts in June/July	Hallé
Snape (The Maltings)	10 days in August	

RICHMONDSHIRE

The market-town of Richmond in North Yorkshire is the centre for a biennial festival – usually held in May or June – of music, drama and literature, plus a variety of sporting activities. Events take place in a number of churches in the surrounding Dales and in the town's own Georgian theatre.

ROSS AND DISTRICT

Professional conductors, orchestras and soloists appear at Ross's Parish Church of St Mary, as do members of music societies from the surrounding Wye Valley. The emphasis in this ten-day event is on choral and orchestral works, though there are also contributions from theatre, film and the visual arts (biennial, late May).

RYE

The festival in this picturesque Sussex town, long since abandoned by the sea, is entirely professional, with some thirty events from chamber recitals to jazz, from live theatre to puppet shows, crowding into a single late summer's week. Other activities include film, lectures, poetry, cabaret and busking. A regular feature each year is the commissioning of new music and poetry (August–September).

SADDLEWORTH

A quadrennial festival that acts as a focus for local cultural and recreational activities in this part of the Lancashire-Yorkshire borderland. It also brings in notable performers – Eva Turner, Gervase de Peyer, Radu Lupu, for instance, and the Allegri and Amadeus Quartets. New music – such as Wilfred Josephs' *Concerto for School Orchestra* – is regularly commissioned and there is a strong emphasis on local heritage (two weeks in September).

SALISBURY

A fourteen-day festival in mid-September centred on the Cathedral, the Salisbury Playhouse and the city's Arts Centre. Policy is to offer a broad cross-section of entertainment, ranging from appearances by artists of international standing to events organized by and involving members of the community.

In 1985, distinguished performers included Giuseppe Sinopoli (conducting Philharmonia forces with Lucia Popp and Brigitte Fassbaender in Mahler's *Resurrection Symphony*), Kyung-Wha Chung (who was soloist with the Bournemouth Symphony Orchestra under Christopher Seaman in a noble account of the Brahms Violin Concerto), Marisa Robles and Peter Donohoe, who gave three recitals in St Thomas's Church, in the first of which he was joined by Jane Salmon (cello) in music by Brahms, Rachmaninov and Rachel Portman – her *Phantasy for Cello and Piano* being a festival commission – while in the second he played Bach and Brahms with Jonathan Rees (violin) and in the third he joined William Stephenson in piano duets. The Academy of St Martin-in-the-Fields directed by Iona Brown played Mozart in the candlelit Cathedral and the Martin Best Mediaeval Ensemble (with the Singers of Trinity College) presented 'The Cantigas of Santa Maria of Alfonso the Wise, King of Castille 1220–1284'. On the lighter side, there were military band concerts (the Grenadier Guards played Handel at the racecourse and accompanied the Dunvant Male Choir in the Cathedral) and a recital entitled 'The A–Z of the King of Instruments' featuring Carlo Curley and Richard Baker.

SIDMOUTH

Founded in 1979, this is an arts festival which combines concerts and master-classes by visiting musicians (the Bournemouth Sinfonietta, the Cantabile Singers) with workshops in such areas as drama, dance, painting and puppetry, and exhibitions of the work of artists and craftsmen from the South-West (two weeks in the latter part of June).

ST IVES

First – in the nineteenth century – came the artists; then, not far behind them, the tourists. Today, the once busy fishing port of St Ives, with its tightly twisting streets and brightly coloured low stone cottages, is a thriving and warm-hearted community, clinging to the north coast of Cornwall at a point where the peninsula is barely four miles across. The influence of painters like Whistler and Sickert, and of their twentieth-century successors Ben Nicholson, Barbara Hepworth and the potter Bernard Leach, is still very much in evidence in the permanent colony of artists that has made the town internationally famous.

The St Ives September Festival, however, is not limited to exhibitions of paintings and sculptures or lecture-demonstrations on the art of the potter. Though it has in some senses sprung from the town's vigorous artistic traditions, it is essentially a family occasion, providing a wide range of events mostly involving performers with strong local associations. There are carnivals, puppets, poets, folk singers, mime artists, films, plays, concerts, interludes in hotels, churches, galleries, schools and – of course – the open sunshine of the streets.

On the musical side, a notable contribution is made by performers from the Prussia Cove International Musicians' Seminar, whose isolated home is only a few miles away, near Marazion on the south coast. In recent years, they have given memorable recitals of chamber music by Haydn, Schubert, Mozart, Elgar and Priaulx Rainier in St Ia Church. Two other groups with close local connections that made appearances in 1983 were the Duchy String Quartet and the Cornwall Youth Jazz Orchestra. The same year, the town's Guildhall resounded to the music of the Brio

Right: The Philharmonia van in front of Salisbury Cathedral in 1983.

Brass Ensemble, a Bedfordshire group which has been making regular tours of the West Country since 1977. While it specializes in the sixteenth-century Venetian repertoire, Brio has also commissioned a number of new works, including John Blood's *Music for St Ives* and Christopher Brown's *Seascape*, both of which were given first hearings at the 1981 festival. A special feature of their 1983 concert was George Lloyd's *Miniature Triptych*, played as a birthday tribute to the composer, who lives in the area. The 1984 season included music and dances from Renaissance Europe, performed by Quodlibet, and also solo guitar recitals by Stephen Gordon.

ST LEONARDS

The St Leonards Festival came into being as recently as 1984 as something of a celebration of civic identity. The town, which has now been all but engulfed by neighbouring Hastings, was founded in 1828 as a fashionable watering-place, thanks to the vision, energy and money of the Scottish builder, James Burton. Burton's efforts were rewarded by royal patronage, starting with the visit, in 1834, of the fifteen-year-old Princess Victoria. The birth of the St Leonards Festival coincided with the 150th anniversary of that event and was marked – appropriately enough – with a ceremony at the town's Royal Victoria Hotel, complete with a marching jazz band.

St Leonards possesses a number of suitable venues for concerts, recitals and exhibitions, including churches, hotels, bars and restaurants. The programme – which lasts somewhat over a week in mid-September – is wide ranging and has attracted a number of distinguished performers. There have been poetry evenings with Adrian Mitchell and Patric Dickinson; talks by Denby Richards and Mark Deller (who was born in the town and whose father, the countertenor Alfred Deller, started his career at Christ Church, Silchester Road); exhibitions (works by four local artists, Prue Theobalds, David Hobbs, Monique and Felix Partridge, and an unusual collection of photographs entitled 'The Parish Priest', in 1984; an exhibition of plans, drawings and artists' impressions of the formative decades of St Leonards, the following year); jazz with the Hot Club of London; folk evenings (the Brian Boru Folk Group, Stevie Waller and Carl Barnwell); recitals by the Rasoumovsky Quartet (playing Beethoven, Schubert, Mozart and Verdi), the Deller Consort, Harold Britton (organ), Yuri Braginsky (violin), the Essenden Consort (in an enterprisingly varied programme of choral music from Scarlatti to Janáček, from Casals to Cole Porter, from Dvořák to Ken Roberts, the group's conductor) and Jenny Miller (soprano). The opening festival even had opera – Rossini's *The Barber of Seville* – performed by a professional cast in the intimate setting of the restaurant Il Boccalino, whose owners, Michael Maurel and Brenda Stanley, are both professors at the Blackheath Conservatoire. The £9 tickets for the opera also included a three-course dinner. The Australian piano duo, Rhondda Gillespie and Robert Weatherburn, gave two recitals in 1984 – a Victorian evening of Brahms,

Mendelssohn, Sterndale Bennett, Sydney Smith, Behr, Rossini and Wagner (arranged Fauré and Messager); and a programme of Bach, Brahms, Liszt (the first performance of two of his *Geharnischte Lieder* in arrangements by Robert Weatherburn) and Robert Matthew-Walker (the première of his *Divertimento on a Theme of Mozart*, Opus 57), culminating in a rousing *Le Carnaval des Animaux* (Saint-Saëns) in which Joan Greenwood was guest narrator.

The St Leonards Festival has got off to a start that promises well indeed for the future.

STOGUMBER

Here's enterprise!

Stogumber is a tiny village (population 610) not far from Taunton, in the heart of Somerset cider-country. It boasts a church, a pub, a school and a village square – all of which play their part in the late-June festival that has been running in Stogumber for the past three years. The festival director is Vera Metters and it was she who started the ball rolling in 1982 with a widely praised production of *Trial by Jury*, in the parish church, that had the villagers asking why there wasn't more music in Stogumber.

Vera Metters with the Vienna Horn Quartet outside Stogumber Parish Church.

So the first, rather cautious, festival came about in 1983. By the following year, it had grown into a packed three days of lively and varied activity. On the Friday evening, St Audrie's School was the setting for a recital by Paul Collins (violin) and Anthony Green (piano) which ranged from Beethoven to Stravinsky. Five major events managed to squeeze into the following day, starting with an informal children's concert in the morning, followed by madrigals and part-songs from the prize-winning Exeter University Singers in church at 3 p.m. At 5.30 p.m., a local garden was thrown open for the festival picnic, ending in time for the recital of Elizabethan words and music given in the evening by Robert Spencer (lute), William Devlin (speaker) and the Amaryllis Singers. (Interval refreshments at this concert were provided at the nearby White Horse Inn, the church bell being rung to warn the audience that the second part was about to begin!) A glorious day's music-making was rounded off at 10 p.m. by jazz in the village square. Sunday afternoon brought what was in many ways the highspot of the festival – a concert of music from three centuries (including Diabelli, Beethoven, Mozart and Bruckner) played by the Vienna Horn Quartet. A festive Choral Evensong brought the three days to a close.

The entire programme was put on without any form of grant, being made possible simply through the hard work and winter fund-raising of a band of dedicated enthusiasts. Stogumber is, indeed, living proof of what can be achieved in the smallest of communities and deserves every encouragement and success.

STRATFORD-UPON-AVON

A high-summer event, lasting about two weeks, in which music takes its place alongside drama, street theatre, puppetry, exhibitions, mime, poetry, dance and fireworks. The emphasis is on entertainment for all tastes and all age-groups (July).

STROUD

For the first ten years of its existence, Stroud was essentially a festival of religious drama. Founded in 1947 by the enterprising and farsighted Netlam Bigg, it sought to bring young people together in the grey post-war years to rehearse and perform plays on religious themes in the local parish church. Over the years, the festival has commissioned many new plays, which are however now given in Stroud's modest theatre rather than in the church. Netlam Bigg was also a talented choral conductor, so it is in no way surprising that, since 1958, when the festival broadened its activities, music should have played an important role.

Stroud, only nine miles from the cathedral city of Gloucester in the green depths of Laurie Lee country, grew to prosperity on the back of the wool trade; and it is perhaps not too fanciful a suggestion that the textile connection is the reason why – like a little bit of Lancashire dropped into the Frome Valley – it should have favoured especially the development of choral singing and brass band music. So strong, indeed, has been the choral element in the festival that a number of important works for voices have been commissioned for Stroud – including Rubbra's *Inscape*, Lennox Berkeley's *Signs in the Dark* (to text by Laurie Lee) and *Orpheus with his Lute* by Michael Hurd. Hurd's opera *The Widow of Ephesus* also received its first performance at a Stroud Festival, as did Antony Hopkins's *Rich Man, Poor Man, Beggar Man, Saint*. Such opera commissions are, of course, very much within the Stroud tradition of encouraging dramatists and composers to provide new works suitable for church performance. Orchestral music written for the festival over the years includes Tony Hewitt-Jones's *Stroud Festival Overture*, Alun Hoddinott's *St Paul at Malta* and Elis Pehkonnen's Symphonic Movement, given by April Cantelo and the Gloucestershire Youth Orchestra.

There has been a happy affinity between Stroud and the Gloucestershire Youth Orchestra, whose members have been regular visitors to the town, giving children's concerts in the afternoons as well as concerts for more mixed audiences in the evenings. In years gone by, other distinguished performers have included the Bournemouth Symphony Orchestra, the Cheltenham Chamber Orchestra, the Academy of the BBC, the Orchestra of St John's, Smith Square, and Rohan de Saram, Ivor Keys, John Lill, Paul Tortelier and Marisa Robles. Apart from the notable commissions, programmes – given in the town's Subscription Rooms or the more cavernous hall at the new leisure centre – have tended to be largely popular in content.

Two highly esteemed offshoots of the festival are the international poetry and composition competitions. The latter, which attracts entries from all parts of the world including the Iron Curtain countries, is for works on chamber scale (in 1984, it was the turn of music for brass ensemble, judged by Philip Jones; in 1985, that of pieces for oboe and piano). Each festival also sees a number of master-classes given by such expert solo performers as Steven Isserlis and Susan Drake.

This highly enterprising venture was, for some time, kept running with the financial support of the Arts Council. In 1984, its grant was discontinued. It is to be hoped that the determination and resourcefulness of the people of Stroud will ensure that the festival itself does not go the same way as the grant.

SWALEDALE

Organized from the North Yorkshire town of Richmond, this festival reaches out into the beautiful and sometimes dramatic countryside of upper Swaledale. Local interests – brass bands, sports, outdoor events – have an influence on the content and there is a strong musical input provided by both local performers and international celebrities (two weeks in May–June).

THORNBURY

A ten-day event which brings together professional outsiders – some well established, others on the brink of a career – and local performers in what is now part of Bristol's suburbia (April).

WARRINGTON

The emphasis is very much on local participation in this major festival in one of Cheshire's new towns. The festival in fact grew out of the celebrations devised in 1972 to inaugurate Warrington's New Town Plan, and has since grown into an event of nearly a month's duration. The area's own operatic and choral societies are kept busy during the period, as is its youth orchestra, but there are also visits from professional groups – such as the Royal Liverpool Philharmonic Orchestra – and individuals, not only from the world of music but representing pretty well every shade of the artistic spectrum (May).

WARWICK

Youth is in many ways the key at Warwick, whose Arts Festival is designed to encourage the participation of local schools and young people's organizations. At the same time, outstanding professional performers are invited to appear in events which are usually built round specific themes – in 1985, Handel and Bach in the context of European music in general, with Weber and Liszt anniversaries spotlit in 1986 (early July).

WAVENDON

Wavendon Allmusic Plan was started in 1969 by the jazz musicians Cleo Laine and her husband John Dankworth, with the idea of breaking down the barriers that exist in the minds of many people between different types of music – jazz and classical, folk and pop. Early supporters of the scheme, which is housed in the old stables adjoining the Dankworth home near Milton Keynes and which takes place year-round, included John Williams, Richard Rodney Bennett and John Ogdon. Activities range from 'mixed concerts' combining jazz items with – say – chamber music, by way of workshop sessions in which performers and young audiences play and sing together, to extended courses at which students can learn more about the various areas of music.

During the months of May, June and July there is an extended festival (the Wavendon Summer Season): events take place in the local church and community centre as well as at the Old Stables and last from early afternoon until well into the night. The variety and quality of Wavendon activities can be gauged from some of the performers who have appeared there in the past – Chris Barber, the Nash Ensemble, Philip Ledger, Ronnie Scott, Dorita y Pepe, Leon Goossens, the King's Singers, the London Chamber Orchestra, Sir John Betjeman and – of course – the Dankworths themselves. Not so much a festival, more a way of life.

WIMBORNE MINSTER

This biennial event was inaugurated as recently as 1981 and it includes concerts and recitals by internationally celebrated performers as well as workshops for young musicians. The Dorset countryside around Wimborne is well supplied with suitable and attractive venues, and past events have included costume recitals in appropriate historical settings (two weeks in June–July).

WINDSOR

The two weeks (plus) of autumn festivity in the Royal Borough have – since their inception in the late sixties – been associated with some truly distinguished names in the world of the arts. Ian Hunter was the first artistic director (succeeded in 1974 by Laurence West), with Yehudi Menuhin responsible for music programming and Hugh Casson for exhibitions of painting and sculpture.

The original plan for the Windsor Festival was to focus an annual celebration of music and the arts on the fine and unusual settings available in the town of Windsor itself and in Eton College, a mere walk away across the Thames. There was generally a festival production at the Theatre Royal and occasional events were housed in the parish church, but most of the music happened in the Royal Apartments and St George's Chapel in Windsor Castle and in the Chapel and School Hall at Eton. This is still very much the pattern, though in 1974 local government reorganization brought about a widening of the borough's boundaries to embrace neighbouring Maidenhead, and festival events have since spread over an area that includes Staines, Cookham and Maidenhead itself.

Sir Yehudi Menuhin, one of the founders of the festival, rehearsing in the Lower Ward of Windsor Castle.

Right: The Waterloo Chamber of Windsor Castle – Sir Adrian Boult and Paul Tortelier at rehearsal.

Below: Curlew River, one of Britten's Church Parables, in St George's Chapel.

Large-scale musical productions are relatively rare here, though the Beethoven *Missa Solemnis* was given an airing back in 1975 by the Windsor Festival Chorus and the New Philharmonia Orchestra conducted by Laszlo Heltay. In the main, festival venues lend themselves more readily to forces of moderate size, such as the English Chamber Orchestra (perhaps in an all-Mozart programme or in a Stravinsky ballet), the Monteverdi Choir and Orchestra (in music written for the Chapel Royal and by seventeenth-century court musicians), the Philip Jones Brass Ensemble and the Menuhin Festival Orchestra (in a programme featuring the first performance of Lennox Berkeley's *Windsor Variations*). Recitals on an even more intimate scale have been given by Ravi Shankar, Janet Baker, George Malcolm, Rubinstein, the Amadeus Quartet and – naturally – Menuhin himself. There is sometimes dance – the London Contemporary Dance Theatre visited one year – and, rather more frequently, opera. Irmgard Seefried appeared with Alexander Young in Purcell's *Dido and Aeneas* and performances of Britten's *Noye's Fludde* and Church Parables have been given amid the magnificence of St George's Chapel.

Additionally, there are lectures, recitals of words and music, and important art exhibitions.

WOOBURN

Wooburn is a *Septemberfest*, an Indian summer celebration of music, drama and poetry that comes just as the beech hangers of the Chilterns are beginning their annual transformation from green to ochre and umber and deepest russet. It describes itself as 'a festival in the Chilterns and Thames Valley' and has, indeed, long outgrown its modest origins in the village of Wooburn, to catch High Wycombe, Eton, Beaconsfield, Marlow and a shoal of intersprinkled villages in its net of performances and displays.

It started in 1967 when the Vicar of Wooburn, the Revd Sidney Hickox, launched an appeal for money to finance essential repair work on his parish church. The appeal impressed his teenage son, Richard, who was on the point of going up to Cambridge on an organ scholarship, and it was he who conceived the idea of a festival.

The mainstay of the Wooburn Festival has always been its close association with the community. It is run entirely by the voluntary efforts of local residents – one of whom, John Shirley-Quirk, was for many years the festival's president. Actors, musicians and artists taking part each autumn come largely from the Thames Valley area, though the festival also benefits from regular contributions by Richard Hickox's own City of London Sinfonia and London Symphony Chorus. It is usually these forces that combine with the Wooburn Singers – a local choir, formed to sing at the festival, whose excellence has led to recordings, broadcasts and engagements at festivals in other parts of the country – in large-scale choral concerts, usually in High Wycombe's spacious parish church. Works performed in recent years include *Belshazzar's Feast* (Walton), the *War Requiem* (Britten), *A Sea Symphony* (Vaughan Williams), the Berlioz *Te Deum*, Elgar's *The Dream of Gerontius* and Geoffrey Burgon's *Requiem*.

Left: Purcell's *The Indian Queen* in the Waterloo Chamber.

Other visiting groups and solo performers since Wooburn came into being have included the Chamber Orchestra of Europe under James Judd, the Endymion Ensemble, the Parley of Instruments (with Roy Goodman and Peter Holman), the Goldberg Ensemble directed by Malcolm Layfield, Richard Lewis, Dennis Matthews, Jack Brymer and Antony Hopkins. There is also a regular jazz spot each year – Ronnie Scott and Humphrey Lyttelton have both made recent appearances – and a special focus on music for young people. In 1984, Emma Johnson, BBC Television's Young Musician of the Year, gave a spellbinding recital of music by Rossini, Brahms and Poulenc in St Dunstan's Church, Bourne End. The same year marked the rebuilding of the organ at High Wycombe Parish Church with a recital by Francis Grier and a performance of the Poulenc concerto by Alastair Ross.

The beauty of Wooburn is that, though it has grown in scale and influence over the years, it is still very much in touch with its roots – Richard Hickox remains its musical director, his mother continues to be a stalwart of the Wooburn Singers and audiences are still made up in large part of residents of the village and its environs.

WORCESTER

Taking place in every conceivable corner of this ancient Three Choirs city, from the Cathedral and Swan Theatre to small pubs and the open streets, 'Worcester Entertains' fosters an enormous range of activities including all areas of the arts, entertainment and sports (six weeks or so in July and August).

WREKIN AND TELFORD

Originally called the Wellington Festival, this well-established event highlights community interests in the fields of music, theatre, the visual arts, dance and a host of other activities, and brings in professionals both to perform and to conduct masterclasses and workshops (two weeks in May).

YORK FESTIVAL AND MYSTERY PLAYS

Though it only occurs once every four years, the York Festival has claims to being one of Britain's largest and most ambitious arts events. Its focal point is the York Cycle of Mystery Plays, dating from the early 1300s, which are presented nightly in the gaunt but spectacular ruins of St Mary's Abbey for a period of about four weeks (usually in June). And for the same four weeks, this exceptional city – its narrow streets sheltering behind massive mediaeval walls and imposing gateways, dominated by the Minster, one of the most perfectly preserved Gothic cathedrals in Europe – erupts in all manner of music, poetry, theatre, film and visual arts, celebrating (as it were) its own celebration.

The first modern revival of the Corpus Christi cycle of mystery plays, which retell biblical events from the Creation of Man to the Last Judgement in the words and

Scene from the 1984 York Festival and Mystery Plays.

dialect of ordinary Yorkshire men and women, took place in 1951 as York's contribution to the Festival of Britain, and the tradition has been established ever since. True to original practice, all but a handful of roles are taken by local amateurs.

Local contributions are also important on the musical front, the University of York's various orchestras, choirs and other ensembles playing a prominent part (in 1973 the New Music Ensemble premièred works by Vic Hoyland and Dennis Smalley, both composers being attached to the university). Other northern regulars include the Northern Sinfonia of England, the BBC Philharmonic Orchestra, the BBC Northern Singers and the Royal Liverpool Philharmonic Orchestra and Choir. Among solo performers from further afield, recent festivals have featured Claudio Arrau, Janet Baker and Paul Tortelier. The Minster is the setting for most of the large-scale concerts, with chamber and solo recitals being housed in some of the city's many ancient halls and churches. There is a lively interest in new music at York, David Blake, Richard Rodney Bennett and Roger Marsh being among the composers whose works have been unveiled there, while both Elizabeth Lutyens and the American, Virgil Thomson, have received special attention. Opera makes the occasional stylish appearance, as when in 1973 William Shield's *Rosina* was staged, or when at a later festival Scottish Opera presented the world première of Thomas Wilson's *Confessions of a Justified Sinner*.

—5—
The Wakefield Legacy

Competitive music festivals are much less popular today than they were in the mid-nineteenth century, when many earnest-minded musicians firmly believed that pitting choir against choir, singer against singer, was the only way to ensure continuing standards of performance. They had, after all, only to point to the vigorous tradition of the Celtic eisteddfod to show how productive friendly rivalry could be. It is, of course, a tradition which is still very much alive in Wales today, the nomadic Royal National Eisteddfod and the international event at Llangollen in particular continuing to attract competitors and audiences not only from all over the principality but worldwide. Over the past twenty years, the North East of England has also acquired a sturdy young eisteddfod, held for one week each July in Middlesbrough.

One of the most influential of the Victorian competitive festivals was the Mary Wakefield, founded in 1885 at Kendal in the Lake District. This biennial event is still going strong (it takes place in mid-May), though the emphasis now is on choral co-operation – choirs from the region coming together to prepare major works for performance rather than vying with each other for winners' medals and silver trophies. A similar transition has taken place at two long-lived festivals in the South of England . . .

LEITH HILL

Leith Hill, steeply wooded and commanding spectacular views of the Surrey farm-lands below, gave its name to a music festival which came into being over eighty years ago in the then sleepy market town of Dorking. The idea behind the festival was that several individual choirs from the area should meet each year in neighbourly competition, as a prelude to combining for an evening concert with professional soloists and orchestra. For the first meeting, in May 1905, the organizers appointed as conductor a young musician by the name of Ralph Vaughan Williams. The success of the venture can be gauged by the fact that, by the time of the outbreak of the First World War, some sixteen choirs had become involved and plans were afoot to launch a children's competition. This development did not actually take place until 1920 – activities were suspended during both wars – two years before the opening

Ralph Vaughan Williams, Gerald Finzi, the composer, and Isidore Schwiller, who was leader of the orchestra for many years, in front of St Martin's Church, Dorking, in 1945. During the war, the Dorking Halls (the festival's permanent home) were taken over for storage purposes by the government and the festival proper was put in abeyance, but concerts still took place at St Martin's.

The first Leith Hill Musical Festival after the war in the Dorking Halls in 1947. The banners are those of the competing choruses.

of what is now the festival's permanent home, the Dorking Halls. On that occasion, a celebratory performance of Bach's *St Matthew Passion* was given, sowing the seed of what has since become a Leith Hill tradition.

Among changes since the 1939–45 war have been the regrettable suspension of children's activities and a shift of emphasis from competition to performance. Recent innovations include the inauguration of the Leith Hill Award, made each year – in the form of an engagement to sing at a festival concert – to a promising young singer from one of the London music colleges, and the performance in 1984 of the festival's first specially commissioned work, John Gardner's Mass in D.

Vaughan Williams's association with Leith Hill as its official conductor continued until five years before his death in 1958. He was succeeded in turn by William Cole and Christopher Robinson, the present occupant of the post being William Llewellyn. 1985 saw Leith Hill, like so many other festivals, paying tercentenary tribute to Bach and Handel with performances of, among other works, the B Minor Mass and *Judas Maccabaeus*. Soloists included Neil Mackie, Adrian Thompson, Penelope Walker and John Noble, as well as Leith Hill Award winners Helen Kucharek, Carol Smith and Carol Green. The orchestra was the Guildford Philharmonic.

The same orchestra accompanies in 1986, when programmes range from Schütz to John Rutter (his *Gloria*) by way of Bach, Bruckner, Honegger's *King David* (Brian Kay as Narrator), Elgar, Vaughan Williams (the *Benedicite*) and Britten.

PETERSFIELD

The Petersfield Musical Festival on the Hampshire-Sussex border was founded in April 1901 in direct emulation of the Mary Wakefield Festival. With the exception of certain war years, it has taken place annually ever since – its eightieth anniversary falls in 1986 – and it is thus the second oldest event of its kind in the country. It was originally, and until well after the Second World War remained, a purely competitive choral festival, providing a focus for a host of small village choirs within reach of Petersfield. But as circumstances have changed, this pattern has been modified and the scope of the festival has, if anything, broadened. It is, however, still a festival for amateur music-makers, arising from the talents and aspirations of local people. Professional assistance comes in the shape of soloists and accompanying orchestras – though the aim is to provide a platform for musicians with local connections wherever possible. It has never been and – as its chairman, the composer Michael Hurd, insists – never will be a 'cheque-book' festival of star names.

As it now stands, the body of the festival consists of two concerts provided by mixed choirs (each of about 150 voices), two identical concerts provided entirely by local schools, and one concert by the Petersfield Orchestra (amateur, with professional stiffening) in which a small group of ladies' choirs (some 70 singers) contributes about a quarter of the programme. There is usually some kind of workshop for young musicians – led in 1984 by Ralph Holmes and the following year by the London Brass Virtuosi – and the 'teachers' either give a concert of their own or appear as soloists in one of the other concerts. Short lunch-time concerts, featuring local musicians, also take place from time to time, as do various exhibitions. The competitive element has all but disappeared. Petersfield has enjoyed a long line of distinguished conductors, from Sir Arthur Somervell, who conducted his cantata *The Charge of the Light Brigade* in 1901, through Sir Hugh Allen and Sir Adrian Boult (who directed from 1920 to 1945) to Sydney Watson, Gordon Mackie, Christopher Seaman, Richard Seal and Mark Deller. The conductor for 1986 is Darrell Davison. Occasional conductors and adjudicators have included Sir Hubert Parry, Sir David Willcocks, Jonathan Willcocks, Sir Malcolm Sargent, Gustav Holst, Donald Tovey, Vernon Handley and Ralph Vaughan Williams. Soloists have included virtually every important name of the day, the help of two local singers, Sir Steuart Wilson and Wilfred Brown, being remembered with special gratitude. The festival takes place in the Petersfield Festival Hall, built in the 1930s by local subscription largely for the purposes of the festival and incorporating the former Town Hall. Plans are afoot to enlarge and improve its already quite considerable amenities. The hall holds about four hundred and is used during the year for many other purposes, including local drama and opera.

The festival has undertaken most major choral works in its time. In the early days the accompaniment was provided by strings and piano, but since the 1920s a largely professional orchestra has been engaged as required. Recent major works include *The Dream of Gerontius*, *The Kingdom* and *The Music Makers* (Elgar), *A Child of Our Time* (Tippett) and the Monteverdi *Vespers of 1610*. The 1986 festival includes Mendelssohn's *Elijah* and Dvořák's Mass in D. Several works have been commissioned over the years – Sir George Dyson's *Agincourt* (1956), Michael Hurd's *Mrs Beeton's Book* (1984) and Judith Bailey's *Seascape* (1985).

Fringe . . . or Frayed Edge?

In 1985, the Cheltenham organizers published a special leaflet listing 'nearly all' the fringe events that they believed would be taking place during the festival period. 'Nearly all', presumably, because they felt their grip on fringe arrangements to be a little unsure. In recent years, fringes have sprouted on almost all the large festivals – Brighton, Cheltenham, Edinburgh, Malvern – as well as some of the smaller ones. Their aim is threefold: to provide official space for local artists to 'do their own thing' at festivals where much time and expense is devoted to the promotion of international celebrities, to widen and intensify the sense of festivity by actively involving more people, and to provide fun and entertainment for family audiences either free or at low cost. As well as extending the standard festival repertoire, fringes explore new areas. Cheltenham's deliberately incomplete list included film, folk dance and music, plenty of jazz, concerts (by Cotswold Brass, the San Francisco Girls' Chorus, the Göttingen Town Choir, pianist David Howells), opera (*L'Elisir d'Amore* in English), practical lunchtime forums involving poets and composers (Ian Jamieson, Paul Dienegri, George Nicholson, Howard Haigh, James Dillon and David Hughes introduced performances of their own music), exhibitions, a flower festival, street entertainment galore, a circus, two musicals, and road and cycle races. Rather a straitlaced batch of events compared with what goes on in some other places.

Indeed, there is a definite streak of anarchy in some fringes – the celebrated Edinburgh fringe actually started life as an exercise in sending up the International Festival. Their massively overfull programmes seem to challenge rather than complement the main event, and – as their very name suggests – they tend to lure audiences away from the principal venues to their own modest premises on the outskirts of town.

So strong have the fringe movements become in some places that festival organizers have expressed deeply felt concern at what they see as a threat to the integrity of their programmes. Fringes, they point out, tend to be anti-establishment and are sometimes given to follies and excesses which damage a festival's reputation. They thin out audiences and lessen the overall impact of a festival by going their own way instead of working to an agreed central theme. They start by benefiting from free festival publicity and end by dominating it. Such views are, however, far from universal and most fringes are now regarded as an essential part of festival activities.

138

–6–

Festivals in London

Fittingly enough, the London festival scene reflects, in the space of a few square miles, the range and richness of events that in the course of the year take place country-wide. There are community-based festivals as at Barnet (lately held in February/March) and Hackney (September/October), Merton (May/June) and Richmond (early June), each with its special emphasis. From the musical point of view, Hackney has proved particularly interesting in the past – with celebrations of Eva Turner (1973) and Joan Cross (1974), the première of John Ogdon's *Dance-Chain*

A free, open-air, late-night concert on the Barbican's lakeside terrace at the 1984 'Summer in the City' Barbican Festival. The City of London Sinfonia, conducted by Richard Hickox, played Handel's *Water Music* before an audience of several thousand.

and appearances by Larry Adler, Ava June, John Brecknock and Nadia Catuse – though in recent years music has had to take its turn (in 1985) with explorations of dance (1984) and theatre (1986). Then again, church and cathedral festivals such as those as Great Witley and Salisbury have their counterparts at Christ Church (Spitalfields), St George's (Hanover Square) and the City of London Festival's productions under the very dome of St Paul's. For the specialist, the spotlight is very much on the contemporary at both the Almeida and Nettlefold festivals; on choral, orchestral and chamber music from the twelfth to the nineteenth century at the Early Music Centre Festival (October) whose concerts – in St John's (Smith Square), the Wigmore Hall and the Queen Elizabeth Hall – are given on original instruments, with style and technique appropriate to the composers' intentions. Opera takes centre stage at Camden, dance at the theatres visited by the international and British artists of the London Dance Umbrella (each autumn). The emphasis is on serving the musical interests of young people at two rather different events – the competitive National Festival of Music for Youth (mid-July) and the prestigious Twentieth Century Music Series promoted each January in the Purcell Room by the Park Lane Group. For those who love to hear music in impressive historic buildings, both the City of London and Greenwich festivals have much to offer, though the latter also has an important community input. Most celebrated of all the capital's festivals is the Promenade Concert season, with its host of visiting orchestras, conductors and soloists of distinction, and its unique atmosphere.

All London festivals have to face the fact that they are in direct competition with the constant and high-quality output of the established concert halls and opera houses. That they have something of their own to offer that cannot be regularly experienced at the Barbican or on the South Bank is demonstrated by their strength and continuity. It is also demonstrated by the fact that in recent years both the major concert halls and the Royal Opera House have initiated their own summer festivals, apparently aimed at attracting younger audiences and also offering an alternative to the Kensington Proms.

The Covent Garden Proms come in two parts: there is a week in late May at the Opera House (the 'Opera Proms') when seven hundred places are made available at low cost from one hour before the curtain rises, and then – in July – there is a special season of ballet staged in the Big Top in Battersea Park.

South Bank Summer Music (started in 1968) is a season of mostly chamber concerts held in the three Thames-side halls – the Royal Festival Hall, the Queen Elizabeth Hall and the Purcell Room – during the latter part of each August. Planning is in the hands of a distinguished guest director who serves for three years – Daniel Barenboim was the first, followed in turn by André Previn and Neville Marriner. In 1981, Simon Rattle succeeded to the task, and the present incumbent, John Williams, took over in 1985.

The Barbican Summer Festival (also in August), with its mainly popular family programmes performed both in the concert hall itself and on the lakeside terrace, is of more recent origin. Its director is currently Richard Hickox.

ALMEIDA

The Almeida Festival takes its name from a theatre (or, more properly, a theatre-club) that in turn takes its name from a little street in deepest Islington. 1985 saw its fifth year of amazing activity lasting for the best part of a month in June and July. Its policy is to introduce to Britain a rich and varied programme of twentieth-century music performed by leading soloists and ensembles from all over the world. It is under the inspired direction of Pierre Audi, assisted by Yvar Mikhashoff and Odaline de la Martinez. Writing in the *Sunday Times*, Paul Driver characterized the Almeida

Left: The Almeida Theatre after restoration of the façade in 1984. *Right:* Virgil Thomson, Conlon Nancarrow and Lou Harrison – three of the American composers who were in residence at the 1985 Almeida Festival.

as 'indisputably our most interesting and enterprising festival', and one that can boast 'efficient organization, a happy and stimulating atmosphere, superb document-ation, and an ideal performance space in the beautifully restored Almeida Theatre itself'.

The 1985 festival fell into four main sections – 'At the tomb of Charles Ives – a celebration of American Experimental Music 1905–1985', 'Aspects of French Contemporary Music, Part 2' (continuing a programme initiated in 1984), 'Hommage à Claude Vivier' and 'New Tangos' – augmented by a number of prestigious one-off events. The American section was by far the most substantial and was highlighted by the presence of six of America's leading composers – Morton Feldman, Philip Glass, Lou Harrison, Conlon Nancarrow, Frederick Rzewski and Virgil Thomson – music by all of whom featured prominently in the festival programmes.

There were first performances by the score, some works being Almeida commissions, others pieces by established composers which for one reason or another had never made it to this side of the Atlantic. The opening concert, for instance, given by Capricorn directed by Oliver Knussen, introduced works by Harrison, Nancarrow and Ives himself (the two Sets for Theatre Orchestra, *Watercolours* and *Four Ragtime Dances*), while the recital of string quartet music by Lejaren Hiller,

Lukas Foss, Ruth Crawford Seeger, Ramon Zupko and Nancarrow given by the Arditti Quartet consisted entirely of UK premières. In another concert, the American chamber group Continuum set new songs by Cage and Crumb and Milton Babbitt's magnificent and complex *A Solo Requiem* alongside lighter scores by Copland, Gershwin and Ives. Each of the visiting composers introduced a programme of his own music, and there were spotlights on the work of John Cage and Roger Reynolds as well as on new departures in jazz and music theatre. Performers included Circle (directed by Gregory Rose), the New London Chamber Choir, Spectrum (under Guy Prothero) and solo performers such as Thomas Halpin (violin), Jan Williams (percussion) and Yvar Mikhashoff himself (piano).

The shorter French section of Almeida 1985 focused principally on Boulez and Debussy (including the first UK performance of *Three Unpublished Mélodies*), but also looked at the work of some less familiar contemporary composers, including Denis Levaillant, Michael Levinas and Pascal Dusapin, performed by the leading French instrumental ensemble L'Itinéraire and Michel Trauchant's Groupe Vocal de France.

'Hommage à Claude Vivier' presented British audiences with their first opportunity to hear the music of this outstanding young Québecois composer who was murdered in 1983, including his pieces for instrumental ensemble (with and without voices) and for chorus, as well as his opera *Kopernikus*. 'New Tangos' featured a series of concerts given by Astor Piazzola and his Quintet as well as a 'tango marathon' in which Yvar Mikhashoff played pieces specially commissioned from composers such as Milton Babbitt, Aaron Copland, John Cage, Michael Finnissy, Oliver Knussen, Karlheinz Stockhausen and Virgil Thomson – a total of fifty tangos by fifty composers!

And, as if all this were not enough, the single events included 'operas for electronics' presented by Electric Phoenix, experimental music by English composers Michael Nyman, Andrew Poppy, Chris Newman and Howard Skempton, and a celebrity recital by singer Hélène Delavault accompanied by Stephen Bishop-Kovacevich.

CAMDEN

Three old LCC boroughs went into the making of Camden, and it was one of them – St Pancras – that originally launched and funded, back in 1954, what has now become the internationally respected Camden Festival. St Pancras, despite being one of the capital's most unprepossessing and deprived areas with social problems galore, has always shown strong interest in and support for the arts – not surprising, since Bernard Shaw was a councillor for many years and gave his name to the borough-owned theatre in the Euston Road.

The festival idea came from V. K. Krishna Menon, with strong backing from that indefatigable champion of community arts, Dame Sybil Thorndike, and its first year saw an emphasis on theatre, visual arts and music, with a high amateur input. The outstanding success of a single performance of Mozart's opera *Il Re Pastore* by Hans Ucko's Impresario Society during that opening season led to the adoption of the exciting and enlightened policy of performing concert or staged versions of rare operas – many of them never before seen in Britain – which has persisted at Camden ever since.

Performances are entrusted to smaller, less well known music groups and opera companies (1985, for example, included contributions by the New London Consort, Abbey Opera, the Chelsea Opera Group and Park Lane Opera), and give young, often unknown musicians the opportunity to try their wings. Indeed, a number of international opera stars have made an early mark at St Pancras/Camden, including Joan Sutherland (in Handel's *Alcina*, 1957), Heather Harper, Pauline Tinsley (especially noted for her Verdi roles) and Kiri Te Kanawa (in Rossini's *La Donna del Lago*, 1969), as well as Thomas Allen, Geraint Evans and Benjamin Luxon.

To date 124 operas from four centuries have been presented and have included world as well as British premières. Of particular interest were the trend-setting revivals of works by Haydn (*Orfeo ed Euridice* 1955, *Il Mondo della Luna* 1960, *L'Infedeltà Delusa* 1964, *L'Incontro Improviso* 1966), Handel (*Deidamia* 1955, *Hercules* 1956, *Alcina* 1957 and 1959, and *Theodora* 1958), Verdi (*Un Giorno di Regno* 1961, *I Masnadieri* 1962, *Ernani* 1963, *Aroldo* 1964, *Il Corsaro* 1966) and Rossini (*L'Italiana in Algeri* 1961, *La Pietra del Paragone* 1963, *Il Turco in Italia* 1965, *Elisabetta Regina d'Inghilterra* 1968, *La Donna del Lago* 1969, *Tancredi* 1971). Modern opera, however, has also been well served with performances of works by Blacher, Milhaud, Menotti, Britten, Tate, Henze, Hindemith, Maconchy, Joubert, Barber, Walton, Stravinsky and Shostakovich, among others. A highlight of the 1984 season was the European stage première of Delius's one-act lyric opera *Margot la Rouge*.

The Camden Festival also presents a good deal of music outside the field of opera. In 1974 it launched a Jazz Week, which now rates among Britain's most lively gatherings, attracting leading virtuosi from the USA and Europe as well as this country. Another innovation was the presentation in 1979 of the first International Music and Dance Week at which artists from all over the world play and sing music from their native lands. 1985, for instance, fielded contingents from Romania, Korea, Ireland, Peru, Spain, Greece and the Gambia.

The popular and successful Events in Historic Buildings series was introduced in 1978; these concerts have explored many of Camden's fascinating buildings with music contemporary to or connected with the date of construction. Old Lincoln's Inn Hall, which dates from 1492, retains all its original fixtures and is the apt setting for Hogarth's fresco 'The Triumph of Justice', has echoed to the sound of groups like the New London Consort (performing domestic, court and theatre music of the sixteenth and seventeenth centuries) and Musica Reservata (in fifteenth-century music for voice and instruments from Burgundy and England). Other regular venues include the Victorian Great Hall of Lincoln's Inn, Gray's Inn Hall (dating from 1556 and bedecked with fine panelling and oak vaulting), the eighteenth-century Court Room and Gallery of the Thomas Coram Foundation in Brunswick Square, and Old St Pancras Church, which has claims to being the borough's oldest building – though it was 'Normanised', as Pevsner puts it, in 1848 – and lends itself well to renderings of mediaeval music by such groups as Gothic Voices and the Martin Best Ensemble.

A recent Camden development has been a specially devised Young Festival, with events designed to appeal to children and young people. In 1985, these included a concert by North Camden Schools' Orchestra, a demonstration of 'The Art of Minstralsye' and performances by the Divertimenti String Orchestra, Highgate Choral Society and Camden Choir, all of which have their homes within the borough.

The aim of the Camden Festival is to appeal to all sections of the community and recent surveys suggest that about half of the 25000 people who support it each year actually live or work locally, though many patrons – particularly those of the more specialized musical events – come from much further afield. It remains an invaluable fixture which takes some of the chill and greyness out of the last two weeks of a London March.

Three London Churches

───────CHRIST CHURCH, SPITALFIELDS───────

It is difficult to imagine a less likely setting for a festival. Commercial Road, E1, is a busy, noisy urban freeway, running through the heart of Jack the Ripper territory – the pub on the corner of Fournier Street is named after the notorious killer. The gutters are awash with cardboard boxes, broken pallet slats and stray cabbage leaves, the flotsam of Spitalfields Market, and, if the breeze happens to be in the wrong direction, the farmyard aromas of Truman's brewery in Hanbury Street invade the entire area. It is an area which has, for centuries, been at the heart of the capital's rag-trade. Originally settled by Flemish Huguenot silk-weavers during the Middle Ages, the nineteenth century saw its development as a ghetto. Today the sweatshops and warehouses are largely in the hands of Bangladeshi immigrants. Christ Church stands, grandly aloof, on Commercial Street itself, opposite the upstart redbrick market building. Its crypt houses a refuge for alcoholics, its forecourt a coffee-stall for market porters.

It was built between 1714 and 1729 and is, architecturally, one of the most important churches in Europe. It was one of six London churches designed by Nicholas Hawksmoor, Wren's personal assistant and an acknowledged master in his own right. Of the six, either radically altered by the Victorians or seriously damaged during the Second World War, only Christ Church has proved to be capable of restoration to its original Baroque splendour. The parish has for many years been severely run down and in 1957, when the roof was declared unsafe, services were discontinued. In 1976, the year of the campaign to save Britain's architectural heritage, a body of Friends of Christ Church was set up, with the aim of reinstating Hawksmoor's original design (the Victorians having been responsible for some unfortunate mutilations) and restoring the fabric of the building. The Friends, realizing that the church possessed a remarkable acoustic, hit on the idea of starting a music festival – not to raise funds for the work in hand, but as a means of drawing people physically into the building, so that they might appreciate its nobility and become involved in its revival.

The Spitalfields Festival, under the artistic direction of Richard Hickox, specializes in Baroque and middle-of-the-road contemporary programmes, and has gained a well-deserved reputation for its enterprise in presenting little performed operas, such as Gluck's *Armide* (produced by Wolf-Siegfried Wagner in 1983) and Handel's *Alcina* (produced by Frank Corsaro in 1985). It is that rare bird – a festival devoted entirely to music whose activities are confined to a single building. Since the removal of the nineteenth-century box pews, the church has lent itself to a variety of seating and performing arrangements, which have been sensibly exploited to the full. At the same time, it is still very obviously a place of worship – though its atmosphere goes beyond conventional churchiness and derives hugely from the massive, almost brooding, architectural presence of Hawksmoor's design. Not surprisingly, in the view of many it is the Baroque programmes that come off best in such surroundings and these are certainly the ones that attract the largest audiences. Regrettably, contemporary music – even John Ogdon's Messiaen recital in 1984 – pulls in only a sprinkling of enthusiasts, and this has tempted the organizers to swing away from the modern towards the Classical and early-Romantic repertoire (1986, for example, sees Weber and Liszt as featured composers). This development comes at a time when the nature of the Spitalfields audience is also changing: what was, in the early days, largely a gathering of architectural and musical cognoscenti from all over London and the home counties is now beginning to include a core of resident East-Enders, and there is no doubt that the community appeal of the festival is becoming stronger.

There is still, however, very much a sense of devotion to a shared ideal. You feel it as you sit, on rather hard seats, your coat wrapped round you against the chilly May evening, your eye wandering up to the high-arched windows as you listen to the London Symphony Chorus sing the Shepherds' Farewell from *L'Enfance du Christ* (Berlioz) with exquisite tone and shading. You feel it, too, as you stroll under the great sunlit portico or queue with penguin-suited performers and market porters at the mobile stall for an interval coffee. It is the ideal of sharing in the bringing back to life, through the power of music, of a great – though neglected – architectural masterpiece. And that is what makes Spitalfields special among festivals.

PICCADILLY

The festival organized around St James's Church, in the heart of fashionable Piccadilly, could not be more different. To begin with, the church itself – a Wren original, lovingly restored after severe bomb-damage during the Second World War, and set in a tranquil courtyard and garden – is to some extent incidental. Though festival events, mostly the musical ones, do take place in its clean-lined, elegant interior, it is only one of a host of Piccadilly venues that are put to use in the course of the season. It has never been the intention of the organizers that their festival should raise money for the church – indeed, they acknowledge their indebtedness to the parish for being prepared to underwrite their losses. Writing in the 1984 festival programme, they had this to say about their vision:

> We started with nothing but a magnificent space in the middle of one of the world's great cities; with nothing but the generosity of several sponsors and the good will of several of our leading artists and entertainers. Usually, festivals are perceived as a ragbag of entertainments – anything to draw crowds and success. For us, the festival is an opportunity to relate the leading art forms, and to direct them into a celebration of a theme which concerns us all. The artist can be the most eloquent interpreter of such a theme. When the various forms unite to explore and create together – music, painting, poetry, theatre, film and laughter – then we have an experience.

It usually falls to the festival director, the artist Peter Pelz, to tease out and explore the possibilities of the individual themes. For 1984, he took his inspiration from the Dunamis project, under whose auspices politicians, philosophers and theologians are invited to St James's to take part in an extended debate on the issue of world peace. The result was a celebration of the Apocalypse – a theme that was illuminated in the work of leading poets, film-makers, satirical artists and composers. A highlight was the first performance of Peter Dickinson's *Mass of the Apocalypse*, specially written for the festival.

Piccadilly is, of course, particularly well endowed with fine buildings and institutions which, since 1984, have played an increasingly important role in the festival. The British Academy of Film and Television Arts (BAFTA), just along the road from the church, has opened its doors for special showings of films by featured directors; the Royal Academy has held exhibitions tying in with festival themes. In 1985, events which had previously been contained – albeit hectically – within a fortnight, were allowed to spread over two months, from May to July, at a more relaxed pace. The result was a festival which has really made its mark on the summer life of the West End. People spend whole days and even days on end moving from event to event: even those who are interested only in one area of activity find their time well filled.

On the musical front, for example, Ivor Bolton – the festival's music director, on loan from Glyndebourne where he is chorus master – organizes a series of lunchtime recitals in the church, given mainly by talented young performers just beginning to make their way in the musical world, as well as more substantial fare in the evenings. The lion's share of the work at the evening concerts is taken by the newly formed St James's Players – a professional orchestra which draws on the London freelance pool – and attendant Choir. The emphasis, as one might expect of a festival based on a great Wren church, is on the Baroque – though modern music, including new commissions, is certainly in evidence. For the future, it is hoped that a place will be found at St James's for opera, while one fascinating possibility is a staged version of Bach's *St Matthew Passion* directed by Elijah Moshinsky.

The Piccadilly Festival is not the place to find the big names, though everything that it undertakes has appeal and interest. This is no doubt partly due to the dedication and professional expertise of the volunteers – many of them practising artists, actors, technicians – who are involved in its planning and day-to-day running. It is not a commercial festival, with an eye on the capital's summer influx of visitors; it is not a religious festival, aiming to attract congregations; it is not a community festival, involving and providing for the cultural needs of local residents. It exists because its organizers have something important and interesting to say; it succeeds because they have found a most effective way of saying it.

ST GEORGE'S, HANOVER SQUARE

Not quite in the middle of Mayfair is Hanover Square, a green oasis of lawns and plane trees within a stone's-throw of the clamour of Oxford Circus. A bronze statue of the younger Pitt and a number of stylish brick house-fronts recall its heyday. The south-east corner of the square is occupied by St George's Church, a grandly ornate building with pillared portico – built by John James during the first quarter of the eighteenth century – which has, throughout its existence, been a favourite setting for society weddings. Lady Hamilton, Shelley, Mary Ann Evans (George Eliot), Disraeli, the Asquiths – all made their marriage vows within its walls. At about the time St George's was being completed, Handel was living and composing just round the corner, in Brook Street. Indeed, for nearly forty years, it was his parish church and he served as one of its Wardens. When Denys Darlow – famous for his work with the Tilford Bach Festival and now director of music at St George's – decided in the late seventies to canvass support for a Handel festival in London, no more appropriate setting could have suggested itself.

The aim of this week-long spring festival is both to give quality performances of Handel's music with the forces and on the instruments for which it was written, and also each year to revive at least one of his choral works that has not been heard live this century. The London Handel Orchestra, which uses Baroque instruments, and the thirty-strong London Handel Choir are all professionals and have gained an international reputation for the quality of their music-making. During the past three or four years, performances of *Solomon*, *The Triumph of Time and Truth* and *Aminta e Fillide* received particularly glowing critical notices. The Handel Tercentenary in 1985 was the occasion for some inspired programme-planning, drawing as it did on Latin motets and Italian cantatas written while the composer was living in Italy, and also on English works dating from the period of his residence in London. Patrizia Kwella and Catherine Denley took part in a Monday-evening concert which included the first London performance of *Daliso ed Amarilli*, another evening was devoted to the rarely heard wedding cantata *Aci, Galatea e Polifemo* (which dates from 1708), while the opening concert was given over to the first complete performance in two centuries of the oratorio *Alexander Balus* (with Gillian Fisher, Patrizia Kwella, Charles Brett, Andrew King and Brian Kay). Another rarity was the music Handel wrote for Milton's *Comus*, for three solo voices, violins and continuo, which only came to light as recently as the late 1960s. The festival concluded with a major, if little played, work that Denys Darlow had already presented at the 1982 festival – *L'Allegro, Il Penseroso ed Il Moderato*, with a star cast including Emma Kirkby and Ian Partridge. Plans for 1986 include revivals of *Jephtha*, *La Resurrezione* and *Clori, Tirsi e Fileno*.

The London Handel Festival is not just an occasion for the Handel specialist or the listener who thrives on new discoveries. It provides a valuable opportunity for the general music-lover to hear Handel's works in authentic performances and setting. And that is relatively rare.

Richard Hickox
AN EXCITING UMBRELLA

Richard Hickox has, in the past few years, risen to eminence as one of Britain's most successful young orchestral conductors. Appointed in 1985 as the first ever associate conductor of the London Symphony Orchestra, he is also director of the London Symphony Chorus, musical director of the City of London Sinfonia and artistic director of the Northern Sinfonia of England – as well as being a regular guest of many other major British orchestras. He is as much at home in the recording studio and the opera house as on the concert platform, and has achieved a considerable international reputation through his broadcasts and appearances as far afield as Russia and the United States.

In spite, however, of the demands placed on him by a schedule which seems to become daily more hectic, Hickox still finds time to be closely associated with a number of important festivals in London and the South West of England. The reason is not hard to find: festivals are, in his own words, 'an exciting umbrella' for his many and various musical interests. He is, in fact, musical director of the Wooburn, St Endellion, Three Spires (Truro), Spitalfields and Barbican Summer festivals – which means that he not only has to be available to perform on home ground, as it were, during the season, but has also to find time throughout the rest of the year to devise programmes, attend planning meetings and squeeze financial blood out of bureaucratic stones. And it is worth remembering that as a planner he is very often working two to three years ahead of the dates set aside for particular festivals.

Hickox's taste for this degree of involvement goes back to the time when, as an eighteen year old, he conceived the idea of mounting a festival to raise funds for the restoration of the parish church of Wooburn in Buckingham-shire of which his father was vicar. 'In those days,' he recalls, 'I did everything from selling tickets to distributing posters to getting the piano tuned.' In a part of the country where festivals were pretty thin on the ground, he set himself the tasks of commandeering suitable houses and halls for his performances, galvanizing friends and neighbours into action and, above all, establishing the all-important goodwill needed for his venture to get airborne. There is a gleam in his eye as he relives the excitement of being in on the start of something entirely new. Even more satisfying, however, is the knowl-edge that his brainchild has grown into a healthy and mature adult. After some twenty years, the Wooburn Festival continues to grow and prosper, performing a very real service in bringing live music and drama to the towns and villages of the High Wycombe area. One of the by-products of the festival has been the formation of the Wooburn Singers, a choir of local amateurs that has achieved a wider reputation through its broadcasts, record-ings and appearances in London and at festivals in other parts of the country. Developments of this sort please Richard Hickox immensely: 'The very best festivals,' he insists, 'are never static. They go on developing, changing, producing new things.' And he cites the example of how four of the young string players in the orchestra he assembles each year for his St Endellion Festival started getting together to play chamber music. Such were the beginnings of the now internationally acclaimed Endellion Quartet.

St Endellion is of all Hickox's festivals perhaps closest to his heart because of its unique focus on music-making as an essentially amateur pursuit. His introduction to the grimly beautiful stretch of countryside just inland from Port Isaac came when he was asked to stand in for the festival's regular conductor. 'It didn't take me long to realize that this was something special – the whole set-up was out of the ordinary. A festival at which professional musicians and amateurs came together from all parts of the country, to live and work together and pay for the privilege of doing so.' At St Endellion, the festival *is* the performers, the audience being more or less incidental. And for Hickox, it is the purest form of festival imaginable.

To Richard Hickox's way of thinking, festivals ought ideally to be concerned with creation, with doing something new or individual in a building that has special qualities or associations. This has been the spirit in which he has approached his work at the festival which takes place each summer in Hawksmoor's magnificent Christ Church, Spitalfields, in the City of London. It was amid the muddle of continuing restoration work inside the church that such distinguished and unrepeatable 'occasions' as the 1981 *Dido and Aeneas*, with Dame Janet Baker, and Wolf Siegfried Wagner's production the following year of Gluck's *Armide* were brought into being. Hickox sees Spitalfields very much as a place in which to develop projects that are a little out of the ordinary; while other festivals during 1985 saw him celebrating Handel and Bach, in his own Christ Church it was Tallis and Butterworth, Cui and Berg.

Richard Hickox is not, however, interested only in his own festivals. As a conductor he spends a good deal of time performing at centres such as Cheltenham and Bath, more often than not with one of his own orchestras. He values very much the fact that festival organizers are willing to spend the time and money in setting up projects that could not be considered in the course of regular concert seasons. 'Only the biggest festivals, of course, have the financial resources to plan and rehearse properly programmes that contain – say – difficult contemporary music or large-scale choral works,' he suggests. 'On the whole, festivals prefer the purpose-built to the adapted model; they create new things rather than pick up what is on offer in an artist's or an orchestra's current repertoire.' And that can only be good for everyone – not least himself. 'I suppose that before all else I'm a special project conductor.' He loves the sheer thrill of the occasion that is special not only to the audience, but to the players and singers as well. He recalls with enthusiasm many an opening concert of the Bath Festival and the unique excitement of playing in front of the deeply attentive Proms audiences.

Hickox admits that as his career advances he is bound to have less time for the festivals that have in some ways nurtured him and with which he has grown up, but he is determined not to lose contact with them altogether. He may have to take a year off from St Endellion or limit the number of his appearances in Truro or Wooburn, but he acknowledges that they are his roots and that he draws a good deal of musical life and energy from his involvement with them. At the same time, he is firm on the point that it can be deadening for a festival to be dominated by one person for too long. 'If that happens, fossilization can easily set in. And I would not like that to come about because of me. Festivals must not stand still. If they are truly to flourish, they must expect to experience healthy change.'

CITY OF LONDON

The 1980s have seen a marked change in the character of London's square mile. At one time, this bustling centre of Britain's commercial life was silent and deserted after office hours and at weekends, but now the opening of the Barbican arts and residential complex has given impetus to a movement to bring people back into the City. The City itself is a fascinating architectural mix, from the forbidding bulk of the Norman Tower to sky-soaring modern buildings of concrete, glass and steel – with, in between, mediaeval livery halls, the grand neo-classical churches of Wren and his successors, and a host of nineteenth-century monuments to Victorian industry and commerce.

The City of London Festival was started in 1962 with the precise aim of – every two years – opening up some of these buildings to a wider public. Such was the success of the venture that it has now become an annual event. Care is taken to match programmes – and these include poetry readings, jazz and lectures as well as classical music of all periods – to the scale and nature of the halls and churches in which they take place. Of course, the mid-July timing must have half an eye on the capital's huge summer influx of tourists, but there are plenty of events – such as lunchtime and early-evening concerts – which cater first and foremost for the thousands who come to the City daily to work. There is also a strong emphasis on London-based performers, both amateur and professional, from the National Westminster Choir, the Priory Festival Choir (based on the Church of St Bartholomew-the-Great) or the St Michael's Singers (from St Michael's Church, Cornhill) to the City of London Sinfonia, the Academy of St Martin-in-the-Fields or one of the major symphony orchestras. International celebrities are by no means lacking, however, and recent festivals have featured appearances by Ingrid Haebler, Cécile Ousset, Igor Oistrakh, Henryk Szeryng, Oscar Shumsky, János Starker, Jorge Bolet and Mitsuko Uchida.

Many of the grandest concerts make use of the vast spaces of St Paul's Cathedral and very often bring into collaboration performers who, in the normal run of a concert season, might not have the chance to work together. In 1980, for instance, Berlioz's *Grande Messe des Morts* was given in circumstances which must have come close to the composer's ideal by a combination of the London Symphony Chorus, the Brighton Festival Chorus and the Philharmonia Orchestra under Sir John Pritchard. Five years later, Sir Charles Groves presided over a performance of the same composer's *Te Deum* in which the forces originally prescribed by Berlioz were supplied by the London Symphony Chorus, the London Philharmonic Choir and a three-hundred-strong children's choir, again accompanied by the Philharmonia. On a rather different scale, but no less effective, was a concert given under the dome of St Paul's in 1981 by the Schütz Choir, the Philip Jones Brass Ensemble and the London Baroque Players conducted by Roger Norrington, in which music for two, three or four choirs or orchestras – including Tallis's 40-part motet *Spem in Alium* – was performed to breathtaking effect.

The London Sinfonietta at Drapers' Hall in 1985 playing Haydn, Mozart and Beethoven.

More intimate, but no less effective, settings for concerts and recitals are the many fine churches and livery halls of the City: choral music in the Chapel of St Peter ad Vincula (where three unfortunate queens – Anne Boleyn, Katherine Howard, Jane Grey – lie buried), in the grand Norman Priory Church of St Bartholomew-the-Great, or at St Giles' Church, Cripplegate, in its splendid isolation among the modern buildings of the Barbican complex; chamber music and solo recitals in the Mansion House or one of the lavishly restored livery halls. Particularly appropriate and delightful was the 1982 'City Music Trail' devised by members of the Guildhall School of Music and Drama, which gave enthusiasts the chance to hear programmes of period music and literature in three Wren churches: early Renaissance pieces in St Mary-at-Hill, Elizabethan and Jacobean lute songs and consort music in St Benet's, Paul's Wharf, and Boyce trio sonatas at St Michael's, Cornhill. Then there was the 'Elizabethan Progress' presented in 1980 by Lyric Arts of London – Dowland, Campion, Morley, Spenser, Drayton, Sidney and Shakespeare in the light, airy surroundings of Painters' Hall. And 'Music for the Crusades' performed in the crusaders' own Temple Church.

In recent years, the festival has shown encouragement for young musicians by playing host to two important special events: the Carl Fleisch International Violin Competition and the Walter Gruner International Lieder Competition, both of which have attracted wide interest among festival visitors as well as among resident musicians. Another area of encouragement has been in the programming of first performances at festival concerts: world, British, or London premières in recent years have included *Still Movement* (Birtwistle), *Epitaph* (John Dankworth), *Key to the Zoo* (Stephen Oliver to a libretto by Miles Kington), *Aria for Ensemble* (Holloway), *Spring Songs* (Wilfred Josephs), *Psalm 4* (Alexander Goehr) and Ruth Gipps's Wind Octet, Opus 65.

And while all these musical events are going on inside the City's historic buildings, out in the tree-hung squares or amid the hubbub of the streets there is free jazz and street theatre and busking.

GREENWICH

Greenwich is a two-week multi-media festival which came into being in 1972 under the enthusiastic patronage of Dame Sybil Thorndike, whose vision of a festival as essentially a celebration has been given faithful and joyful life by the local organizers ever since. It has not simply been a matter of starting proceedings with a bang – fireworks and the National Centre for Orchestral Studies Symphony Orchestra launching into Tchaikovsky's *1812 Overture* in the Cutty Sark Gardens – it has also been a case of encouraging the people of Greenwich to become full-bloodedly involved at every level and in every sphere of activity promoted by the festival, be it dance or music, ethnic or family events, exhibitions, films, poetry, theatre or sport. For, as well as presenting programmes by internationally celebrated performers, Greenwich is strong on employing local amateur talent and on fuelling mini-festivals within the various communities, such as Abbey Wood, Plumstead, Eltham, that make up the borough. Since succeeding Dame Sybil as patron in 1975, Prince Philip, who as well as being Duke of Edinburgh is also Baron Greenwich, has repeatedly voiced his support for an organization which combines the involvement of up to 150 local groups presenting their own activities with the traditional pattern of arts and entertainment by professionals. And it is fitting that Greenwich should, of all places, be the focus for this kind of venture, containing within its borders not only such famous tourist attractions as the Royal Naval College and the great hall of Eltham Palace, but also vast swathes of often dreary urban development.

The 1980s, with the increasingly acute unemployment problems they have brought to the borough, have seen a socially aware council intensifying its efforts to provide, through the festival, some alleviation of the pressures placed on so many of its residents. The festival itself does not work each year to a theme in quite the rigorous way, say, Piccadilly does, though 1982 saw it contributing to the 'Maritime England' celebration, the following year to the Pepys anniversary, and 1984 to London's anti-racism campaign.

On the musical front, Greenwich is fortunate in having a number of outstanding buildings in which to hold performances. Audiences at concerts given in the Chapel of Wren's classically elegant Royal Naval College have the opportunity of devoting their interval break not, like lesser mortals, to queuing for lukewarm coffee, but to taking in the magnificence of the Painted Hall of 1704. The Georgian Ranger's House, which overlooks Blackheath and was once the home of the Ranger of

Left: The Chapel of the Royal Naval College – a performance of Mendelssohn's *Elijah* in 1985.
Right: Opening of the Greenwich Festival aboard the *Cutty Sark* in 1985.

Greenwich Park, is ideal for chamber recitals and also contains the important Suffolk Collection of Tudor and Jacobean paintings. Nicholas Hawksmoor's fine, though heavily restored, Parish Church of St Alfege, Greenwich, and the great five-hundred-year-old banqueting hall of Eltham Palace also lend themselves to music-making on all but the very grandest scale. Performers in recent years have included Clifford Curzon, James Galway, Claudio Arrau, Kyung-Wha Chung, Alfred Brendel, Yehudi Menuhin and Henryk Szeryng, together with groups such as the English Chamber Orchestra, the City of London Sinfonia and the Royal Philharmonic Orchestra, while excellent local contributions have come from the Blackheath String Orchestra, Eltham Choral Society and the Choir of the Royal Naval College. The 1984 festival included a violin-making competition designed specifically to encourage British craftsmen, along with workshops, displays and concerts.

From the start the festival has been keen to commission new music – including a string quartet by Anthony Milner, Robert Walker's Chamber Symphony, Stephen Oliver's *Bad Times* (a dramatic sequence for baritone and string quartet) and Carl Davis's Clarinet Concerto – and to give other first performances. New choral and chamber works by John Tavener, Michael Berkeley and Paul Patterson have found generally appreciative audiences in Greenwich, Patterson being 'featured composer' in 1985. One of the most exciting festival occasions in recent years was provided by Simon Halsey's Cambridge Opera Group, which took over the Chapel of the Royal Naval College for evocative new productions of Britten's three Church Parables.

NETTLEFOLD

Music-lovers from North London are advised that inoculations and emergency rations are not required to cross the Thames – there are very frequent train connections from Victoria and London Bridge . . . and bar and catering will be available at the hall throughout each evening.

It was, indeed, in an effort to change South London's image as a cultural wilderness that composers Simon Desorgher and Lawrence Casserley organized a new music festival at Lambeth's Nettlefold Hall during October 1984. They already had some experience of the hall, which is situated in Norwood High Street and backs on to the South Metropolitan Cemetery, through the performances there of their own work and that of other composers in one-off concerts. Pleased with its acoustic responsiveness and ambience, they decided to run a pilot festival offering a rich variety of music and music-theatre over three consecutive weekends. Each of the six evenings was made up of two concerts, the earlier (starting at about 7.30 p.m.) by an artist or ensemble renowned for the performance of exciting and innovative music, the later (at 9.30 p.m.) being a short presentation of work from electronic music studios around the world. Lambeth Council supported the venture by providing the hall and other facilities, and the organizers undertook fund-raising to pay performers' fees.

Tube Sculpture – Simon Desorgher (*left*)
and Lawrence Casserley on (probably) the largest pan pipes in the world.

The concerts were by turns witty, adventurous and stunning. Circle (an instrumental group formed in 1979 as counterpart to the vocal ensemble Singcircle) played Stockhausen, Globokar, Cage and Holliger; the bass clarinettist, Harry Spaarnay, gave première performances of works by – among others – David Bedford, Luciano Berio and Karel Goeyvaerts; Tube Sculpture – a group which includes Desorgher and Casserley themselves – unveiled a gigantic set of computerized pan pipes (comprising over 150 pipes, the largest being fifteen feet in length) which was not only blown but also used as a percussion instrument and resonator. At the other end of the scale was a recital on the *shakuhachi*, or Japanese flute, by Yoshikazu Iwamoto, who played both traditional *honkyoku* solos and highly contrasted modern works. Other concerts were given by Melvyn Poore (tuba) and Vocem, a group of singers with a strong sense of theatre.

Such was the success of the venture that it was repeated in 1985. Highlights included a concert given by Jane Manning of music by Tristram Cary, Simon Desorgher and Priaulx Rainier; the London première, given by Philip Mead, of Stockhausen's Piano Piece No. 12; Hugh Davies and Hans Karsten-Raeke in a concert on 'invented instruments' – including the first performance of a piece by Davies himself with dancers and amplified costumes; and Barry Guy (double bass) in a programme of improvised music with guitarist Derek Bailey.

A really lively – and not too straight-faced – festival, which seems set fair for the future. Things are looking up in Norwood!

THE PROMS
THE BBC HENRY WOOD PROMENADE CONCERTS

When is a festival not a festival? There are some who maintain that by no stretch of the imagination can the Henry Wood Promenade Concerts be called a festival, however loosely. There are others who assert as strenuously that they are in fact the biggest music festival in the world (in 1984, they attracted live audiences totalling over 200,000 people and reached broadcast audiences of some 100 million).

On the one hand, the arguments go that the Proms quite often buy in performances prepared for other occasions (for the Edinburgh Festival, for instance, or for Glyndebourne), that they offer no positive encouragement to 'local' talent or amateur performers, that they supply no special need – London hardly being reliant on a single concentrated burst of musical activity in high summer to rescue it from 'cultural backwater' status – and that their vast scale (in 1985, there were sixty concerts in the course of eight weeks) makes it difficult, if not impossible, for any coherent single design to be developed.

On the other hand, it is pointed out that the Proms are nothing if not a sustained and intensive period of music-making – surely qualifying as a festival on that score alone – originally timed to fill the summer slack period when little else of musical note was going on in the capital (though a measure of their success in drawing audiences – and regular audiences at that – may be seen in the comparatively recent establishment of rival 'festivals' at both the South Bank and Barbican concert halls).

Then again, the Proms offer the opportunity for Londoners to hear a galaxy of international soloists and ensembles, many of them unavailable in this country at other times of the year. They encourage new music and frequently commission works from both emerging and established British composers, and – while not espousing particular schools or musical causes – present a wide spectrum from mediaeval to minimalist. They are identified very largely with one much loved, if not acoustically perfect, building in the shape of the Royal Albert Hall and – perhaps most important of all – they generate an enormous sense of excitement and celebration in their relatively young audiences, as witness the banners, the streamers, the funny hats and the emotional involvement of the Last Night. Comradeship, great good spirits, utter devotion to the Proms ideal and profound attentiveness to and appreciation of the programmes on offer are perennial characteristics of the 'promenaders' – many of whom queue night after night to pay a modest ticket-price for the privilege of standing through a Mahler symphony or Stravinsky ballet, and who think nothing of camping overnight outside the arena entrance in order to secure the best possible vantage point from which to enjoy the first or last night festivities.

Sir Henry Wood was by no means the inventor of promenade concerts – they were in fact a French importation originally designed as popular entertainments at which people could come and go as they pleased. The idea was to attract large audiences by making the occasions relatively informal and by programming music that was generally familiar and accessible – waltzes, marches, operatic arias and cornet solos together with the occasional overture or concerto. Sir Henry's first series of Proms – held in the recently opened Queen's Hall in 1895 – immediately stiffened the 'serious' element by devoting the first half of each concert to the symphonic repertoire, to Bach or Wagner or the less familiar Russian composers. It also set a fashion with an unprecedented crop of new works – there were no fewer than twenty-three first performances during the eight weeks of that opening season. Every concert of the series was played by Wood's own orchestra, with which, by means of regular rehearsals and the close commitment of its members, he raised the standard of orchestral playing in the capital. He engaged many well-known and well-loved solo performers, but he also made it his policy to 'bring on' talented young players and singers on the threshold of their professional career.

There have been significant changes in the Proms format over the years: in 1985, some twenty orchestras took part, with over forty conductors; semi-staged opera is now a regular crowd-drawer; since the destruction of the Queen's Hall during the blitz, the Royal Albert Hall has become the home of the Proms, though occasional concerts and recitals take place elsewhere in London; and since the late twenties every series has been financed and masterminded by the BBC and is now broadcast in its entirety to radio listeners throughout the world. But many of Wood's original objectives have been maintained – the role of the Proms for many as a semi-official musical education, for instance, is as strong as ever, John Amis going so far as to suggest recently that what was once a sixth-form guide is now more in the nature of a university degree course.

A glance at what happened in 1985 illustrates pretty well what the newcomer to this grand musical institution can expect. There was, of course, plenty of new music – notably first performances of Anthony Payne's *The Spirit's Harvest*, Malcolm Williamson's *Three Poems of Borges* (sung by Heather Harper) and Robin Holloway's Viola Concerto with Rivka Golani as soloist. There were also several notable second or third performances – those occasions on which composers so much depend and for which the Proms have become a special vehicle in recent years. Then there was a series theme, a celebration of American music including hearings of Steve Reich's *Desert Music*, William Schuman's Seventh Symphony and Walter Piston's Second, Charles Ruggles's *Sun-Treader*, Elliott Carter's Piano Concerto and *Penthode*, Roger Sessions's *When Lilacs last in the Dooryard Bloom'd*, as well as pieces by Griffes, Barber, Bernstein, Ives, Copland and Gershwin. There were performances of works most definitely not found in regular London concert-programming: Lutoslawski's Third Symphony (conducted by the composer), Prokofiev's Fourth, Gerhard's cantata *L'alta naixença del rei en jaume*, Harrison Birtwistle's *Secret Theatre*, Stenhammar's Second Symphony and Peter Maxwell Davies's Third. There were star conductors, soloists and ensembles – what other festival could boast a cast embracing Boulez, Abbado, Mata, Haitink, Klee, Maazel, Rattle, Slatkin, Tennstedt; Fassbaender, Ludwig, Vickers, Ashkenazy, Accardo, Ogdon, Cherkassky, Harrell, Frankl, Gelber, de Larrocha, Norman, Lill, Brendel, Mutter; the Chamber Orchestra of Europe, L'Ensemble Intercontemporain, the London Symphony, London Philharmonic, Philharmonia, Royal Philharmonic, BBC Symphony, BBC Philharmonic, Hallé, Pittsburg Symphony and Swedish Radio Symphony Orchestras? Large-scale choral works came in the shape of *Messiah* in the Mozart orchestration, Mahler's *Resurrection Symphony*, Walton's *Gloria*, the *St Matthew Passion* (given in authentic style by Andrew Parrott's Taverner Choir and Players), *La Damnation de Faust* by Berlioz and the *Choral Symphony* of Beethoven in its traditional final-Friday slot. There were specialist programmes from the Monteverdi Choir and English Baroque Soloists under John Eliot Gardiner, the Hilliard Ensemble (singing Pérotin and Machaut), the Nash Ensemble, Lontano playing Berio, Stockhausen and Jonathan Harvey under the direction of Odaline de la Martinez, the London Classical Players (conducted by Roger Norrington) and a group presenting Japanese imperial court music.

A catalogue of Proms achievements over the years would occupy a book in its own right. But it would be foolish to pretend that all concerts are unfailingly interesting, or all performances uniformly well prepared. Man shall not live on caviar alone, and there have been bread-and-butter days in the Albert Hall as elsewhere. There are years when the programming seems occasionally perverse and evenings when the playing is distinctly lack-lustre. But, to end where we began, at their best the Proms are stupendous, and if they do not represent festival music-making at its most meaningful and exciting, then perhaps it is time we started redefining a few terms.

Right: Dame Janet Baker rehearsing for the Glyndebourne Festival Opera production of Gluck's *Orfeo ed Euridice* at the 1982 Proms. *Far right:* The Taverner Choir rehearsing the Monteverdi *Vespers of 1610* at the 1983 Proms.

Left: Sir Charles Groves rehearsing with the BBC Symphony Orchestra in 1984.
Below: Promenaders outside the Royal Albert Hall.

_7_
Moveable Feasts

Several British festivals are of a distinctly peripatetic turn of mind. Designed to bring festival delights to communities scattered over a wide (and usually rural) area, they wander from village to village, leaving an exhibition here, a choice recital there. Church Stretton and South Shropshire, for example, serves a couple of hundred square miles of border marches, while the Vale of Glamorgan travels the Thaw and Ely Valleys, west of Cardiff, making music in a succession of castles and churches. No matter how widely they may roam, however, such festivals generally have some sort of central base – Music in East Kent, which brings concerts to houses and halls the length of the Stour Valley, calls the pilgrim church at Boughton Aluph its home. There are two important music festivals, however, which for one reason or another are very much of no fixed abode . . .

————STATELY HOMES MUSIC FESTIVAL————

The Stately Homes Music Festival was the brainchild of Douglas Reed, a lively young entrepreneur who cut his teeth, so to speak, as an arts administrator in Greenwich. Inspired by the abundance of fine settings for musical performance within the borough – he was responsible among other things for launching the Royal Naval College concerts – he conceived the idea of canvassing the owners of great houses up and down the country to see what interest there might be in a music festival centred on their homes. The response was overwhelmingly favourable and the festival, which started in a quiet way in 1980, is now firmly established. In 1985, twenty-seven concerts were scheduled between early June and mid-October, taking in buildings as magnificent, different and geographically distant from each other as Leeds Castle in Kent, Hopetoun House in Edinburgh, Penhow Castle near Newport, Gwent, and – for the first time – Castletown House, near Dublin.

While admitting that his festival differs from others in that it has not sprung from the needs or wishes of a particular group of people in a particular location – he confesses to having 'imposed' it where conditions seemed most favourable – Reed is quick to point out that it does have a good deal in common with more conventional ventures. For instance, it has an important fund-raising function, proceeds from

concerts being channelled back to the charitable trusts responsible for the maintenance of individual houses, to help with restoration work and running costs. It also
provides more than just concerts. The ticket-price of a festival concert entitles the
visitor to access to the grounds of the house or castle, a conducted tour with a
special eye to the architecture and artistic treasures to be found there, the concert
itself with champagne during the interval, and, in most cases, a reception attended
by both owners and performers. Buffet suppers are available at extra cost, as are
picnic hampers, whose contents are consumed, Glyndebourne-fashion, in walled
gardens or wooded parks. The sense of occasion is heightened by the forewarning
that 'black tie is the usual dress for all concerts'. The Stately Homes Music Festival
also makes a point of noting birthdays and celebrating the achievements of great
men. And there is something rather special about marking the five hundredth
anniversary of the founding of the Tudor dynasty in 1485 with music at Penhow or
Dorney Court, near Windsor, or Handel's three hundredth birthday in the elegant
surroundings of the Georgian Drawing Room of Chiswick House.

The festival's staple is the performance of early and Baroque music in the sort of
settings for which it was originally composed. Many of the houses have music rooms
or ballrooms with acoustics ideally suited to groups such as the Deller Consort,
Musica Antiqua of Cologne, the Purcell Quartet or the Academy of Ancient Music.
Some also have libraries in which a wealth of manuscript or early printed scores
await discovery and performance – as has already happened in the case of Longleat
and Hengrave. 'In almost every sense but the literal one,' as Douglas Reed vividly
explains, 'these houses come to life and sing to us.' That is not to say that Romantic
or modern music is banned: Mendelssohn and Britten have their place, but they are
distinctly overshadowed by Tallis and Wilbye, Purcell and Handel.

Balance and discretion are important features of SHMF presentations. Extra
staging and lighting are kept to a minimum – apart from anything else, to avoid
damaging valuable floors or overtaxing venerable wiring – and concerts are frequently
given by candlelight. The problems of traffic noise, which beset some festivals which
use beautiful but inadequately insulated old buildings for their concerts, are generally
absent, most of the houses in question being well distant from major roads. Disturb-
ances, if any, tend to be of a different sort – as when a recital at Luton Hoo seemed
fated to be drowned out by aircraft taking off and landing at nearby Luton Airport.
A phone call to the authorities from the owner of the house led to the diverting of
planes for the duration of the concert – as much an acknowledgement of the airport's
being built on land leased from the Luton Hoo estate as of the prestige of the
festival! On another occasion, performance of a Beethoven slow movement was
interrupted by the nine o'clock chimes of what seemed like a hundred independent-
minded clocks.

The Stately Homes Music Festival is a flourishing concern. In 1984, ninety per
cent of all the tickets available for its concerts across the country were sold. It attracts
large numbers of visitors from abroad, especially tourists from America, Japan and
the European continent. Even so, on average half of those who attend individual

Above: The English Concert playing at Apsley House on the north side of Hyde Park Corner. It was bought by the Duke of Wellington in 1817 and now houses the Wellington Museum.

Left: Firle Place in Sussex, home of the Gage family since the late fifteenth century, was rebuilt in the eighteenth century from the original Caen stone. Concert evening takes place each year in early September. *Inset*: Supper in the garden at Gorhambury House in Hertfordshire.

concerts come from within a radius of twenty-five miles of the host houses. A number of owners have been inspired by this fact to promote their own more extended festivals – as at Leeds Castle and Wingfield College in Suffolk. Reed does not mind this for a moment: he likes to feel he is a trail-blazer and in any case there are plenty of moated granges and echoing halls throughout the country still so far untapped for their musical potential. 1985 saw his first foray into Eire. He would like to develop that particular territory more fully in the coming years – and rumour has it that he is already turning a beady eye in the direction of France.

English Bach Festival

If ever there were a misnomer it is the 'English Bach Festival', which is no longer a purely English venture, no longer focuses its main spotlight on Bach and is no longer a festival in the conventional sense. That it is, however, one of the most precious jewels in the crown of British musical life and that it remains – as it always has been – the darling of the critics, there can be no question.

It was founded in 1963 by the vivacious Greek keyboard player, Lina Lalandi, employing the magnificent halls and chapels of Oxford – both ancient and modern – as settings for performances of the music of both Bach and his contemporaries and also of the present day. It was, from the beginning, a highly prestigious undertaking, which attracted the full-hearted support of Albert Schweitzer as its honorary president and gave to the music-lovers of Oxford, that first glorious May, performers of the calibre of Jascha Horenstein, Nathan Milstein, Ernst Haefliger and Pierre Fournier. Unfortunately, however, in the long run Oxford proved indifferent to the sumptuous fare it was being offered. A Gérard Souzay recital of French *mélodies* in Christ Church Hall was greeted politely but unenthusiastically; the great Teresa Stich-Randall was lured from the States to sing cantatas to a half-empty Playhouse. So, in the early seventies, Miss Lalandi moved part of her operation to London – she subsequently abandoned Oxford altogether – in search of more appreciative audiences. The move was a considerable success, especially since it favoured a widening of the festival's activities in the sphere of contemporary music: the list of composers whose works have received British, if not world, premières at EBF concerts includes Messiaen, Skalkottas, Xenakis, Berio, Stravinsky (the festival's second president), Bernstein (its third), Stockhausen, Walton, Lutyens, Ligeti, Dutilleux and – somewhat unexpectedly – Roussel and Ravel. As the critic William Mann declared at the time, 'Oxford's loss is London's gain'.

Today, the English Bach Festival is pre-eminently an international Baroque opera company, specializing in lavish productions with authentic instruments, Baroque dance and splendid costumes copied from original designs. It no longer observes a set season, but mounts its productions, divertissements and other concerts throughout the year, both in this country and in the great palaces and theatres of continental Europe. If it can be said to have a home, that home is now the Château of Versailles, where it is the resident opera company. Anyone who has seen one of the EBF's Baroque productions – and they started in the Oxford days, with grand costume entertainments at Blenheim – will know of their concentration on eye- and ear-catching stylishness. Their object is to present the stageworks of Handel or Rameau not as museum pieces, but with high panache, as living masterpieces. The festival tends not to engage star performers in the way it did in the sixties, instead aiming to bring on young – principally British – musicians by encouraging them in their specialisms. The English Bach Festival Orchestra is made up of players from the London freelance pool and largely overlaps with the Academy of Ancient Music and the London Baroque and Monteverdi Orchestras.

The main burden of dreaming up, organizing and financing the festival activities still falls on the shoulders of the indefatigable Lina Lalandi. No detail is too insignificant for her attention – from vetting a Thames riverboat for an anniversary performance of Handel's *Water Music*, to following up and engaging promising singers, to booking hotels and arranging transport. 'That Miss Lalandi,' the Steward of one of Oxford's senior colleges was heard to complain when she positively insisted – against his wishes – on shifting the massive wooden dining tables and benches in

English Bach Festival – Baroque dancers in 'Divertissement' at the Banqueting House, Whitehall.

readiness for a recital, 'she never takes "no" for an answer.' With typical energy, she is already looking at how the festival might develop over the coming years and is planning to 'move into Mozart'. Her great desire is to present Mozart's operas as the composer himself saw and heard them – using fresh young voices singing at eighteenth-century pitch and accompanied by period instruments. Her first venture, planned for 1986, is likely to be *Così fan Tutte*.

Seldom can there have been such a consensus of critical praise for a festival as there has been for the EBF and the vision that inspires it. 'Flamboyant', 'intrepid', 'ever inventive', it has been called – 'the most adventurous', 'our liveliest and most versatile institution'. Certainly, since its inception it has had a profound influence on the planning of concert programmes and the staging of opera, and it has left a remarkable legacy of authentic performances of Baroque music on record – mostly, however, issued by a French company. And it has achieved all this against enormous financial odds, without regular commercial sponsorship or major public funding.

It does not matter one iota that the English Bach Festival is a hybrid, that it is no longer a festival in the usual sense of the word. What does matter is that it continues to reflect – as it has always done – a true festival spirit and achievement.

—8—

Some Scottish Festivals

In Edinburgh, Scotland can boast one of the largest, liveliest and most truly international festivals in the world. But the Scottish capital is not the only place north of the border where music and celebration meet.* Perhaps inspired by Edinburgh's success, festivals have sprung up in many parts of the country during the past thirty-odd years, from northernmost St Magnus in the Orkneys to Dumfries (each Whit Week) in the South.

Most of the activity is confined to the east coast (Aberdeen, with its own 'Bon-Accord Festival' in June and an International Youth Festival in early August, St Andrews, Perth, Dunkeld and Birnam) or to the Central Lothian region. Here, the diversity is enormous. On the one hand are festivals set in historic old burghs such as Stirling and Dunfermline, dominated by their proud castles or abbeys, full of royal associations. Stirling (early August) is notable for its encouragement of Scottish artists and traditions, for its choral concerts and celebrity recitals – past visitors have included John Ogdon, Shura Cherkassky and Annie Fischer – while Dunfermline is centred on its organ competition. On the other hand, there are several festivals which have emerged from the bleaker suburbs of the major cities of Glasgow and Edinburgh. They are largely community affairs, offering local inhabitants the chance to develop their creative talents and to participate in a grand kaleidoscope of activities – Easterhouse (each summer) on the periphery of Glasgow, Monklands (from April) in Airdrie, Wester Hailes (June) and Craigmillar (early June) in deepest Edinburgh.

Craigmillar was once described by its own festival society as a 'huge concrete jungle of pre- and post-war housing built without any thought of the other resources necessary for community life'. Indeed, the purpose of the festival has been to give the area some kind of cultural identity and by this means to improve the social lot of those who inhabit it. A special feature each year is the 'community musical' – written and scored as well as performed and directed by Craigmillar folk – dealing with some burning local issue. *The Time Machine*, for example, took as its theme the uproar caused by plans to route a motorway through the district.

In 1983, Glasgow acquired its own city-wide Mayfest, which runs for two weeks and is devoted to both popular theatre and music, with international as well as

* See also the entry on Proms in the Regions, page 120.

166

Scottish input. As for the west coast, stretching from the Solway Firth northwards to the aptly named Cape Wrath – all it has to offer in its hundreds of miles of moor and mountain, sea lochs and islands, is to be found in the little town of Ayr.

AYRSHIRE

The Ayrshire Arts Festival, centred on the seaside town of Ayr in deepest Burns country, started in 1983 as a fully professional event supported by the Scottish Arts Council, the local district council and a number of Ayrshire businesses. Unfortunately, it tried to run before it could walk, and in 1984 made a huge financial loss. The result was a decision to change policy somewhat and to encourage the participation of local performers to a greater extent – especially talented youngsters working under the direction of professionals. This bore fruit spectacularly in 1985 with the production of Richard Rodney Bennett's one-act opera *All the King's Men*, and the bringing together of over a hundred schoolchildren to perform in public (some for the first time) with a professional orchestra.

Other musical events in the 1985 festival – which lasted for a week in mid-May – included concerts by the Ayrshire String Orchestra at the aptly named Dansarena, where audiences sat on cushions on the floor to listen to Bach, Handel, Scarlatti's *Salve Regina* and Matyas Seiber's *Four Greek Songs* (in which the mezzo soloist was Marilyn de Blieck); by the Ayrshire Youth Jazz Orchestra and Junior Fiddle Orchestra; by the BBC Scottish Symphony Orchestra under Brian Wright in a popular programme of Johann Strauss, Beethoven's *Eroica* Symphony and Bruch's First Violin Concerto, with Christopher Warren-Green as soloist; and – on the lighter side – by Harvey and the Wallbangers.

For the rest, there was a cavalcade to the celebrated racecourse, kite-flying on Low Green, a folk night, drama productions, busking competitions and exhibitions of paintings (including Ben Nicholson and William Crozier) and photographs.

A worthy festival that has now probably found its level and combines the best of local talent with outside 'names'.

DUNKELD AND BIRNAM

The Dunkeld and Birnam Festival's logo is made up of three elements, each a reminder of the history of this particular corner of Perthshire: to the left a square tower, to the right a forest tree and linking them a seven-arched bridge. The tower is that of Dunkeld Cathedral, now largely a pleasantly belawned ruin somewhat withdrawn from the main part of the town. Only the fourteenth-century choir is intact and serves as Dunkeld's parish church. The tree represents the village of Birnam, whose wood's famous walk to Dunsinane so unnerved Shakespeare's Macbeth. And, joining them across the silvery Tay, is the fine bridge that Telford built in 1809.

The purpose of the festival, founded in 1978, was to build another kind of bridge between Dunkeld and Birnam. About that time, a new bypass was opened which diverted both traffic and visitors away from the villages, leaving local people fearing that, unless something were done to enhance community spirit, cultural stagnation would soon set in. The answer was to be a festival of the arts, lasting four days each late June, with the aim of focusing attention on the area by means of concerts, drama, exhibitions and other forms of entertainment.

Music comes in various guises at Dunkeld – promenade organ recitals in the Cathedral (most musical events take place there or at Murthly Castle, a few miles to the east along Strathtay), Scottish music, dance, jazz, choral and chamber concerts, opera – many of the performers being based in Scotland. The opening festival featured the Scottish Wind Ensemble (members of the BBC Scottish Symphony Orchestra) in Mozart, Hummel and Gounod. Two years later saw a visit from Cantilena, a chamber group of fifteen members drawn from the Scottish National Orchestra. In 1981, Ian Wallace made a welcome appearance (as did Leon Goossens), while the following year a programme of eighteenth-century Scottish music proved a popular attraction. 1984 included the Scottish Chamber Orchestra in a selection of Corelli, D'Indy, Wassenaer, Rossini and Haydn, as well as singers from Scottish Opera performing Schubert, Brahms and Janáček. The most recent festival, in 1985, featured performers from south of the border, in the shape of Pavilion Opera (in *Don Pasquale*) and Kaleidoscope in a programme of music by 'Mozart and Friends', alongside the Cramond Dancers and Ron Gonella playing classical Scottish fiddle music.

Of the other festival events, perhaps the most prestigious are the art exhibitions (housed in the Cathedral) which originated well before the festival itself came into being. Recent years have seen Turner watercolours, Stubbs drawings, and paintings by Alexander Nasmyth on display. This is a festival well suited to the pleasant villages that have given it life. It serves a very real community function, and if it is unlikely to be able to expand its activities in coming years, it is to be hoped that there will be no falling off in its high standards.

EAST KILBRIDE

The town of East Kilbride lies to the south of Glasgow in the Strathclyde region of Scotland. Its festival, inaugurated in 1980 with the aim of providing a programme of entertainment for all tastes over a broad spectrum of the visual and performing arts, takes place for about a week between June and August.

Most of the musical events are held in the Village Theatre or Ballerup Hall, named after East Kilbride's Danish twin-town. Ballerup itself has a biennial arts festival and in recent years cultural links have been established leading to the exchange of performers between the two festivals. East Kilbride's programmes feature both local artists and those with a wider national reputation. In 1985 the Glasgow Opera Group presented Wolf-Ferrari's comic opera *Dr Cupid* and the local film society sponsored a showing of Carlo Saura's flamenco ballet version of Bizet's *Carmen*. Visiting celebrities included Kenneth McKellar and Julian Lloyd Webber, while the Edinburgh Quartet gave two 'cushion concerts' and the Antics Community Dance Company presented a programme of contemporary dance. Jazz, folk and drama were also strongly in evidence.

EDINBURGH

The Edinburgh International Festival came into being in 1947, while the shadows of the Second World War still hung heavily over a Europe united only in its drabness and austerity. It owes its origins to the vision and determination of a small group of enthusiasts (among them Rudolf Bing, then general administrator of Glyndebourne Opera) who felt that it was no good just sitting around waiting for the clouds to lift – a means had to be found of breaking through them, of raising people's spirits and giving them confidence in the future. And the means they hit on was a festival – a great celebration of the arts to rival the best the Continent had to offer at Salzburg and Bayreuth.

To begin with, Bing thought that his festival ought to be nearer London – at Oxford, perhaps, or Cambridge. But the apathy he encountered in both these places, combined with his first impressions of Edinburgh, convinced him that the Scottish capital was ideal for his purposes. It was well supplied with halls, theatres, galleries; it was historically and architecturally interesting in its own right; there was no shortage of hotels and boarding houses to accommodate visiting performers and audiences. And its site was spectacular: for Edinburgh is built, like Athens (to which it is frequently likened), on a number of steep and imposing crags. From the narrow winding streets of the Old Town you can gaze out over grey roofscapes or up at beetling mediaeval tenements. The more level, central area of the city – the New Town – was developed during the late eighteenth and early nineteenth centuries, and contains many fine examples of Georgian and early Victorian neo-classical architecture.

Bing's first festival was in keeping with this magnificent setting. There was to be no question of modest beginnings rising to more ambitious heights as, in due time, reputation was established and confidence increased. Bing began at the top. He engaged the Vienna Philharmonic Orchestra with Bruno Walter as conductor and invited Elisabeth Schumann and Kathleen Ferrier to sing. Schnabel, Szigeti, Primrose and Fournier made their breathtaking quartet début. Opera travelled north in the shape of productions of Mozart's *Le Nozze di Figaro* and Verdi's *Macbeth*, while the cast for the ballet *The Sleeping Beauty* included Margot Fonteyn, Beryl Grey and Frederick Ashton. The drama contribution included productions staged by the Old Vic Company and the French Compagnie Jouvet de Théâtre de L'Athénée. Over the years, the basic pattern established by Bing in 1947 has been augmented with film, revues, art, street-theatre, jazz, pageantry, pipers, and festivals of books and architecture – not to mention the celebrated Edinburgh fringe, an informal and independent 'festival within the festival' providing hundreds of shows, concerts and exhibitions in little theatres, halls, streets and squares all over the city.

From a musical point of view, Edinburgh's great strength lies in its ability to attract to Scotland for three weeks each August the very finest orchestras, opera and ballet companies, and solo performers from all over the world. There have been some truly memorable occasions: 1951 – the first performance of the Verdi *Requiem* in Britain since the war with the La Scala Orchestra and Chorus under Victor de Sabata and soloists Renata Tebaldi, Fedora Barbieri, Giacinto Prandelli and Cesare Siepi; a series of concerts, the same year, by the New York Philharmonic Orchestra

Left: Edinburgh's Usher Hall – Simon Rattle conducting the Philharmonia and the Festival Choir.
Right: The first fireworks concert at the Edinburgh Festival in 1982 – Trevor Pinnock conducting the Scottish Chamber Orchestra and Chorus.

conducted by Bruno Walter and Dimitri Mitropoulos; Beecham conducting Strauss's *Ariadne auf Naxos* in its original version, then – at his wife's insistence – donning a steel helmet to direct Handel's *Firework Music*, complete with firework display and cannon, on the Castle Esplanade; 1959 – the Royal Opera, Stockholm, in *Die Walküre* with Svanholm, Nilsson, Söderström and Meyer in the principal roles; the visit of the Leningrad Symphony Orchestra in 1960; Stokowski conducting Schoenberg's *Gurrelieder* the following year. In the festival's first thirty-two years, no fewer than sixteen foreign opera companies gave performances, including those from Hamburg, Stuttgart, Belgrade, Prague, Frankfurt and Florence. Visiting orchestras have included the Israel Philharmonic under Mehta, the Chicago Symphony (Solti and Giulini), the Boston Symphony (Ozawa), the Vienna Philharmonic (Abbado and Böhm), the Concertgebouw (Haitink and Kondrashin), the Leipzig Gewandhaus Orchestra (Masur), the Orchestre de Paris (Barenboim) and all the major British orchestras. Among soloists that have been heard at Edinburgh are some of the great post-war names – Schwarzkopf, Vishnevskaya, Fischer-Dieskau, Holliger, Pollini, von Stade, Curzon, Argerich, Rostropovich, Pavarotti, Verrett, Bishop-Kovacevich, Fischer, Galway – while a number of distinguished composers have come to the city to hear or to conduct performances of their works – among them Petrassi, Dallapiccola, Tippett, Křenek, Penderecki and Lutoslawski.

Not everything that flowers during Edinburgh's high summer, however, is transplanted from foreign soil. The Scottish National Orchestra has taken part in many festival performances – notably under the baton of Sir Alexander Gibson – and the Scottish Chamber Orchestra and Baroque Ensemble have come to considerable eminence in recent years. A notable milestone was passed with the formation – in 1967 – of Scottish Opera, which has been responsible for several fine productions – Berlioz's *The Trojans* with Janet Baker and Helga Dernesch among them – while among the outstanding successes of the Edinburgh Festival Opera was the 1975 *Figaro* in which Ileana Cotrubas sang Susanna, Heather Harper the Countess, Teresa Berganza Cherubino, Dietrich Fischer-Dieskau the Count, and Sir Geraint Evans Figaro himself. Among Scottish composers who have been commissioned to write specially for the festival are Iain Hamilton and Robin Orr. 1967 also saw the inauguration of the Edinburgh Festival Chorus, trained by Arthur Oldham, which has been the mainstay of many exciting choral and orchestral concerts and has earned the high praise of such eminent conductors as Karajan, Abbado and Kertesz.

To bring matters up to date, a glance at what went on during the 1985 season reveals that there has been no lowering of standards or narrowing of focus. Three opera companies were in residence: Opéra de Lyon under John Eliot Gardiner gave performances of Chabrier's *L'Étoile* and Debussy's *Pelléas et Mélisande*; Les Arts Florissants presented a Baroque double-bill (Charpentier's *Actéon* and Rameau's *Anacréon*); and Connecticut Grand Opera was responsible for Gian Carlo Menotti's *The Consul*. Notable among the dance companies were the Paris Opera Ballet and Scottish Ballet, the latter joined by Nureyev in *La Sylphide*. Visiting orchestras included the Orchestre National de France (under Charles Dutoit, Thomas Fulton and Christoph Eschenbach – the latter conducting a programme in which Martha Argerich played Ravel's Piano Concerto in G and Michel Béroff his Left-Hand Concerto); the New Symphony Orchestra of the USSR (Rozhdestvensky); the Pittsburg Symphony (Maazel); the London Philharmonic (Tennstedt) and the Philharmonia (Sinopoli). Soloists included Lucia Popp, Andras Schiff, Jean-Philippe Collard, Steven Isserlis and Sir Yehudi Menuhin (who took part as soloist in Bach's Violin Concerto in E in an unusual Scottish Chamber Orchestra concert which also included Nureyev dancing to the music of the Third Cello Suite).

Noël Goodwin
PERSEVERE!

As a music critic, for many years with the *Daily Express* but more recently freelance, Noël Goodwin's experience has been chiefly of the larger, more prestigious British festivals. That is not because he takes a superior view of what goes on at Newbury or Haslemere or Fishguard, or rates their festivals as less important than Edinburgh or Bath – on the contrary, he recognizes the immense debt owed to festivals all over the country for injecting new vigour into its musical life, and especially for encouraging new compositions. The narrowness of his focus has been, rather, the direct result of the small (and contracting) amount of space generally made available in the national newspapers for music reviews. 'When – at the height of the season – you have ten or twelve festival concerts happening on the same day in different parts of the country,' he points out, 'you have to go for the one that you believe will command the widest interest among your readers. And the "big four" – Edinburgh, Aldeburgh, Bath and Cheltenham – have a pretty good track record for putting on programmes that make you sit up and take notice.' At the same time, he admits that the availability of newspaper space often depends on the musical enthusiasm of the editor: if he is keen and aware of what is going on around the country, then the column inches can sometimes become less scarce.

Goodwin has always welcomed the call to pack his bags and set off for festival-land, not only because of the musical delights that might be awaiting him there, but also because it provides a break from his London routine. He appreciates the foresight of organizers who have cultivated their festivals in tranquil or inspiring surroundings, though he has sometimes missed the convenience and facilities that the capital provides. He recalls his visit to Aldeburgh's Jubilee Hall to hear the first performance of Britten's opera *A Midsummer Night's Dream* in 1960. A magical evening. But the professional critic cannot sit back and wallow in the magic quite in the way an ordinary member of the audience might – he has a job to do: 'I started writing my notice during the second interval (actually, I found a place to sit on the beach, which wasn't too bad) knowing that I would then only have to add a couple of concluding paragraphs at the end of the performance, before telephoning London to catch my deadline. I don't think the performance ended all that late, but by the time I had rounded off my review, hunted out a call-box, read the piece over to the copy-taker, and eventually made my way back to my hotel, I found myself well and truly locked out!'

So festival atmosphere is not a thing that influences Noël Goodwin very much. He recalls concerts that had a special kind of excitement – Mahler's Eighth Symphony or Schoenberg's *Gurrelieder* on a festival-opening Sunday night in Edinburgh, really rocking back audiences that were just not accustomed to musical canvases of such vast scale – but by and large he has made it his business not to be affected by the buzz of the occasion. 'I'm there to serve the music, to listen to it, to concentrate on it before all else. The atmosphere doesn't count for much, whether it is one of barely contained enthusiasm or the very opposite. I am always optimistic, but if I have to write deflatingly about a concert or recital that has everyone else present turning cartwheels, there will be a reason given.' That said, he firmly believes that reviews have an important role to play in focusing public attention on festivals and what they are trying to achieve. Newspaper and TV and radio coverage does a good deal to generate interest and encourage support. In addition, critical attention helps keep performers working to the highest pitch of excellence of which they are capable. 'Festivals cannot afford to allow the sense of celebration with which they so often surround themselves to provide an excuse for inferior or jaded music-making. We should support festivals because they are attempting the new and interesting and because they are aiming high in every respect, not just because they are festivals and – maybe – worthy. To do the latter would be to employ dangerously double standards.' If the music and the performance are right, however, he does sometimes develop a special sympathy for certain festivals. Aldeburgh is a case in point: he speaks with affection of the first performances of Britten's three Church Parables in Orford Church, occasions on which he experienced outstanding pleasure and felt entirely at one with his surroundings.

Goodwin is more than a little suspicious of festivals which grow out of a sense of competition, of keeping up with the Joneses – where municipal pride inspires a town to mount an annual event in order not to be outdone by a near neighbour. That is the sort of festival, in his eyes, that soon becomes flabby and lacking in direction. 'If, on the other hand, the organizers can identify something that is really worth doing, and can work to achieve it, then the operation is infinitely worthwhile.' Festivals should not be afraid to make demands on their audiences – including the critics. He sums up his feelings with a rueful grin and an anecdote about Edinburgh: 'It was at one of those rather gruelling morning concerts – a programme of Schoenberg quartets in Leith Town Hall. I must confess that I was beginning to flag a little, when my eye drifted upwards to the civic coat of arms fixed high over the proscenium arch. Complete with a motto that said it all – "Persevere"!'

PERTH

Late May, 1985, and the city of Perth is astir with activity: a flurry of early visitors is poised for excursions along Strathtay, to one or other of the romantic castles in the vicinity and especially to Scone Palace which houses the famous King's Stone of Destiny. But there is also plenty to be doing in Perth itself, for just now we are at the height of the festival season.

Orchestral concerts in the City Hall are a major attraction this, as every, year: the London Mozart Players conducted by Yan-Pascal Tortelier in Beethoven, Mendelssohn, Schumann (his Piano Concerto played by the gifted Canadian, John Kimura Parker) and Mozart; the Scottish Chamber Orchestra with Barry Tuckwell as horn soloist cum director playing Mendelssohn, Gow (the first Scottish performance of *Janus*), Mozart (the K447 Horn Concerto) and Beethoven's *Pastoral* Symphony; the Scottish National Orchestra under Neeme Järvi in an evening of grand opera, with guest soloists Heather Harper, Rosa Mannion, Ann Howard, Arthur Davies and Donald Maxwell; the Academy of St Martin-in-the-Fields directed by Iona Brown in two all-Bach programmes which include the complete Brandenburg Concertos; and the BBC Scottish Symphony Orchestra, with the Scottish Philharmonic Singers, under Sir David Willcocks in a celebration of English music from Handel, via Parry and Elgar, to Walton and Britten. Another popular venue for festival music is the ancient St John's Kirk of Perth which houses midday concerts by pupils from a number of local schools, a flute recital by Susan Milan, a performance of Bach's Mass in B Minor by the John Currie Singers and Orchestra and a lecture-recital by George Malcolm – as well as being the evocative setting, each evening, for the festival production of T. S. Eliot's *Murder in the Cathedral*, whose events took place about the time St John's was founded.

Concerts and recitals also take place out of town, in the Long Gallery of Scone Palace (Susan Milan playing Bach and Vivaldi accompanied by the Scottish Baroque Ensemble directed by Leonard Friedman) and at Battleby House, Redgorton (the Classical Piano Trio one evening, guitarist Angel Romero another). As well as all this, the twelve-day festival (founded in 1971) also includes organ recitals (Jane Parker-Smith in virtuosic Vierne, Dupré, Germani and Liszt), Scottish fiddle music, military bands, dance bands (the Joe Loss Orchestra), cabaret, a Perth walkabout, a feast of film and art exhibitions.

ST ANDREWS

The inspiration for this winter festival – it is held every other February – came from the undergraduates of St Andrews' ancient university, and though town and gown co-operate in keeping a fatherly eye on it, the day-to-day running (programming, publicity, financing and box-office management) remains in the hands of a committee of students. In one sense, the festival is a gesture of goodwill from the university to the town that has given it house-room since 1410 (it is Scotland's oldest seat of learning), though it also attracts visitors from further afield and care is taken to help them find accommodation. Most of the festival events take place in university halls and theatres, which are conveniently close to each other in the centre of the town.

Music – both classical and contemporary – plays an important role at St Andrews, though theatre, dance, exhibitions and films also draw appreciative audiences. Past performers include the Scottish Baroque Ensemble, the Scottish Chamber Orchestra, Scottish Opera, the Alexander Roy Ballet, John Williams, Julian Lloyd Webber, the Kodály Quartet, the Northern Sinfonia Orchestra and Magma (a French five-piece group led by Christian Vander, specializing in contemporary repertoire). The 1985 festival gave a warm welcome to the BBC Scottish Symphony Orchestra under James Loughran on the one hand and – on the other – to Ronnie Scott, who was the star attraction at a mini jazz festival-within-the-festival. It was also joined, for its first two days, by the Scottish Student Drama Festival which did plenty to add to the liveliness of the occasion.

ST MAGNUS

The St Magnus Festival, now happily a regular fixture in late June each year, very nearly failed to get started at all. Which is scarcely surprising when one considers the financial and logistical problems of setting up a major cultural venture in so remote a spot as the Orkney Mainland and attracting to it performers and audiences not only from all parts of the islands but also from as far afield as Glasgow or London. But the great enthusiasm and perseverance of the local organizing committee, coupled with Peter Maxwell Davies's dedication and foresight as artistic director, ensured not only that the festival got off the ground, but that it has grown and prospered. In fact, the very first season, in 1977, had as its centrepiece the première of Maxwell Davies's chamber opera *The Martyrdom of St Magnus*, which the BBC recorded in Kirkwall.

Kirkwall, the Orcadian capital, with its bustling harbour, its high-gabled houses and the red and yellow sandstone St Magnus's Cathedral, is one of the two main festival centres. The other is the fishing and ferry port of Stromness, sheltering in a safe bay on Hoy Sound, some dozen miles to the west. Singers and instrumentalists from schools, choirs and amateur orchestras from the Kirkwall and Stromness districts make a major contribution to festival activities and, in 1982, appeared in as many as eleven out of a total of twenty-two events. It is for these same performers that much new music is provided each year, particularly by Maxwell Davies, but by other composers as well. In the festival's first five years, twenty new works were commissioned, of which half were designed specifically for local groups (including Davies's *The Two Fiddlers* for Kirkwall Grammar School, his *Le Jongleur de Notre Dame* prelude for Stromness Academy Wind Group, the *Kirkwall Shopping Songs* for Papdale Primary School and *The Rainbow* for Stromness Primary School).

St Magnus caters for a broad range of tastes, with exhibitions, poetry, jazz and rock, film, Scottish (especially Orcadian) music, theatre and mime as well as classical and contemporary music. The 1985 festival was typical. Ben Nicholson and Ian MacInnes were the featured artists, Edwin Morgan the resident poet. The Orkney County Drama Group put on a number of performances of Brecht's *The Caucasian Chalk Circle* with new music especially written by local composer John Gray. The opening concert, in St Magnus's Cathedral, featured the Festival Chorus, the Cathedral Choir and the Orkney Orchestra in a programme which included Britten's *Rejoice in the Lamb*, Dvořák's Mass in D and Martin Dalby's Two Liturgical Canticles. The following day, a special schools' concert brought together performances by children of different age groups of Michael Hurd's *Little Billy*, Paul Patterson's *Rebecca* and a new rock operetta by Douglas Watt and Fiona Menzies entitled *David and the Giant Philistine*. Other concerts were given by two visiting ensembles, the Scottish Chamber Orchestra (conducted by Nicholas Cleobury) and The Fires of London. The former group gave an all-British programme – Delius, Holst, Elgar, Maxwell Davies (his Sinfonia Concertante) and Edward Harper's specially commissioned *Fantasia V – Passacaglia on EH3 7DC* – plus a Classical/Romantic programme which included the Tchaikovsky *Rococo Variations* in which Ralph Kirshbaum was the solo cellist. The Fires played Maxwell Davies (including the first Scottish performance of his work for cimbalom, *Image, Reflection, Shadow*) and Schoenberg in Stromness, and in Kirkwall an all Maxwell Davies concert, in which Mary Thomas appeared as soloist in *Miss Donnithorne's Maggot* and Tom Yang danced the *Vesalii Icones*. In addition, there were recitals by Ralph Kirshbaum with Ian Brown, Marjorie Bruce (organ), the Fires of London trio and John Gray (clarinet) with James Gray (trumpet and guitar). This last recital, given one lunchtime in the Academy Hall in Stromness, included music by Boulez and Maxwell Davies, and John Gray's own festival commissions for trumpet and for clarinet, guitar and tape. Other festival visitors came in the shape of two Norwegian choirs who gave concerts not only in Kirkwall but also on the islands of Shapinsay, Flotta and Hoy.

St Magnus may well be the most northerly and remote of British festivals, but – largely thanks to its artistic direction – it is no backwoods affair; on the contrary, it is a living demonstration of what can be achieved by inspired leadership and the enthusiastic participation of an entire community.

_9_
Festivals with Young People in Mind

Whether singing the latest Maxwell Davies at Kirkwall or busking on the fringe at Cambridge or Cheltenham, young people make an enormous impact on festivals throughout the country. They come as choirs – cathedral, school, university – and as instrumentalists – members of regional youth orchestras or emerging soloists (Young Musicians, perhaps, of this year, next year . . .) – and they bring to their performances a bright-eyed enthusiasm which is at once engaging and moving. Edges may not always been tooled to perfection, there may be the occasional sour, or at least unripe, note. But such considerations take second place to the fact that the music is there, and _they_ – in their blazers or jeans or surplices or crisp white blouses – are making it. So all credit to the festivals, great and small, that place a special accent on youth, that give the kids from the local comprehensive a hearing alongside the deft London professionals.

There are a few festivals that focus even more closely on the talents and commitment of youth. At Milton Keynes (mid-October), for instance, a festival which takes a pride in commissioning new work and creating opportunities for young artists from all disciplines, there is particular emphasis on involving young people between the ages of five and eleven years. At Deal, the festival is built round a series of masterclasses conducted by distinguished visitors. At Aberdeen, Harrogate and Shrewsbury, music is seen as a means of furthering international understanding, while at Cleveland and at the Llangollen Eisteddfod sweet harmony goes hand in hand with friendly competition. In London, just before the Proms get under way, in mid-July, there is the National Festival of Music for Youth, whose objective is to provide a platform for young musicians at all stages of their development – from primary school to university. Every form of instrumental ensemble is represented. For those rather further along the professional road, there is another event on the London calendar. The Park Lane Group Young Artists' Series, held in the Purcell Room each January, presents the young and gifted in programmes made up exclusively from the wide range of twentieth-century music.

Two festivals, both coincidentally born in Kent, have actually grown up in schools. Canterbury's 'King's Week' (mid-July) is the older of the two, having been founded in 1951 by Canon F. J. Shirley, and is designed to take place in and around the

School and Cathedral precincts. The majority of the events are performed by pupils of the King's School – up to three plays each year, plus a jazz concert, two symphony concerts and a serenade in the Cathedral cloisters. Distinguished visitors from outside – including, in the past, Larry Adler, George Malcolm, the Dudley Moore Trio, the Allegri String Quartet, the King's Singers, the London Mozart Players and the Academy of St Martin-in-the-Fields – also take part. The pattern at Sevenoaks is rather similar.

—ABERDEEN INTERNATIONAL YOUTH FESTIVAL—

The granite city on Scotland's east coast is a long way from Switzerland, where the International Youth Festival had its beginnings in 1969, under the auspices of the International Youth Foundation. When the festival moved to Scotland in 1973, it was taken under the wing of the Aberdeen City Council, where it has continued to thrive ever since. The object of the festival is to provide an opportunity for young musicians and dancers to live together for a two-week period, to rehearse, perform, get to know Scotland, make friends and learn about different cultures. They are housed in the halls of residence of Aberdeen University's two fine and historic colleges – King's, founded in 1495, and Marischal (1593, but extensively restored during the nineteenth century) whose great Perpendicular façade has earned it the reputation of being one of the world's most splendid granite buildings. Festival time is early August, when the city is at its brightest and the scent of roses rises from spacious parks and roadside flowerbeds, and when visitors from near and far throng the narrow cobbled streets that weave around King's College, with its celebrated Crown Tower, and the dignified mass of St Machar's Cathedral.

Most festival activities within Aberdeen itself take place in the recently restored His Majesty's Theatre, the Music Hall and the Mitchell Hall auditorium of Marischal College. Visiting groups are not, however, confined to the city for the festival fortnight, but travel throughout Scotland to give concerts and displays. On 10 August 1984, for example, a San Francisco dance troupe was performing in Peterhead, the Palo Alto Chamber Orchestra was in Callander, Inverurie Town Hall was the setting for a colourful concert by the Woodtrin Steel Band from Trinidad, a Polish Schools' Chamber Orchestra was in Kirkintilloch, the Strasbourg University Orchestra was playing in Dunblane Cathedral, a dance group from Sri Lanka was performing before an audience in the Pitmeddon Garden at Ellon, while another, from the Philippines, was in Lochgally.

Back in Aberdeen, the sense of occasion is enhanced by an opening festival parade, a firework spectacular with music and a number of celebrity concerts. In recent years, guest performers have included the Scottish Chamber Orchestra under Kenneth Jean, Isobel Buchanan, Olivier Munoz, dancers from the Scottish Ballet, Nigel Kennedy, Christopher Adey, the Edinburgh Quartet, Antony Hopkins and Nicholas Braithwaite.

The festival is essentially non-competitive: each visiting group gives at least one

The University of the Philippines Concert Chorus at Crathes Castle, Banchory, in 1985.

concert in Aberdeen itself and its members have the chance to enrol for a variety of master-classes in the music and dance schools that are held during the festival. Music school students, all aged between twelve and twenty-one, are also invited to audition for the Festival Orchestra and Chorus, which are put through their paces at a final gala concert by a distinguished guest conductor. The 1984 concert was conducted by Christopher Seaman and consisted of Beethoven's *Egmont Overture*, Brahms's Second Piano Concerto (with Krystian Zimerman) and pieces by Debussy and Elgar. Although competition is not the central point of the International Youth Festival, there are three major competitions held each year for which individuals or groups may enter. These are the Skene Aberdeen Music Award (for the most outstanding young musician taking part in the festival), a Chamber Music Competition and the Mary Garden Memorial Prize (for the most outstanding singer).

The Aberdeen International Youth Festival is a truly rich and colourful occasion, with music and dance of all kinds performed to a high degree of excellence. The programmes chosen by the participating groups are far from conventional or unexciting. In 1984, a chamber orchestra from Katowice in Poland complemented their offering of Bach, Handel and Haydn with Lutoslawski's *Five Dance Preludes for Clarinet and Orchestra* and Karlowicz's *Serenade for String Orchestra*; a Japanese male-voice choir performed Paul Creston's *Missa Solemnis* as well as introducing Japanese folksongs and *The Bells*, a piece by Tokuhide Niimi; and a cello ensemble from Italy played Cirri, Rossini, Popper, Prokofiev (*Canti Armeni* for an orchestra of cellos) and Villa-Lobos. Nor are large-scale concert works avoided: the National Youth Orchestra of Scotland played Mahler's First Symphony, Canada's Calgary Youth Orchestra gave Dvořák's Seventh and the Oakland Symphony Youth Orchestra Ives's

179

Second. Then again, audiences at the concert given by the Camerata of the University of Maryland had the chance to hear idiomatic performances of contemporary American choral music, while those who supported the Sibelius Lukio Choir were treated not only to pieces by the Finnish master but also to works by living composers. All in all, the Aberdeen International Youth Festival is a feast not just for the participants but for anyone who loves music and is keen to seek out fine performances.

CLEVELAND INTER-TIE
CLEVELAND'S INTERNATIONAL EISTEDDFOD

Cleveland Inter-TIE is a week-long festival which takes place every other year in late July. It combines competitions for amateur performers from all over the world with evening concerts which bring together talented competitors and visiting professional musicians. The festival started in 1966 and was held in a complex of tents and marquees set up in ICI's Teesside recreation ground. In later years, it moved to a more central site – the Prissick School Base in Middlesbrough, on which the organizers pitched one of the largest tents in Europe, capable of housing over 4000 people. Today, the main concerts are held in Middlesbrough Town Hall, which – together with Teesside Polytechnic – also hosts the competition sessions.

The competitions cater for large and small choirs, solo singers, instrumentalists, folk groups and folk dancers, and their international flavour is reflected in the fact that in 1984 small, mixed-voice choirs came to sing Morley and Saint-Saëns (together with pieces of their own choice) from Czechoslovakia, Turkey, Singapore, the Philippines, West Germany and Romania, as well as from various parts of the United Kingdom. There were youth choirs from Singapore and Hungary, folk singers from Spain, France, Switzerland, Canada, Poland and Portugal, male-voice choirs from Reading, Bratislava and Ankara, tenor soloists from Italy, Wales, Singapore and Yugoslavia. Many of these visitors took part in the 'international concerts' held during the week not only in Middlesbrough itself but also in neighbouring towns such as Hartlepool, Stockton and Guisborough.

Each festival brings together distinguished professional adjudicators – such as Jean Allister, Havelock Nelson, Noël Cox, Kristian Lange and the Czech composer Antonin Tucapsky – as well as guest performers for the evening concerts. The very first Inter-TIE in 1966 had its crowning moment in a performance of Beethoven's *Missa Solemnis* with the Huddersfield Choral Society in full cry. Two years later, the newly formed Inter-TIE Choir was joined by the Royal Liverpool Philharmonic Orchestra conducted by Sir Charles Groves in Haydn's *Creation*, while subsequent festivals have featured performances of *Gerontius* and *Elijah*. Orchestral concerts also find their way into the programmes – in 1978 the Cleveland Youth Orchestra played the Dvořák *New World Symphony* and was joined by Raphael Wallfisch in Elgar's Cello Concerto. The 1984 festival included visits from the BBC Concert Orchestra under Iain Sutherland in a programme of light music and the BBC Philharmonic Orchestra under Günther Herbig, with Boris Belkin as soloist in the Tchaikovsky

Cleveland Inter-TIE – members of Le Gai Farandolaire from France
performing in Victoria Square, Middlesbrough.

Violin Concerto. Other guest performers that year included The Spinners, The Grand Union and Yullyo Akhoe, a group of singers, dancers and instrumentalists from South Korea. Perhaps the festival's greatest coup has been to enlist the enthusiastic support of Elizabeth Schwarzkopf, who sang during the 1966 season and paid a return visit in 1974.

Cleveland Inter-TIE boasts a lively fringe, a multitude of activities being organized in department stores, hotels, schools, parks and the open streets before, during and after the festival week.

DEAL

The first Deal Summer Music Festival was held in 1982, the result of the vision, determination and musical knowledge of the Swedish pianist, Lennart Rabes. The two-week festival, held in mid-August when the town is at its sunniest, takes the form of a series of master-classes at which young instrumentalists are coached by distinguished musicians from this country and abroad, together with concerts and recitals given by both 'masters' and 'pupils'. Deal, which lies six miles along the coast north of Dover, was once an important Cinque Port, under the protection of Henry VIII's squat, rose-shaped castle. Its neat Georgian and Victorian streets, these days a popular haunt of weekending Londoners, contain several venues well suited for festival use – among them the Royal Marines' Concert Hall, the Astor Theatre, St George's Church and the Quarterdeck (situated appropriately close to the sea, opposite the pier).

Steven Isserlis (*left*) with a cello class in 1984.

The esteem in which the festival has come to be held in the short time it has existed is reflected by the help it has received from well-known artists who have donated performance fees to support its activities. In 1982, the oboe master-class directed by Evelyn Rothwell was a considerable attraction, as were those in the following two years led by Steven Isserlis (cello) and Roger Raphael (violin). Among eminent soloists who have given recitals at Deal are Lydia Mordkovitch, Moura Lympany, Lennart Rabes, Claus-Christian Schuster and Janet Hilton. A highlight of the 1984 season was the concert at which Ronald Smith played Balakirev's B flat Minor Sonata, Chopin's twelve Opus 10 Études, a selection of Alkan's shorter pieces and *Pictures at an Exhibition* by Mussorgsky.

The following year, for the first time the festival opened with an orchestral concert – consisting of works by Weber, Beethoven and Elgar, given by the Lydian Orchestra under Jonathan Butcher – and included a 'light classical' evening introduced by Gabriel Woolf in which star performers let their hair down in such pieces as Rossini's Duetto for Cello and Double Bass (Steven Isserlis was joined by Chi Chi Nwanoku), Poulenc's *Babar the Little Elephant* (Gabriel Woolf accompanied by Claus-Christian Schuster) and Alan Ridout's *Story of Ferdinand the Bull* (Woolf and Lydia Mordkovitch).

The Deal Summer Music Festival has also distinguished itself in the course of its brief life by including in its programmes the first British performances of a number of works – not all of them particularly new. In 1982, Lennart Rabes played Berwald's *Fantasia on Two Swedish Folk Melodies* and Henning Mankell's Fourth Ballade, while Steven Isserlis and Peter Evans unveiled the Ballade for Cello by Patrick Piggott, who was present at both rehearsals and performance.

The Deal Festival, now under the musical direction of Steven Isserlis, has clearly identified and filled an important gap in British musical life. It is to be hoped that it will continue its training and encouragement of young musicians for many years to come.

HARROGATE
—— INTERNATIONAL YOUTH MUSIC FESTIVAL ——

The Harrogate International Youth Music Festival is the older sister of the one held each July in Shrewsbury. Each Easter up to thousand young people come from all parts of the world to take part in concerts and displays both in Harrogate itself (including the Royal Hall, the Harrogate Centre and a number of schools, churches and hotels) and further afield – in 1984 groups appeared in Knaresborough, Ripon, Leeds and at Harewood House.

The Berger and Nesoddtangen Skolekorps from Norway
performing in the Harrogate Centre at the 1985 Harrogate International Youth Music Festival.

The festival is entirely non-competitive and the participants come together not to be judged, but to further the spirit of international exchange. A typical recent programme listed choirs, orchestras, bands and dance groups from Belgium, Canada, Denmark, Germany, Hungary, the United States of America and the United Kingdom. As well as giving individual performances, groups have the opportunity to take part in choral and jazz workshops, in which pieces are studied in preparation for one of the gala evening concerts. Each group takes part in a minimum of four performances. Participants stay with families in the Harrogate area, giving them the chance to sample the British – and, indeed, the Yorkshire – way of life. This is very much a festival for performers, though it brings a good deal of colour and enjoyment to its host town each spring.

LEEDS – CITY OF LEEDS
————COLLEGE OF MUSIC FESTIVAL————

The City of Leeds College of Music offers both full- and part-time foundation and diploma courses and a range of evening classes for instrumentalists and singers of all levels of attainment. It also provides an advanced diploma course in jazz and light music. Since 1966, the college has held an annual festival, usually in the early spring, which serves as a focal point for much of the year's practical work. In many ways the festival can be regarded as an open week when parents, friends and members of the general public can experience a representative cross-section of the work in which the college is involved. In addition to its other functions, it has the extremely valuable role of encouraging students and staff to work together to the highest standards in the preparation and staging of a major event.

The range of festival music has always been extremely wide, embracing, in addition to the staple fare of the traditional classics, works of an experimental nature and examples of music from other cultures. Originally, jazz and light music also had their allotted place, but since 1983 they have been made the subject of a specialist festival earlier in the year. The grandest concerts are given at either end of the festival week in Leeds Town Hall under the direction of Joseph Stones, director of the college and the festival's founder. The college symphony orchestra and choral society are always heavily involved in these, giving students a collective opportunity to prepare works which, because of their scale, are not over-frequently exposed as part of the standard concert repertoire. These have included Berlioz's *Grande Messe des Morts* and *Te Deum*, Mahler's Second and Fifth Symphonies, Janáček's Sinfonietta, the Verdi *Requiem*, *Carmina Burana* (Orff), *King David* (Honegger), *The Dream of Gerontius*, Holst's *Hymn of Jesus* and the Beethoven *Choral Symphony*.

The college also manages to mount occasional first performances, having been responsible for that of Havergal Brian's *Concerto for Orchestra* as well as Jeffrey Lewis's *Strata* and *Fanfare with Variations*. A particularly felicitous piece of programming one year brought together Bruckner's F Minor Mass and *Das Lied von der Erde* by

Mahler, with visiting soloists Barbara Parry, Barbara Robotham, Alexander Young and Frederick Westcott.

Elsewhere in the week there are opera workshops, solo and chamber recitals, performances of student compositions, choral concerts and a look at the contemporary scene. All in all, a lively occasion which benefits enormously from the enthusiasm and sparkle of the students who work so hard for its success.

LLANGOLLEN
—— INTERNATIONAL MUSICAL EISTEDDFOD ——

For a week each July, all roads lead to the Welsh town of Llangollen. Singers, instrumentalists and dancers – many of them in their teens and twenties – from all over the world come together to engage in friendly competition, join each other in a number of international concerts and be entertained by professional performers from this country and abroad. The object of the eisteddfod, founded in 1947, is to advance public education in the fine arts and by that means to play a part in the preservation of peace, setting aside politics and ignoring the barriers of class, colour and creed that elsewhere divide man from man. The atmosphere of mutual understanding and goodwill is enhanced by the beauty and serenity of the setting – the festival ground being situated outside the town in a natural amphitheatre formed by the gently rolling hills. The main performing area is a huge marquee set up in the centre of the ground and surrounded by smaller tents and booths catering for the every need of competitors and visitors alike.

The 1985 festival opened in style with a concert shared by the Band of the Royal Marines' School of Music and the King's Singers, who sang groups of folk songs, close-harmony numbers, madrigals and chansons, as well as Gian Carlo Menotti's *Moans, Groans, Sighs 1981 (or A Composer at Work)*. After the grand opening, the daily pattern is for morning and afternoon competitions to be followed each evening by concerts in which choirs, dance-troupes and instrumentalists, joined by one or two well-known professionals, entertain each other. Recent visitors at these occasions have included Fou Ts'ong (playing Scarlatti and Chopin), the Bulgarian bass Assen Vassilev, Michael Rippon, violinist Hidako Udagawa, American soprano Jo Ann Pickens and Julian Lloyd Webber. The eisteddfod usually – though not always – comes to a blazing conclusion with a large-scale choral work: recently Owain Arwel Hughes has brought the Hallé Orchestra and the Huddersfield Choral Society to Llangollen to sing *The Dream of Gerontius* (1983, with soloists Bernadette Greevy, Kenneth Woollam and Benjamin Luxon) and *Messiah* (1985, with Rita Cullis, Alfreda Hodgson, Howard Haskin and Stephen Roberts).

—— SEVENOAKS ——

The Sevenoaks Summer Festival started, in the form in which it exists today, in 1972. Based on and partly underwritten by the town's famous public school, its aim is to present as broad a range as possible of the performing and visual arts for the people of Sevenoaks and the young in particular. The varied programme is put on at a time – the height of the summer and the end of the academic year – when the atmosphere is ideally suited to a cultural enterprise of this kind. The encouragement to be adventurous was originally, and has remained, a vital element in the festival planning: while not forgetting the connoisseur and those with specialist interests, the Sevenoaks Summer Festival has always served as an enjoyable introduction to the arts for the novice and the uninitiated. A wide range of performing levels is included, from talented school pupils and students, through gifted local amateurs, to aspiring young artists fighting for a foothold on the professional ladder, and top-class virtuosi with international reputations.

Most events take place on the Sevenoaks School campus – in the purpose-built Sackville Theatre, the Aisher Hall, the Little Theatre or the Johnson Library – though St Nicholas's Church is used for choral and orchestral concerts.

The 1985 festival was typical in its music programming: Julian Lloyd Webber (cello) in recital with Gordon Back; the Philip Jones Brass Ensemble playing music from Henry VIII to Michael Berkeley, John McCabe and Lutoslawski; Emma Johnson – the 1984 BBC Television Young Musician of the Year and a former music scholar at Sevenoaks School – in a programme including Brahms's Trio for Clarinet, Cello and Piano; the Coull Quartet playing works by Haydn, Shostakovich and Schubert; a Bach/Handel Tercentenary Concert featuring the Corydon Singers under Matthew Best (another past pupil); and programmes by the Yehudi Menuhin School Orchestra, by the Lydian Orchestra (a body made up of young musicians from the area) and by talented solo performers as well as choral and instrumental ensembles from Sevenoaks School. On the lighter side, there were appearances by Peter Skellern and Georgie Fame, while dance programmes featured the talented English Dance Theatre Company and the all-male Phoenix Dance Company. The festival also included drama, mime, revue, lectures, expeditions, films and a variety of children's events.

SHREWSBURY
───── INTERNATIONAL MUSIC FESTIVAL ─────

For one week each July, Shrewsbury is the setting in which hundreds of amateur musicians and dancers of all ages and from all over the world join together to learn about each others' music and cultural traditions. Like its sister festival which takes place each Easter in Harrogate, this is a strictly non-competitive event. The days are filled with recitals and displays both in local schools, churches and hotels and also in the open air, on the Grand Parade or in the Market Square, by choirs, mime groups, instrumentalists, bands, folk dance ensembles. In the evenings, there are concerts in which visiting groups join together to perform pieces rehearsed in the course of festival workshops.

A performance of massed bands, led by E. Jon de Revere, in front of Shrewsbury Castle at the Shrewsbury International Music Festival.

The 1984 festival brought together performers from Belgium, Canada, France, Germany, Israel, Italy, Norway, the Philippines, Poland, Switzerland, Taiwan, the United States of America, Yugoslavia and the United Kingdom. Participants all stay either with local families or, in larger groups, in schools: gaining some experience of the British way of life is regarded as an important aspect of the festival experience for the overseas visitors.

Programmes are planned on thematic lines ('Across Three Continents' or 'East meets West' or 'Song and Dance') and care is taken to provide contrast – boy singers from Flanders and a church choir from Washington flanking a wind ensemble from Essex under the direction of the London Symphony Orchestra's Denis Wick, or a pot-pourri of folk dance, close harmony and music by a concert band. Special features also include benefit concerts given in aid of local charities and the participation of visiting choirs and ensembles in church services in the area. In 1984, for example, the French Chorale de Sète assisted in the Abbey, an American Presbyterian choir at St David's Presbyterian Church and a Canadian band played at the Roman Catholic Cathedral.

— 10 —

Some Specialist Festivals

Opera at Buxton, at Camden, at Glyndebourne (of course!); Handel at St George's, Hanover Square; Bach in East Cornwall (St Germans) and West Surrey (Tilford); the organ shaking the rafters in Bath or Dunfermline, Manchester or St Albans; British music proclaimed at Keele and Peterborough; church music celebrated at Ashwell, Edington, Norwich and by the Southern Cathedrals – many and varied are the special tastes for which individual festivals cater. More generously served than most are the early and contemporary music scenes: on the one hand, there are events like London's Early Music Centre Festival (during the second half of October) and Mark Deller's Stour Music; on the other, Colchester (April/May) with its guiding principle of introducing hitherto unperformed new works, and the capital's young but adventurous Almeida and Nettlefold festivals. However, not all early music festivals are alike either in scale or in approach – the same being true of those which espouse the contemporary cause. Each has its own flavour, its own outlook and – as the following survey makes clear – its own personality.

Ancient . . .

BOXHILL

Cleveland Lodge, a fine country house in the shadow of Boxhill in Surrey, was the home that, until his death in 1946, the eminent mathematical physicist Sir James Jeans shared with his Austrian-born wife, Susi. Shortly after being widowed, Lady Jeans – a brilliant keyboard player with a profound love of early music – decided that she wanted to do something for the neighbourhood in which she lived, and this bore fruit in a Festival of Britain concert she organized in 1951. The programme on that occasion was typical of what the Boxhill Festival has become famous for, in that it included first modern performances of 'mislaid' works by important composers of past centuries: a mass by John Dunstable and a Haydn Double Concerto for Violin and Harpsichord.

Following the success of this initial venture, in 1954 Susi Jeans joined forces with Stephen Manton in the organization of the Mickleham and Westhumble Festival, which attracted musicians of the calibre of Thurston Dart, Leon Goossens, Matyas

Seiber, Antony Hopkins, Alfred Deller and Julian Bream to perform both in the local church and at Cleveland Lodge. The Jeans-Manton collaboration lasted for twelve years. In 1966, the first Boxhill Festival took place in the austere, high-ceilinged music room which Sir James Jeans had himself designed for its special acoustic properties. Capable of seating an audience of nearly a hundred, it houses an important collection of organs, harpsichords and clavichords, which feature prominently in festival performances.

The repertoire is largely made up of rare music uncovered by Lady Jeans or her friends in the course of their musicological researches, and played by them in authentic style. The music is mainly of Renaissance or Baroque origin and includes neglected pieces by composers of repute – Handel, Telemann, Vivaldi, J. S. Bach – as well as those by more minor figures such as J. I. Mueller, Georg Muffat, Sir William Herschel and A. W. Bach. Not, however, that music has to be obscure to be heard at Boxhill: the tercentenaries of Bach and Handel were marked in 1985 with performances of the *Goldberg Variations* and a number of well-known concertos by both composers.

The atmosphere of this exquisite little festival, which – not surprisingly – now casts its audience net much wider than the local community, is essentially relaxed and friendly.

The Gabrieli Quartet and Robert Simpson who composed a quartet
for the centenary of the birth of Sir James Jeans (Susi Jeans standing to right of fireplace).

HASLEMERE

Haslemere can claim to be one of the most celebrated and influential festivals not only in this country but throughout the world. It is also one of Britain's oldest – it first opened its doors in 1925 – and most unusual, in that members of a single family have been its driving force for over six decades.

Arnold Dolmetsch, who though born in France was of Swiss origin, devoted his life – much of it spent busily travelling to and fro across the Atlantic – to reviving interest in early music and musical instruments. In his late sixties he decided to call a halt to his journeys about the world and let instead the world come to him, and with this in mind he instituted a festival at Haslemere, the quiet Surrey town in which he had settled with his family in 1917. The Haslemere staple was from the start, and has remained, the unjustly neglected music of past centuries – in particular the sixteenth, seventeenth and eighteenth – idiomatically performed on period instruments, both original and faithfully reconstructed in the family workshops. Leading figures in the world of the arts, such as Bernard Shaw, Wanda Landowska, Isadora Duncan, Ezra Pound and W. B. Yeats, became Haslemere devotees. In 1932, Percy Grainger described the festival concerts as 'the most liberal musical education I have ever witnessed'.

The Dolmetsch ideal has always been to present early music not as some kind of museum relic, but as an art form as alive and meaningful today as it was to the society that first produced it. That is not to say that scholarship or authenticity has been ignored. On the contrary, much of the music played at Haslemere has come from the Dolmetsch Library, which contains many priceless early manuscripts and original printed editions. Each year has seen first modern performances of music that has been long lost; during the festival's first decade over twelve hundred pieces were played, of which a thousand or so were new to modern listeners. In 1984, works by Albinoni and Benda were revived as part of the sixtieth birthday celebrations.

Responsibility for the Haslemere Festival now rests with Carl Dolmetsch, Arnold's second son, who took over as artistic director on his father's death in 1940, and it is he who heads the family ensemble that plays the bulk of each July's concerts. Each year also sees the participation of eminent guest artists as well as some younger performers on the threshold of their careers. Singers and instrumentalists who have appeared at past festivals include Elizabeth Harwood, Alfred Deller, Robert Spencer, Paul Esswood, Anthony Camden, Sheila Armstrong, Jennifer Bate and Iona Brown.

Arousing the interest of young people in music of all kinds has always been a particular Dolmetsch mission and most years there have been special children's concerts and lectures at which Carl Dolmetsch introduces a variety of early instruments – recorders, viols, lutes – and the music composed for them. In 1984, there was also a revival of sixteenth-century court dances, originally researched by Arnold's wife, Mabel Dolmetsch, and performed by Lucy Graham's Renaissance Dance Company of London.

The range of music played at Haslemere has always been wide and attractive.

The first festival included an all-Bach concert (with keyboard and recorder concertos, string sonatas and pieces from 'The 48' – a programme that was repeated in 1984) and a healthy dose of music from the English golden age. Typical Haslemere seasons might feature evenings devoted to Mozart and his contemporaries, or vocal and instrumental works by Scarlatti, Geminiani and other members of the Italian School, or choral music by Tudor composers. Whatever the offering, however, the things that make this festival special are its continued dedication to an ideal and the infectious sense of enjoyment and involvement which reaches out from the members of one remarkable family to the audiences for whom they play.

YORK EARLY MUSIC FESTIVAL

The *Guardian* has described the York Early Music Festival as 'an event of the first importance, with an unequalled range of ambitious and novel programmes'. The festival came into being in 1977 and immediately established a national reputation for itself. Lasting for two weeks in mid-July, it takes place in three out of every four years – giving way in the fourth to the York Festival and Mystery Plays. Its aims are to explore the enormous repertoire of music from mediaeval to Classical (up to about 1750) and to recreate as closely as possible the sounds that the composers of that

The Rose Consort of Viols at Beningbrough Hall
(National Trust) near York – part of the 'Beningbrough Extravaganza' in the 1985 festival.

music would themselves have known. Concerts and recitals are given on period instruments – or on careful reproductions – and in authentic style, in some of the splendid historical settings that the buildings of York and its environs have to offer. A further aim is to demonstrate that early music is fun and is for everyone, both on a local and a national scale. There is an extensive fringe which is incorporated into the main programme and which involves large numbers of local people in events ranging from stained glass working to storytelling, mediaeval drama to Renaissance cabaret to sixteenth-century dance classes.

Most years the festival works to a theme: when, in 1982, the celebration was of the 250th anniversary of Haydn's birth, the aim was to put the full range of the composer's work into perspective. The works played included, on one hand, the keyboard sonatas (Karen Evans used a piano, David Kershaw a clavichord, Richard Burnett a fortepiano) and, on the other, the large-scale choral works (the *Nelson Mass* and *Salve Regina* given by local forces under Peter Seymour with a solo line-up of Yvonne Seymour, Catherine Denley, Joseph Cornwell and Philip Lawson; *The Creation* entrusted to the Classical Orchestra conducted by Alan Hacker, with Yvonne Seymour, Adrian Thompson and David Thomas). The Fitzwilliam Quartet gave a recital which included the D Minor, Opus 103, and *Lark* Quartets; further keyboard pieces turned up in harpsichord recitals by Trevor Pinnock and Bradford Tracey; Yvonne and Peter Seymour included six of the English canzonets and the cantata *Ariana a Naxos* in their Mozart-Haydn song recital; and Michael Laird played the Trumpet Concerto in a Classical Orchestra concert which also included the *London Symphony*. But 1982 was by no means undiluted Haydn. Other programmes celebrated Schmeltzer, Biber and Muffat; English choral and consort music of the Tudor period; music from the early sixteenth-century Viennese court of Emperor Maximilian I; Bach harpsichord concertos; the Monteverdi *Vespers of 1610*; a pot-pourri of Baroque violin music and an oboe recital which brought together music by Marais and Kalliwoda, Birtwistle and Saxton.

The 1985 festival took as its 'theme' the extraordinary number of composers whose ter- and quatercentenaries fell that year: Bach, Handel, Scarlatti, Tallis, Schütz and George Jeffreys. Performers included the German Baroque group, Musica Antiqua of Cologne; Baroque Brass of London; the Salomon Quartet; and Gothic Voices – not forgetting the perennially excellent Yorkshire Bach Choir and Baroque Soloists. As in previous years, there were special early music workshops for children, plus a Baroque dance workshop (presided over by Belinda Quirey) and – in the beautiful grounds of Beningbrough Hall – a final 'extravaganza' with fire-eaters, jugglers, jousts, masques, a mediaeval treasure-hunt and a plethora of musical activities. York Early Music days are full to overflowing, and enthusiasts find their time well and truly occupied.

A typical Saturday in 1985 started with the Salomon Quartet playing a Classical programme in the restored mediaeval Guildhall at 11 a.m.; two hours later, a brisk trot away at All Saints' Church, the Chapter House Choir sang the first notes of their selection from Byrd, Tallis and Victoria; Caspar the Storyteller regaled an audience made up of both young and old with tales from the Arthurian cycle in the Museum Gardens at 2 p.m. Those with enough energy to get back to the Guildhall for six in the evening could hear and see Estampie in a costumed recital of Renaissance music from 'court, chamber and street'. The main concert of the evening, however, was at the Church of St Michael-le-Belfry where the Yorkshire Bach Choir and Baroque Soloists under Peter Seymour gave a performance of Bach's B Minor Mass – while for those who preferred to end their crowded day with drama, the Lords of Misrule were engaged in a double-bill of *Everyman* (in original Middle English) and *The Blessed Apple Tree* at the Micklegate Arts Centre.

. . . *Modern*

CHELTENHAM

The Cheltenham International Festival of Music, as it is now known, came into being in 1945 as a direct result of the anxiety of Cheltenham residents to keep their town on the map. Its original importance as a spa and health resort had been declining for some years, and now the National Health Service seemed about to bury it for good. How, then, to keep visitors coming to the place? How to let the

Cheltenham Festival 1957: (*left to right*) William Wordsworth (the composer), Michael Kennedy (critic and author of *The Concise Oxford Dictionary of Music* and biographical studies of Vaughan Williams, Elgar and Britten), Mrs Kennedy, and Ralph and Ursula Vaughan Williams.

world know that Cheltenham still existed? The answer they came up with might at first glance have seemed an unlikely – not to say eccentric – one: genteel, conservative Cheltenham was to be the home for a festival of contemporary music. But it was from the start – and remains – a resounding success. What the organizers did was to identify a distinct gap in British musical life and set about filling it.

Originally occupying ten days at the height of the summer season, in 1980 the festival was extended to a fortnight and began to include in its programmes music from the Classical and Romantic repertoire alongside the strictly contemporary. The esoteric musical press had something of a field day, accusing the organizers of abandoning their principles. But, in fact, the quantity of new music played was not reduced at all – the number of concerts was simply increased, making room for Brahms and Schumann alongside Tippett and Birtwistle. That said, there is a good deal of truth in the notion that Huddersfield stands in 1986 where Cheltenham stood in 1945 as contemporary music flag-bearer. The position can perhaps be best summed up in the words of Cheltenham's festival organizer, Jeremy Tyndall, who suggests that if Huddersfield is the place to go to hear *radical* new music, Cheltenham continues to hold its corner as champion of the *classical* new music. His festival is not exclusively for the specialist contemporary music lover: it aims to offer the more adventurous element of the general concert-going public the opportunity for intellectual stimulation and involvement. Even if, after a concert in Cheltenham Town Hall, audiences go away uncertain or disturbed, they will at least have responded in some measure to the sounds of the twentieth century. And that is what the organizers are after.

But how to avoid putting people off in the first place? How to draw them to listen to new music? That is where star performers and balanced programming have their part to play: if the visitor to Cheltenham has misgivings about the difficulty of some of the music he will encounter, these will almost certainly be offset by the knowledge that he will have the chance to hear internationally known soloists and ensembles in performance and that the contemporary diet will be complemented with music that is both familiar and palatable to him.

The opening concert of the 1983 festival illustrates the working and success of this policy very clearly. The season marked the eightieth birthday of the festival's president, Sir Lennox Berkeley, and the opening piece was a set of sixteen variations on a theme from his opera *Ruth* specially commissioned from sixteen young composers who had at one time or another been his pupils. This was followed by Webern's Passacaglia and Berkeley's own Flute Concerto. James Galway, who had been engaged to play the latter piece, also volunteered to play the Flute Sonata by Poulenc in Sir Lennox's orchestration – a very happy and appropriate suggestion – and it was decided that this should open the second half of the concert. The evening was rounded off with Brahms's *St Antoni Variations*. The concert cost something in the region of £15000 to put on – so it could in no way have been expected to make a profit, in spite of the fact that it attracted a capacity audience. But the sense of occasion – the opening night, Berkeley's birthday, the new commission, the appear-

Tribute to Lennox Berkeley on his eightieth birthday in 1983: Sir Lennox (*centre*) with some of the sixteen composers who contributed a variation on the Reapers' Chorus from his opera *Ruth*. His son, Michael Berkeley, is on his left.

ance by James Galway – was immense. Nor did the music, though largely modern and unfamiliar, make excessive demands on the listeners, whose response was warm and enthusiastic. The evening was typical in every respect of what the Cheltenham Festival has come to represent in recent years.

Cheltenham, for all that it is promoted jointly by its own arts festival company and the local borough council, is not a community festival. Its aim is not, unlike its counterparts in Chichester and Exeter, primarily to provide for the musical needs of the local residents, though at least half of its box-office revenue comes from music-lovers who live within a fifty-mile radius of the town (which, of course, includes the cities of Birmingham, Bristol and Oxford). 'The Cheltenham Festival,' Jeremy Tyndall points out, 'could have happened anywhere.' It is not a product of the town or its surrounding area or the tastes of the people who live there. It does not raise money for local causes or employ local musicians. It draws, instead, on funds made available by the Arts Council, the borough council and private sponsorship to provide an important national forum for music which might otherwise, if left to the regular concert seasons of the large orchestras, never be performed. There are occasions – it would be odd if there were not – when the musicians, hired at great expense, find themselves playing to half-empty halls. It is not, however, financial success that concerns the festival organizers, so much as artistic integrity. 'In our opinion, the music we programme deserves to be heard and to be acknowledged. If we don't do it, there are precious few other organizations that will.'

The festival has always had a reputation for commissioning new works from both emerging and established composers: 1985, for example, saw the unveiling of

Cheltenham Town Hall was the setting for this concert by the Stockholm Sinfonietta conducted by Jukka-Pekka Saraste with soloist Christian Tetzlaff (violin) in 1985.

Graham Whettam's *Symphonic Prelude* and Robin Holloway's Harp Concerto. It is also strong on programming hitherto unperformed works that it has not been responsible for commissioning, especially if they fit into the thematic scheme being adopted for the particular year. Second, third and later performances of recent music also feature in Cheltenham concerts, though the planners are sometimes less enthusiastic about mounting these, because they attract less of the critical and media attention on which the festival to some extent relies. A first performance gets the critics down from London, very often secures BBC coverage, has a sense of occasion – usually with the composer in attendance at both rehearsals and performance. Such things keep a festival like Cheltenham very much in the public eye. A second performance, while important to the composer and interesting in itself, is in many ways just another performance.

Cheltenham is a town of festivals, yet it is in some respects not a festival town. In the course of the year, festivals of one sort or another follow each other in rapid succession, the music festival taking its turn with the rest. Yet there is seldom much sign elsewhere in this spacious, elegant town that great things are going on in the Town Hall on Imperial Square or in the Pittville Pump Room. Visitors may come from Europe or the United States or Japan to attend one of the most prestigious concerts of the musical year, while the locals know little or nothing of what is happening. However regrettable that might be, it in no way alters the fact that the townsfolk of Cheltenham have on their very doorsteps, for two summer weeks each year, one of the most exciting and innovative music festivals in the world.

Teresa Cahill and Robert Saxton
TRIALS AND TRIUMPHS

Festivals have meant a great deal to Teresa Cahill and Robert Saxton in their respective careers as singer and composer, and they talk with both affection and amusement about their experiences. One thing in particular on which they agree is that the best festivals are like people – each having its own distinct personality – and that they have an uncanny way of mirroring in their pace, programming and mood the places which give them birth.

Teresa Cahill speaks warmly of Malvern, whose countryside and atmosphere and devotion to Elgar and all his works make it for her just what a festival should be. She recalls the heady emotion of a particular Malvern concert: 'It was *King Olaf*, in the Winter Gardens, with Vernon Handley conducting. The reception was tumultuous and we all, soloists, chorus and orchestra, got our share of audience acclaim – except Tod Handley who seemed reluctant to take his own, well-deserved bow. In the end, we managed to push him out on to the platform alone; but when he got there, instead of acknowledging the applause, he picked up Elgar's score and held it high above his head for everyone to see – as if to say "It's not me you should be clapping, but Elgar's music and genius." The audience, of course, went wild – I really thought the old cliché about bringing the house down was about to come true. It was all very moving.'

Aldeburgh has similar memories, though rather lower-keyed, for Robert Saxton – who, as a precocious nine year old had written to Britten and been summoned to the Red House for lessons. He was pleased when, in 1984, Oliver Knussen asked him to choose and introduce a programme given by members of the London Sinfonietta in the intimate setting of the Jubilee Hall. 'It was a memorable occasion for me – I think I knew personally most of the people in the audience. And it was especially good to get back to something of the modest scaling of earlier Aldeburgh festivals; definitely *not* Snape-glossy and star-studded. Actually and very satisfyingly run on a shoestring.' For Saxton, this was festival music-making at its most purposeful – a sharp contrast to the emptiness of another recent occasion at a well-known international festival, where audience apathy and lack of any real festival spirit led to Rostropovich playing to a mere hundred people in a hall capable to holding many times that number.

Festival inadequacies sometimes have a more personal impact on Teresa Cahill, who has experienced any number of inconveniences both behind the scenes and on stage: icy vestries with poor lighting, no hanging space or mirror, no room to lay out make-up, and which have to be shared by male and female soloists; or that particular brand of hospitality which is known in the business as 'festival hostility' – 'You know the sort of thing: you're met off the train by some complete stranger who tells you that you're not as pretty as your picture and that last year they had so-and-so singing for them (implying that they don't expect you to be as good).' And the settings chosen for festive concerts sometimes call for prolonged exercise of the stiff upper lip. She remembers sitting in the pulpit of Westminster Abbey, for example, clutching a hot-water-bottle throughout one particular Elgar celebration, and recounts, more in sorrow than anger, her experiences at a well-meaning new festival whose organizers had never arranged a solo recital before. 'To begin with, they had arranged it out of doors, in the romantic ruins of an old abbey, with a tarpaulin over the performing area in case of bad weather. That in itself was just as well because it poured for most of the concert. What made things worse, though, was that the water collected in the tarpaulin above my head and eventually began to cascade in a heavy curtain between me and the audience. I was vaguely aware that there were people listening to me somewhere out there, but how much they heard I really don't know. At least they will have heard the accompaniment though, because the organizers – for reasons best known to themselves – had supplied Roger Vignoles with an amplified electronic grand piano!'

Teresa Cahill has, however, a lasting love and respect for music festivals, in spite of the fact that they sometimes entail as many trials as triumphs. Like many another young singer, she owes an immense debt to the training she received with the Glyndebourne Festival Opera, and she speaks appreciatively of the contribution to British musical life made by those émigrés from Europe – Strasser, Gui, Busch, Ebert – who during the forties and fifties set and maintained the superlative standards of performance for which Glyndebourne has become a byword. 'People say that Glyndebourne is not the place for big names, but it's worth remembering that many of today's great singers – Pavarotti, Freni and Sutherland among them – got their early experience and encouragement there. It's a wonderful nursery and we all owe it so much.'

Like many another young British composer, Robert Saxton values festivals especially as platforms for new music. He has been composer-in-residence at Huddersfield and recently had new pieces performed at Harrogate (his *Traumstadt* was played by the Koenig Ensemble), Cheltenham and the Proms, where in 1984 Sir John Pritchard with the BBC Symphony Orchestra introduced his *Concerto for Orchestra*. Both he and Teresa Cahill agree on the special character of the Proms audience, whether it is erupting enthusiastically at the end of a Beethoven Ninth or *Elijah*, or listening with rapt attentiveness to something entirely new and untried. 'They must surely be the most amazing and rewarding audience in the world – festival or no festival – and that's really saying something!'

HUDDERSFIELD CONTEMPORARY MUSIC FESTIVAL

Since its inception in 1978, the Huddersfield Contemporary Music Festival has established itself as one of the most important events in the musical calendar. For a short while, until the arrival of the infant Almeida and Nettlefold festivals in London, it was the only British festival devoted specifically to contemporary music.

Its guiding genius is Richard Steinitz, music lecturer at Huddersfield Polytechnic, who has worked miracles in securing the funding and attracting the audiences to enable what was originally a modest five-day event to double its length and triple its scope. His policy has been to present new music in the best possible light, wooing audiences with concerts that are so varied, stimulating and brilliantly performed as to persuade them that the pilgrimage to Huddersfield is worth any amount of time and effort. He wants them to see that, far from being tedious or difficult, today's music has – at its best – a powerful directness, a revelatory vigour that makes it as spiritually and emotionally satisfying and as entertaining as great music has always been. The festival is promoted jointly by Kirklees Leisure Services and Huddersfield Polytechnic and performances are shared between the 150-year-old St Paul's Hall – a modestly elegant auditorium which used to be the Polytechnic's campus church – and a number of other venues scattered in the near vicinity. A feeling of intimacy and involvement is very much part of the festival's special appeal.

The history of Huddersfield has been punctuated with remarkable coups. The opening season in 1978, for instance, made headlines by attracting the American composer, George Crumb, to make his first-ever professional visit to Britain to lecture and attend performances of a number of his major scores, including the solo Cello Sonata (played by Rohan de Saram), *Black Angels* for electric string quartet (given by the Gaudeamus Quartet), *Voice of the Whale* and *Dream Sequence* (performed by Dreamtiger) – the last of these pieces receiving its European première. The 1983 festival featured a visit by Crumb's fellow-countryman, Elliott Carter, in his seventy-fifth year (the Arditti Quartet played his Second and Third Quartets, The Fires of London his *Triple Duo* and *Night Fantasies*, and the BBC Philharmonic Orchestra under José Serebrier his First Symphony), while the European tradition was represented by Hans Werner Henze, who – among other things – conducted *The Miracle of the Rose* and *Cantata della Fiaba Estrema*, and supervised the first staging of his *Labyrinth* (1951) by the Northern Music Theatre.

Other notable visitors to Huddersfield have included Henri Dutilleux, Iannis Xenakis, Harrison Birtwistle, and – in 1984 – Maurice Kagel and Peter Maxwell Davies. Such 'personal appearances' have had a magnetic effect. 'As with a one-man art exhibition, concentration upon a single composer can,' Steinitz points out, 'deepen and enrich one's understanding through the presence of many complementary aspects of his vision.' But that does not mean that the festival lacks variety: on the contrary, 1984 alone included performances of over sixty compositions by forty-five living British composers.

In 1985 the festival celebrated the sixtieth birthday of the Italian composer, Luciano Berio, with performances of his Sequenza II for Harp (soloist Francis Pierre, to whom Berio dedicated the work), *Circles*, one of the most inventive avant-garde scores of the 1960s, and *Folk Songs*, in which the BBC Symphony Orchestra and Singers were conducted by Berio himself.

Francis Pierre, dedicatee of Berio's Harp Sequenza which he played at the 1985 Huddersfield Festival.

The percussion trio Le Cercle from Paris playing *Tribadaboum* by Vinko Globokar at the 1984 Huddersfield Festival.

A recent development has been the festival's bold and exhilarating presentation of music-theatre, exploring the drama that is part of the very nature of music and the tendency that music has to merge with art forms such as movement and gesture. Memorable occasions have included Gemini's double-bill of Nigel Osborne's *Vienna, Zurich, Constance* and Margaret Lucy Williams's *Struwwelpeter*, Northern Music Theatre in Kagel's *Kontra-Danse* and Maxwell Davies's haunting *Vesalii Icones* with Tom Yang and The Fires of London.

The Huddersfield Contemporary Music Festival has, in the short space of eight years, established itself as a national institution. To quote the *Observer*, this is 'no milksop provincial affair defining as contemporary anything since Tchaikovsky, but a proper display of modern music'. Critics have been unanimous in hailing the festival's enterprise and vision in providing audiences with the opportunity to hear live and in as near-ideal conditions as possible a full and rich cross-section of the music of our time.

——Leeds Twentieth Century Music——

Leeds Twentieth Century Music Week is a child of the eighties. A biennial festival, it is next due to appear in 1987. Its philosophy is to present a miscellany of major currents in the music of this century rather than concentrating on any one style or school. Stravinsky rubs shoulders with Rachmaninov, Henze with Albéniz. Walton shares programmes with Webern, Berio with Ravel. There are jazz sessions, chamber recitals, concerts including large-scale symphonic works, organ recitals, lectures, first performances, electronic workshops – the aim being both to suit and surprise all tastes. In 1983, the festival included a string quartet competition, designed to inspire a new look at an established musical form.

The main programmes take place of an evening, though some talks and recitals occupy mid-morning and afternoon slots. Leeds Town Hall, the Clothworkers' Hall of Leeds University and the Institute Gallery at the City of Leeds College of Music are the principal venues. Each year works to a central theme – in 1983, the focus was on the rise of modernism from the perspective of pre-First World War Vienna. Mahler's Fifth and Tenth Symphonies dominated the week (the former given by Andrew Davis with his Toronto Symphony Orchestra, the latter by the City of Birmingham Symphony Orchestra under Simon Rattle, in a programme that also contained Britten's *Sinfonia da Requiem*) and Schoenberg, Berg and Webern were well represented, while papers were presented on the achievement of Schreker, Szymanowski and Zemlinsky. On a rather different tack, the Leodian String Quartet appeared with Jack Brymer in Bliss's Clarinet Quintet and the Leodian Wind Quintet played music by William Mathias and Malcolm Williamson. Another chamber group, Anemone, explored more radical contemporary repertoire – Vic Hoyland's String Quartet and Harrison Birtwistle's *Silbury Air*.

The central thread of the 1985 programme was French music, from Debussy and Satie, by way of Varèse and Milhaud, to Messiaen. Indeed, the week culminated in Messiaen's *Des Canyons aux Étoiles*, given by the London Sinfonietta conducted by Elgar Howarth, while an earlier recital by Peter Hill was devoted to the same composer's *Catalogue d'Oiseaux* and Jane Manning included his *Poèmes pour Mi* in a recital which featured British premières of pieces by Simon Emmerson, Melvyn Poore and Alison Bauld. Ravel's Quartet in F was the concluding work in a recital by the Lindsay String Quartet, Milhaud's Symphonies 1–3 featured in a pair of concerts by the Music Department Orchestra of Leeds University, and Debussy's *En blanc et noir* was played by Julian Dawson-Lyell and Andrew Ball. There was also music by Berlioz (the *Corsaire* Overture opened the concert by the BBC Philharmonic Orchestra under Edward Downes), Poulenc, Satie, Pierné, Koechlin – and Jane Parker-Smith included pieces by Dupré, Widor and Duruflé in her Town Hall organ recital.

Leeds Twentieth Century Music Week has a good deal to be said for it – interestingly balanced programmes, intelligent overall planning, first-rate performances. But one of its most welcome and surprising characteristics is the fact that –

thanks to the generosity of its principal sponsors, the City of Leeds College of Music, the Music Department of Leeds University and the City of Leeds Leisure Services, admission to about half the events each year is entirely free.

NORWICH FESTIVAL OF
——————CONTEMPORARY CHURCH MUSIC——————

This is a very new festival, the first having been held as recently as 1981, the second two years later. It is at present uncertain whether a biennial or triennial pattern will evolve, but 1986 has been earmarked for further activities. The artistic directors of the festival are Peter Aston (Professor of Music at the University of East Anglia) and Michael Nicholas (organist of Norwich Cathedral), who set out with three interlinked aims for their undertaking. These were (and are) to provide a focus for new church music, to stimulate more composers not merely to write for the Church but to do so in genuinely contemporary style, and to encourage the performance of such music both professionally and by amateurs. The festival strikes a fair balance between workshop sessions and concerts, with the daily choral services in Norwich Cathedral forming an integral part of the programme. Distinct themes also link the various events of the three days and, as a special feature, there is a composers' competition, the winning entry for which is performed in the course of the festival.

In 1983, Gregory Rose (director of Singcircle) lectured on vocal techniques in contemporary music, there was a seminar on the question of what the Church asks of composers and Alan Wilson rehearsed his Norwich Service (a festival commission) at a choral workshop. There was also an exploration of electro-acoustic resources in an electronic studio at the Music Centre of the University of East Anglia. Electronic music featured prominently during the festival, not least at Singcircle's concert of music by Richard Orton, Jonty Harrison, Luciano Berio and Jonathan Harvey. At a second concert, given by the Canterbury Cathedral Choir, music by Poulenc, Messiaen, Maxwell-Davies, Patterson and the festival's president, Lennox Berkeley, was performed. Richard Orton's Mass for Voices, Tape and Organ, another festival commission, was given a first hearing at Sung Eucharist in the Cathedral on the final day, while music by Giles Swayne, James MacMillan (the competition winner), Peter Aston and Gordon Crosse was performed at other services in the course of the festival.

Though a number of festival events take place in other buildings – notably at the university and in the United Reformed Church Hall – part of the fascination of these three July days is to hear avant-garde compositions in the sharply contrasted setting of Norwich's exquisite mediaeval cathedral. A mind-focusing experience.

Festivals in Wales

Music runs in the veins of the Welsh – so much so that it might be supposed that the majority of them can sing before they have learned to speak. From Sunday chapel, from mid-week village hall or working-men's club, the melancholy-sweet strains of the male-voice choir echo down the valleys to stir the soul as it did Elgar's nearly a century ago. We have Wales to thank for some of today's finest singers – Margaret Price, Gwynneth Jones, Helen Watts, Stuart Burrows, Geraint Evans, Gwynne Howell – and, in William Mathias, Alun Hoddinott and Daniel Jones, for some of our most prolific composers.

Welsh festivals are not very great in number, but they have a proud record of pursuing their objectives – such as bringing music to far-flung communities, encouraging native Welsh composers and performers, nurturing young and emerging talent – in the most whole-hearted fashion imaginable. They mostly blossom on the edges of the principality – at Cardiff, Llandaff, Llantilio Crossenny, Rhymney, Swansea and in the Vale of Glamorgan in the deep South; clinging to the western seaboard at Barmouth and Fishguard; at Llangollen, with its international eisteddfod, and St Asaph in the North. The Welsh-language Royal National Eisteddfod (early August) travels about the country with its five-thousand-seat pavilion and its annual programme of competitions, concerts, plays and pageants (Rhyl in 1985, Fishguard in 1986). In the heartland, little seems to be stirring, except for one September week at Llandrindod Wells and at Presteigne, on the very border with England, where Michael Berkeley is active and enlightened president.

BARMOUTH

Gŵyl Celfyddydau Y Bermo – the Barmouth Arts Festival – started life over ten years ago, dedicated to concentrating into two September weeks a variety of cultural activities to suit all tastes and ages. The little Merioneth seaside town, with its famous railway viaduct and child-beckoning sands, nestles beside the cliffs of Dinas Oleu and looks out on some of the most dramatic mountain scenery in the British Isles.

The festival, catering principally for the local community, is centred on the town's Dragon Theatre and usually opens with speeches, a concert and a civic reception, complete with buffet. Chamber groups dominate the musical side of things, the players coming both from the region and from further afield. In recent years, the Paganini Trio (guitar, viola and cello), the Intermezzo Piano Quartet and the Fine Arts Brass Ensemble have been engaged to perform. Recitalists have included Richard Greenwood (piano) playing a programme of Bach, Schubert, Beethoven and Chopin, and David Cowley (principal oboe of the BBC Welsh Symphony Orchestra) accompanied by Bryan Evans. Opera on a similarly intimate scale usually takes up a night or two – one year it was the enterprising Pavilion Opera with its company of young singers that gave performances of *Don Pasquale* and *The Marriage of Figaro* to piano accompaniment; on another occasion, the London Operetta Ensemble (including Elizabeth Bainbridge and Dennis Wicks) sang Gilbert and Sullivan. Sometimes dance gets a look in, as when in 1984 the Welsh company, Jumpers, gave a programme ranging 'from art to popular'.

Other regular features at Barmouth are children's entertainments, lectures, Welsh evenings, exhibitions and organized afternoon walks up into the splendours of those high, wild hills. A small festival with modest objectives, but one that gives a good deal of thought to its planning and a good deal of pleasure to the folk who cling to this craggy edge of Wales.

CARDIFF

The Cardiff Festival radiates its glow in late November and early December each year, just when the Welsh winter is beginning to settle in. It was founded in 1967 with composer Alun Hoddinott and pianist John Ogdon (for the first two years) as joint artistic directors. Based on the Music Department of University College, Cardiff, it was conceived both as an extension of the work of the department and also as a means of widening the musical horizons of a then rather blinkered Welsh capital. The five concerts of the 1967 season were housed in the Reardon Smith Lecture Theatre of the National Museum of Wales, the City Hall and the New Theatre. The lack of concert halls both large and small within the city was very obvious and limited the scope of the festival in a number of directions. However, the high standards of this initial venture were immediately reflected in concerts by artists of the calibre of John Ogdon, Cleo Laine, John Dankworth and the City of Birmingham Symphony Orchestra under Hugo Rignold.

Artistic policy for the future was also laid down at this time – varied programmes by international artists (these, over the years, have included Vladimir Ashkenazy, Clifford Curzon, Louis Kentner, Radu Lupu, Vlado Perlemuter, Stephen Bishop-Kovacevich, Stuart Burrows, Victoria de los Angeles, Geraint Evans, Peter Pears, Margaret Price, Julian Bream, John Williams, Wanda Wilkomirska, Bronislav Gimpel, Ida Haendel, Ruggiero Ricci, Paul Tortelier and Barry Tuckwell); a high proportion of twentieth-century music set in its historical and chronological context; the encouragement of composers, established and young, Welsh and non-Welsh, achieved by the commissioning of new works (these have included pieces by Malcolm

Arnold, Michael Berkeley, Peter Racine Fricker, John Gardner, David Harries, John McCabe, John Manduell, William Mathias, John Metcalf, Alan Rawsthorne, Humphrey Searle, Grace Williams and Malcolm Williamson), the programming of premières (Britten, Maxwell Davies, Hoddinott, Ogdon, and Randall Thompson); and the performance of works rarely found in the traditional concert repertoire. The Cardiff Festival also seeks to encourage young (especially, though not exclusively, Welsh) artists, to use the gifts of musicians resident in Cardiff and its environs, and to draw into the orbit of festival activity young people within the area – a recurring feature has been the use of school choirs and orchestras in festival concerts.

In 1968, the festival made a modest expansion with a total of eight concerts and new venues at Cardiff Castle and Eglwys Dewi Sant. There were no fewer than eight first performances and special seminars included discussion of their works by Peter Maxwell Davies and William Mathias. The first major growth, however, came in 1970 with the opening of University College Music Department's new building, containing a purpose-built concert hall with seating for five hundred, an organ and two grand pianos. That year, the festival presented opera for the first time (the Welsh première of Stravinsky's *The Soldier's Tale* given by the London Sinfonietta and artists from the National Theatre). The ensuing years have seen a consolidation of the festival in the musical life of South Wales and an increase in the number of concerts given under its umbrella. Of particular importance has been the opening, in 1982, of Cardiff's St David's Hall, arguably one of the finest concert halls in Europe and one that is capable of housing works on the grandest scale (such as Mahler's *Resurrection* Symphony, given in 1984 by the London Symphony Orchestra

St David's Hall, Cardiff, opened in 1982,
is one of the finest concert halls in Europe and capable of housing works on the grandest scale.

and Chorus with Benita Valente and Maureen Forrester under the direction of Gilbert Kaplan).

Recent years have also seen expansion in the areas of workshop experience (Oliver Knussen and Stephen Walsh presided over a composers' day in 1982, while two years later there was a programme of seminars, lectures and demonstrations culminating in a concert of music by George Benjamin) and festival participation by locally based groups, schools and youth organizations (West Glamorgan Youth Orchestra, Cardiff University Choral and Orchestral Society, South Glamorgan Youth Orchestra and Choir). This has in no way stemmed the flow of major professional ensembles that have come to perform at Cardiff: as well as most of the important British orchestras there have been several foreign visitors, including the Württemberg Chamber Orchestra, the Berlin Radio Symphony Orchestra, the Polish Radio Symphony Orchestra, the Radio Telefis Eirann Symphony Orchestra, the USSR State Symphony Orchestra, the Stuttgart Philharmonic and the Oslo Philharmonic, under such eminent conductors as Rudolf Kempe, André Previn, Andrew Davis, Wilfried Boettcher, Neville Marriner, Ivan Fischer, Yevgeny Svetlanov, Sir Georg Solti, Mariss Yansons and Eduardo Mata.

FISHGUARD
GŴYL GERDD ABERGWAUN

Fishguard Festival sprang to vigorous life in 1970 and almost immediately launched on a policy of commissioning major works from distinguished composers – Desmond Bradley, Alun Hoddinott, Daniel Jones, John McCabe, William Mathias, Trevor Roberts, Richard Rodney Bennett – several of them with strong Welsh connections. It was the brain-child of John Davies, conductor of the Dyfed Choir, and it is he who has masterminded its triumphant development ever since.

Fishguard itself is an unexpected, yet at the same time natural, setting for so ambitious a venture – a picturesque port, its wide cliff-sheltered bay is haven for the ferries that ply the Irish Sea. The festival takes place in late July, when tourist traffic is at its peak and when the surrounding Pembrokeshire coastline, with its dramatic alternation of towering headlands and peaceful coves, is at its most appealing. The concert hall at Fishguard School is the setting for most of the concerts and recitals, though local churches also play their part and large-scale choral works (including the Verdi *Requiem*, *The Dream of Gerontius*, *Messiah*, Bach's B Minor Mass, as well as Mathias's recent *This Worlde's Joie*) are given in the magnificent surroundings of St David's Cathedral, a dozen or so miles down the coast. As well as music, Fishguard regularly features poetry, film and the visual arts, and crams up to fifteen major events into its eight-day duration.

Native Welsh performers have always been popular with Fishguard audiences – Sir Geraint Evans, Gwynne Howell, Margaret Price, the BBC Welsh Symphony Orchestra and, of course, the Dyfed Choir with John Davies himself – but there is nothing parochial about the festival, and visitors are as likely to encounter the LSO, the Bournemouth Symphony Orchestra, the Academy of St Martin-in-the-Fields with Berglund or Kegel, Hickox or Willcocks, and soloists of international note such as Peter Frankl, Mayumi Fujikawa, Maurice Hasson, Rafael Orozco, Cristina Ortiz, Cécile Ousset, Michel Béroff and Gyorgy Pauk. Jazz and popular music are also well served, past performers including Larry Adler, the Pasadena Roof Orchestra, the Swingle Singers and Stan Tracey.

The Fishguard pattern incorporates music to suit all tastes, with the exception of opera – which does, however, make an appearance on film. St David's choral concerts usually begin and end the season (in 1985 a programme including the Bach *Magnificat* started the proceedings and *Messiah* with the Royal Liverpool Philharmonic Orchestra and soloists Marie McLaughlin, Alfreda Hodgson, Keith Lewis and Gwynne Howell rounded them off), but purely orchestral evenings also play an important part in the festival programming. Recent years have seen John Georgiadis presiding over a Viennese concert; Maurice Handford conducting Mathias (*Dance Overture*), Brahms (the First Piano Concerto with Peter Donohoe) and Beethoven; and Herbert Kegel giving the first performance of Desmond Bradley's Symphony No. 3 in a programme with the BBC Welsh Symphony Orchestra that also included works by Mendelssohn and Brahms. Chamber music and solo recitals also have their place in the week's activities – from the Fitzwilliam Quartet playing Shostakovich, Borodin and Beethoven, via Michael Collins (clarinet) and Ian Brown (piano) in a mixed bag of high Romantic and accessible modern, to Michel Béroff in Bach, Schumann and idiomatic Debussy.

It could be said that, except in the area of its commissions, Fishguard is not greatly innovative in its programming. But that is not necessarily the point: like a number of other festivals (notably Newbury), it exists to bring outstanding musicians and high standards of performance to an area of the country that might otherwise be culturally forlorn. And it is none the worse for that.

LLANDAFF

Llandaff, once a proud cathedral city in its own right, is now part of the suburbs of the Welsh capital, Cardiff. Its festival was founded in 1958, at the instigation of the Friends of the Cathedral, to coincide with the restoration of the Lady Chapel and Sanctuary of the ancient building, which had been severely damaged during the Second World War. The festival runs for eight days in early June and for many years was responsible for filling serious gaps in the musical life of the region. The Cathedral itself has always been the main focus of activities, the organizers undertaking the complicated task of erecting staging against the West Door, and turning the seating round to face it, to create an adequate auditorium for both chamber recitals and large-scale choral and orchestral works. Significantly, the first two festivals were known as the Llandaff Cathedral Festival of Music and the greater part of the programmes were designed to suit the venue. There were organ recitals by Jeanne Demessieux and Francis Jackson, concerts (which included organ concertos) by the Philomusica of London, performances of Handel's dramatic oratorios *Esther* and *Jephtha*, of Christopher Fry's play *The Firstborn* (involving the Student Theatre Company of the Welsh College of Music and Drama), and of Cherubini's *Requiem* by the Treorci Male Choir.

The change of designation to the Llandaff Festival in 1960 did not, however, lead to overnight secularization of the programmes. For some years, there continued to be a regular flow of religious works, many of them specially commissioned – *Heaven cannot hold Him* (the life of Christ in words and music devised by the Ven. J. G. James, Archdeacon of Llandaff) and *The Race of Man*, a music-theatre work combining music, word and dance, by Alun Hoddinott. Similar works were commissioned from William Mathias (his masque *St Teilo*, 1963), Owain Arwel Hughes (*St Francis*, 1965), Daniel Jones (the oratorio *St Peter*) and Grace Williams (*Missa Cambrensis*).

It was not until 1966 that the principal emphasis at Llandaff came to be on concert performance – the big symphony orchestras from London, Liverpool, Bournemouth, Birmingham, Manchester and Cardiff itself (under such conductors as Sir Adrian Boult, Sir Charles Groves, Kurt Sanderling, Norman Del Mar, Walter Weller, Paavo Berglund and Seiji Ozawa) dominating the programmes in the Cathedral, and international stars drawing capacity audiences both there and at other venues throughout the city – Claudio Arrau, Henryk Szeryng, Robert Casadesus, Tamás Vásáry, Moura Lympany, Geraint Evans, Janet Baker, Christian Ferras, Geza Anda, Artur Rubinstein, Victoria de los Angeles, Yehudi Menuhin, Isaac Stern, Julius Katchen, Paul Tortelier, Josef Suk, Lazar Berman, John Lill.

Since 1982 and the opening of Cardiff's grand new St David's Hall, the festival organizers have been faced with the twin facts that the Cathedral is no longer the only or the best place in the city in which to listen to orchestral music and that much more music is available in Cardiff today than was the case in the late 1950s. Concerts are still mounted under the imposing gaze of Epstein's figure of Christ in Majesty, but there has been a shift back to performances which underline the Cathedral's spiritual and cultural contribution to the life of the area. In 1983, for instance, a major event was the enacting of Britten's Church Parable *The Burning Fiery Furnace* by the Llandaff Cathedral Choral Society and the Cambridge Opera Group, while the Choir of Christ Church, Oxford, came to sing Taverner, Byrd, Bach, Walton, Messiaen and Hoddinott. In the future, sacred choral concerts, cathedral music and religious music-drama will form the nucleus of festival planning under the newly appointed director, George Guest. It is to be hoped that there will be no cutting back on new commissions and first performances under the new dispensation, and that many new pieces will be added to a list which already includes symphonies by Daniel Jones, William Mathias and Robin Orr, Alun Hoddinott's Organ Concerto, Mathias's Harp Concerto and David Harries's Piano Concerto, as well as many smaller-scale works.

LLANTILIO CROSSENNY

It was the much-loved conductor Mansel Thomas who, in 1961, laid the foundations of this charming little festival held on the first weekend in May at the twelfth-century Church of St Teilo at Llantilio Crossenny. What started life as a single carol concert has grown into a tapestry of chamber and orchestral music interwoven with poetry and opera.

Proceedings begin on the Thursday evening with a recital of vocal or instrumental music; this is followed on Saturday by an evening of staged opera – for many years in the capable hands of the Handel Opera Society of London, whose conductor, Charles Farncombe, is now the festival's artistic director; Sunday afternoon is given over to an orchestral concert given by players from professional symphony orchestras and soloists of international standing. The range of music is wide, from Handel to Beethoven, Mozart to Poulenc, Schumann to the moderns, with new works (such as Mansel Thomas's *Cri'r Wylan*) occasionally taking the limelight.

Michael Berkeley
NEW MUSIC: THE LIFEBLOOD OF FESTIVALS

For the past few years, composer Michael Berkeley has been president of a modest music festival in the Welsh town of Presteigne. He sees it not as a vehicle for the performance of his own work, but as an opportunity for bringing all kinds of people together to make music. The festival employs amateur talent to the full – and is especially fond of involving children – along with imported professionals. But he does not regard the latter as a prop for amateur musicians to lean on: 'The experience of working as a group,' he insists, 'is a very valuable one for both sides.' As a composer, he enjoys writing for amateur performers: 'It focuses the mind and makes you think very carefully about what you are trying to do and how best to achieve it.' But this should not be interpreted as any kind of talking down to his singers and players – 'Far from it. I don't believe a composer should ever lower his artistic sights just because his performers are not paid-up, full-time professionals. That would be death.'

Though his own music is played at Presteigne, Berkeley is anxious that new music by local and other living composers should feature largely in the programmes, as well as music from other centuries. He believes firmly that all music festivals – no matter how long or recently established and whatever their scale of operations – should feature new music. 'New music is the lifeblood of festivals; without it they cannot hope to survive.' He has, indeed, been commissioned to write new pieces for a number of the more venerable institutions, including the Three Choirs, Cheltenham and Edinburgh – though he had an unfortunate experience with the powers that be at Edinburgh over one particular work. This was a piece originally commissioned for the festival by the Scottish Chamber Orchestra, of which Berkeley was at the time composer-in-residence. When he was about half way through its composition, the city fathers decided that it should be dropped from the programme on the grounds that Edinburgh audiences were not yet ready for 'modern' music – music as modern as his, at any rate. Though he was upset about it at the time, Berkeley looks back on the incident with wry amusement: 'You see, they replaced my piece with Strauss's incidental music to *Le Bourgeois Gentilhomme*. That says it all!'

Berkeley, like many other composers, prefers working to deadlines, and festivals, which have to take place at a specific pre-announced time, are better at enforcing these than concert seasons which may provide up to six months' flexibility. He enjoys commissions which involve particular soloists and the opportunity to work out technical details with them in the course of composing; he speaks fondly of his collaborations with Julian Bream, Robert Cohen and Michael Thompson. He is not, however, greatly influenced by the acoustics of the hall or church in which his first performances are to take place, pointing out that what works well in one setting may fall very flat in another. 'And what composers are looking for these days are not first performances – though they are, of course, important – so much as second, third and fourth performances.'

Many young composers depend on festivals to get their works heard and their names familiar with the public. It does not matter whether or not the performance itself is of the highest polish, that the players might ideally have had longer in rehearsal to master the work. What is much more important,

Berkeley feels, is that they are all making music together – and that includes the composer in his capacity of non-playing adviser. He had his own break in the mid-1970s when his oboe concerto was put on during the Burnham Market Festival, in Norfolk. It was, he feels, a considerable landmark in his early career, and one which helped chart his later development.

The coming together of performers and composers is, to Berkeley, an integral part of the festival atmosphere, which he believes to be quite distinct from that of more routine musical encounters. The sense of community, very often strengthened by a particular geographical location, is very important – and that frequently draws in the audience as well, creating for them a closer relationship with the acts of creation and performance than might otherwise be possible. He illustrates the warmth of festival relationships with an anecdote about the occasion when his father, Sir Lennox Berkeley, and fellow-composer Sir William Walton were both at Aldeburgh to supervise productions of one-act operas. In order to illustrate a particular point to his performers, Berkeley Senior sang part of his score to Walton's piano accompaniment. 'It was hilarious. I think the only thing they succeeded in demonstrating was that my father was probably the worst singer in the world, and that William was the worst pianist!'

Of course, festivals have their shortcomings: 'Some are too elitist – in a social sense. Others do nothing to push forward musical frontiers. Few actually make any money. And there is a side to almost all festivals which is faintly pretentious, faintly absurd – as was brought out beautifully by some of the things that went on in Stephen Pile's Nether Wallop Festival.' But Michael Berkeley believes that they have a very clear and valuable part to play in British musical life. 'I don't know what we would do without them.'

RHYMNEY VALLEY
GŴYL GELFYDDYDAU CWM RHYMNI

The Rhymney Valley runs due north from castle-crowned Caerphilly, cutting its way – like its near neighbour, the Rhondda – into the gaunt flanks of the Brecon Beacons. The festival which takes its name from the valley was founded with the aim of bringing 'quality' events and performances to as many people as possible within reasonable distance of their homes, while at the same time recognizing and encouraging the considerable talent of individuals and organizations within the area. It is a nomadic festival that wanders up and down the valley, pausing its performing caravan in Bargoed or Ystrad Fawr or Ystrad Mynach or indeed Caerphilly itself for a concert, opera, recital or play before moving on to some other community.

Finances have been a problem and a number of changes have had to be made in recent years in the name of economy. For one thing, what was once an autumn festival has been shifted to high summer in order to catch bigger audiences – in 1985 it occupied the first two weeks of July, with a few isolated events scattered over October and November. Then there has been a cut-back in the number of venues (in 1984, the entire festival was held in Caerphilly) and in the number of imported items.

In some ways, Rhymney's heyday was in the early eighties, when a single season contained visits from the BBC Welsh Symphony Orchestra under Gyorgy Lehel (playing Mozart and Beethoven, with Erich Gruenberg as solo violinist), the Endellion String Quartet in Wolf, Weber and Mendelssohn, the Opera Players (who staged a spirited *Carmen*) and the Chamber Choir and Orchestra of the Welsh College of Music and Drama in an interesting programme of Holst (the *Rig Veda* Choral Hymns), Vaughan Williams, Barber, Bruhns and Vivaldi – together with recitals by local musicians and first performances of festival commissions by Neil Day (his Three Sketches for Guitar) and David Nevens. Since then, though programmes have included concerts by visiting professionals (the Oxford Pro Musica and Janáček Wind Ensemble in 1983, London Chamber Opera in Offenbach's *Pepito* and Sullivan's *Cox and Box* the following year), the focus has been more on local talent and a generally less interesting musical diet. It seems likely that this will be the pattern for the future.

ST ASAPH

A few miles down the road from the coastal resorts of Colwyn Bay, Rhyl and Prestatyn, the cathedral village of St Asaph may at first seem a somewhat unlikely place to start a major professional music festival. To begin with, North Wales is scarcely the most densely populated area of Britain, and the Welsh – enthusiastic musical amateurs that they are – take a lot of convincing that importing professionals to perform for them is a worthwhile exercise. None the less, under the aegis of the North Wales Arts Association and Welsh Arts Council and the thoughtful artistic direction of the composer William Mathias, St Asaph first opened its doors to festival audiences in the early 1970s. At first, there was just a handful of events in the middle of a week, but it was not long before demand permitted expansion and today the festival lasts for seven full days (Sunday to Saturday) each late September, with concerts every evening and on four mornings. The success of the venture can be measured by the fact that audiences come from a wide area, encompassing not only mid-Wales but also the border counties, Cheshire, Lancashire and the Wirral.

There is a careful balance between large-scale orchestral concerts and chamber recitals, between native Welsh performers of high calibre and the best available from outside the principality, between standard musical fare from Renaissance to Impressionist and new works, many of them commissioned for the occasion.

All concerts are held in the modest but acoustically comfortable Cathedral. Originally founded in the sixth century, the building as it stands today dates mostly from the thirteenth and can hold something over eight hundred people. Staging does not present too many problems in the light, roomy nave, but those of the audience unlucky enough to have to sit in the aisles sometimes find a pillar or two blocking their view.

There are generally three orchestral concerts in the course of the week, the orchestras mostly being those that can find their way to St Asaph without too much difficulty – the City of Birmingham Symphony, the Hallé, the Royal Liverpool Philharmonic and the BBC Welsh Symphony – though there have also been recent visits by the London Mozart Players and the City of London Sinfonia. Programmes tend to be middle-of-the-road, with occasional outbursts of the exciting or unexpected: Bach, Beethoven and Rimsky-Korsakov favourites one evening, Berlioz, Mendelssohn and Tchaikovsky potboilers another – then, out of the blue, Messiaen's *Turangalila* Symphony, Bartók's First Violin Concerto, a cleverly contrived mixture of Beethoven (the three *Leonora* Overtures) and Sibelius (the Third and Seventh Symphonies), or a newish work by Hoddinott or Mathias himself. Soloists at these concerts are usually of the first rank – Jean-Bernard Pommier, Eugène Sarbu, Marisa Robles, John Lill, Alicia de Larrocha, Cécile Ousset, Kyung-Wha Chung and Peter Frankl.

Chamber concerts and solo recitals also play an important part in St Asaph programming, and there have been notable visits by Tamás Vásáry, Peter Donohoe, Peter Katin, Nigel Kennedy (with Peter Pettinger), Jack Brymer, Osian Ellis and the Gabrieli, Alberni and Lindsay string quartets. There are always two organ recitals in the course of the seven days by such eminent performers as Gillian Weir, John Scott, Roy Massey and Peter Hurford. Visiting choirs also make a valuable contribution, whether they be from St John's College, Cambridge, Chetham's School of Music, Manchester, or the Sankt Annae Gymnasium in Copenhagen.

New works of all kinds make their bow each year at St Asaph, from major orchestral pieces to works for solo harp (David Harries, Paul Patterson), clarinet (Trevor Roberts), organ (Derek Bourgeois, Kenneth Leighton, Mervyn Burtch) or guitar (Dalwyn Henshall).

There is a great sense of occasion at festival time in St Asaph. While everything is designed to run like clockwork, there is also a nicely informal strain in the way audiences and performers can meet to talk music in pub or street or festival club. There is also a strong determination on the part of the organizers to maintain the highest standards, to live up to the expectation of those who now travel sometimes great distances to attend festival concerts. What might have looked like a gamble in the early seventies seems to have paid off.

SWANSEA
GŴYL GERDD A CHELF ABERTAWE

The Swansea Festival combines international gloss with a serious concern for things Welsh and the encouragement of young musicians and audiences. You cannot get much glossier than a festival which includes in a single season – as Swansea did in

1984 – concerts by four of the major London orchestras, plus the Vienna Symphony, the Hallé, the BBC Welsh Symphony and the London Mozart Players under such musical globe-trotters as Tennstedt, Sawallisch, Skrowaczewski, Chailly, Simonov and Ashkenazy.

On the other hand, it is difficult to find a more Welsh festival than one that regularly includes a contribution by the truly national Welsh National Opera company (in 1983, they put on a gala concert which included Acts 3 and 4 of *Carmen*; the following year, they gave a week of staged performances at the newly refurbished Grand Theatre, including *The Merry Widow*, Verdi's *Ernani*, *La Bohème* (Puccini) and Martinu's *The Greek Passion*) or that has a policy of commissioning new works each year, mainly from Welsh composers. The music comes in all shapes and sizes, from song cycles (like Grace Williams's *The Billows of the Sea*, first given in 1969 by Helen Watts with John Streets) to string quartets (David Harries's Second in 1968, played by the Dartington Quartet; David Wynne's Fourth, premièred by the same group four years later) to large-scale orchestral works (such as Hoddinott's *The Sun, the Great Luminary of the Universe*, given by the LSO under Vernon Handley in 1970, or Daniel Jones's Eighth and Eleventh Symphonies, or William Mathias's Third Piano Concerto which was unveiled in 1968 by the BBC Symphony Orchestra under Moshe Atzmon, with the composer as soloist). Choral commissions – indeed choral concerts of any kind – are surprisingly rare at Swansea, though a cantata for chorus, orchestra and three solo voices by John Metcalf was given at the 1985 festival by BBC forces under the direction of Richard Hickox.

Swansea is essentially a professional festival, which aims to bring the brightest and best of performers to South Wales for three weeks of intensive music-making each October. Though local amateurs do sometimes appear in the concerts, it is not the festival's policy to build programmes specifically around them. On the other hand, the organizers do make a point of engaging young musicians, those embarking on a professional career and especially those who are themselves of Welsh origin. There are also concerts for children and, from time to time, master-classes conducted by members of London orchestras.

The festival is designed very much to appeal to the local community, which both forms the backbone of its audiences and – through local industry – sponsors and supports its activities. This being the case, the programmes reveal a distinct adventurousness and lack of conservatism in the tastes for which they cater. Of course, there *are* the Beethoven Eighths and *Eroicas*, the Tchaikovsky piano concertos, the Rachmaninov *Paganini Variations* and the Dvořák *New Worlds*, but equally you will find – alongside the new commissions – a Mahler Sixth, a Bruckner Fifth, an evening of Maxwell Davies (1983 included *Image, Reflection, Shadow*, a new piece *Birthday Music for John* – the dedicatee being John Carewe, conductor of The Fires of London – and a staged performance of *Le Jongleur de Notre Dame*), a Shostakovich Tenth or an *Also Sprach Zarathustra*.

Most concerts take place in the golden acoustic of the Brangwyn Hall, the concert room of Swansea's fifty-year-old Guildhall, with its busy and colourful murals by

The London Mozart Players performing in the Brangwyn Hall at the 1982 Swansea Festival.

Sir Frank Brangwyn. Chamber music also sounds well here (the Delmé, Medici and Amadeus Quartets have all given recitals during recent festivals) and the great organ attracts devotees from all over South Wales to listen to performers of the calibre of Lionel Rogg, Christopher Robinson and Flor Peeters.

The festival package is rounded off with jazz, film, dance and poetry.

──────── VALE OF GLAMORGAN ────────

The Vale of Glamorgan lies to the west of Cardiff – good country through which the Thaw and the Ely rivers flow, invaded long ago by the Normans and dotted with many fine historic buildings. The festival which takes its name from the district, though based at St Donat's Castle, spends a fortnight or so each late August wandering its way through the valleys, presenting chamber concerts and recitals in such places as Beaupré Castle, St Illtyd's Church (Llantwit Major), and the churches at Cowbridge, Llancarfan and Penmark. At St Donat's itself – now the United World College of the Atlantic – the Bradenstoke Hall (a magnificent fourteenth-century structure, actually transferred from Bradenstoke Priory in Wiltshire) and fifteenth-century Tythe Barn provide the settings for some half of the events.

The founder and present director of the festival, the composer John Metcalf, has made it his aim both to bring performers of international stature to the area and to encourage the composition and playing of new music. Visits by the Orchestra of St John's, Smith Square, the London Mozart Players, the Moscow Virtuosi, the Allegri and Delmé string quartets, the Nash Ensemble, the John Alldis Choir, the Baccholian Singers, Michel Dalberto, Jack Brymer, Peter Katin, Louis Kentner, Radu Lupu, Fou Ts'ong and Tamás Vásáry bear witness to his success in achieving the first of these aims, while a glance through past programmes recording first performances or first Welsh performances of pieces by Berio, Crumb, Henze, Jolivet, Enesco, Maxwell Davies, Musgrave, Souster and Xenakis is sufficient reminder that he has never let up on the second.

In recent years, the festival has turned its attention increasingly to music-theatre and experimental music-drama, and there have been notable visits from the Rosemary Butcher Dance Company with Dreamtiger and the Nuremburg Opera Studio. In 1983, the festival set up its own Music-Theatre Ensemble to provide new productions for the Vale which might subsequently be toured elsewhere in Wales and England. The company, which included Oliver Knussen, Mary King and the dancers Eberle Pringle and Frank Rozelaar-Green, gave the première of Michael Finnissy's *Vaudeville* and performances of Stravinsky's *The Soldier's Tale* and a Satie extravaganza entitled *Gymnopediae and the Black Cat*.

The Vale of Glamorgan Festival also makes substantial use of soloists and ensembles resident in the area (such as the Atlantic College Madrigal Group, the Welsh Brass Consort, the Welsh National Opera Chorus, the Welsh Philharmonia, Anthony Hose, Richard Armstrong, Brian Noyes, Julian Smith and Julian Moyle) and of young artists not yet fully established in the musical profession.

The festival balance is between concerts by small instrumental ensembles (in 1984, John Harle's Berliner Band played music by Hanns Eisler, Michael Nyman, Dave Heath and Gary Carpenter; the Moscow Virtuosi performed Bach, Shostakovich and Tchaikovsky; and the Albany Brass gave a programme of Penderecki, Metcalf, Malcolm Arnold and Martin Davies) and chamber and solo recitals (Dennis Lee in Szymanowski's *Shéhérazade*, Chopin's B flat Minor Sonata and pieces by Debussy; Suzanne Murphy; the Medici String Quartet playing Strauss, Schoenberg and Tchaikovsky; Tamás Vásáry; and – at Ash Hall, Ystradowen – Enid Luff (piano), Rachel Payne (mezzo soprano) and Nancy Ruffer (flute) in a programme of British, French and Japanese music).

Though the festival is music-based, there are also exhibitions of art and photography, poetry programmes and jazz.

Index and Festival Addresses

Addresses and telephone numbers are the most recent available though, since many festivals are run by unpaid volunteers from their own homes, some changes are inevitable. Some of the festivals listed are biennial or less frequent (see Festival Calendar).